BUILDING EFFECTIVE TECHNICAL TRAINING

BUILDING EFFECTIVE
TECHNICAL TRAINING

How to Develop Hard Skills
Within Organizations

William J. Rothwell
Joseph A. Benkowski

JOSSEY-BASS/PFEIFFER
A Wiley Company
www.pfeiffer.com

JOSSEY-BASS/PFEIFFER

A Wiley Company
989 Market Street
San Francisco, CA 94103-1741
415.433.1740; Fax 415.433.0499
800.274.4434; Fax 800.569.0443

www.pfeiffer.com

Jossey-Bass/Pfeiffer is a registered trademark of Jossey-Bass Inc., A Wiley Company.
ISBN: 0-7879-5595-7

Library of Congress Cataloging-in-Publication Data

Rothwell, William J.
      Building effective technical training: how to develop hard
      skills within organizations / William J. Rothwell Joseph A.
Benkowski.
         p. cm.
      Includes bibliographical references and index.
      ISBN 0-7879-5595-7 (alk. paper)
      1. Employees—Training of. I. Benkowski, Joseph A. II.
      Title.
      HF5549.5.T7 R6573 2001
      658.3'12404—dc21
             2001004594

Printed in the United States of America

We at Jossey-Bass strive to use the most environmentally sensitive paper stocks available to us. Our
publications are printed on acid-free recycled stock whenever possible, and our paper always meets or
exceeds minimum GPO and EPA requirements.

Acquiring Editor: Josh Blatter
Director of Development: Kathleen Dolan Davies
Editor: Rebecca Taff
Senior Production Editor: Dawn Kilgore
Manufacturing Supervisor: Becky Carreño
Cover Design: Blue Design

Printing 10 9 8 7 6 5 4 3 2 1

DEDICATION

From William J. Rothwell: This book is dedicated to my beloved wife, Marcelina Rothwell, and my beloved daughter, Candice Rothwell, the two most important women in my life.

From Joseph A. Benkowski: This book is dedicated to my wife, Karen, and our sons, Brian, Gregg, and Marc, our daughter, Jill, her husband, Steven Donarski, and our wonderful grandchildren, Victoria, Samuel, and Alexandra.

CONTENTS

List of Exhibits   ix

Acknowledgments   xii

Preface   xiii

PART I   FOUNDATIONS OF EFFECTIVE TECHNICAL TRAINING   1

Chapter One   What Is Technical Training?   3

Chapter Two   What Are the Characteristics of Effective
                   Technical Training?   32

PART II   PLANNING AND MANAGING THE TECHNICAL TRAINING FUNCTION   69

Chapter Three   Establishing an Organizational Plan for Technical
                   Training   73

Chapter Four   Leading and Managing the Technical Training
                   Department   107

PART III KEY ISSUES IN TRAINING COURSE DESIGN 121

Chapter Five   Basic Principles of Instructional Systems Design   123

Chapter Six   Identifying Technical Training Needs   143

Chapter Seven   Preparing Technical Training Programs   176

Chapter Eight   Determining and Using Delivery Methods   192

Chapter Nine   Evaluating Technical Training   218

PART IV SPECIAL ISSUES IN TECHNICAL TRAINING 227

Chapter Ten   Using Vendors and Managing Original Equipment
                  Manufacturers   229

Chapter Eleven   Operating Apprenticeship and Safety Training
                  Programs and Working with Unions   241

Chapter Twelve   Achieving Results with Alternatives to Technical
                  Training   268

PART V CONCLUDING THOUGHTS 279

Afterword   Lessons Learned from Experience in Technical
                  Training   281

APPENDICES 287

Appendix I   Assessing and Building Competence as a Technical
                  Trainer   289

Appendix II   Guidelines for Technical Training Development and
                  Delivery   292

Appendix III   Examples Representing the Work of an
                  Organization's Strategic Planning for Technical
                  Training Committee   310

Appendix IV   A Written Questionnaire to Assess Technical Training
                  Needs   320

References   338

About the Authors   347

How to Use the CD-ROM   349

Index   353

LIST OF EXHIBITS

1   The Organization of the Book   xix

2   Part I Within the Scheme of the Book   2

1.1   Worksheet to Assess Level of Management Support for Technical Training   15

1.2   Distribution of Respondents by Industry   22

1.3   Distribution of Respondents by Size of Organization   23

1.4   Distribution of Respondents by Job Function   24

1.5   Perceived Reasons Why Organizations Sponsor Technical Training   25

2.1   Perceived Characteristics of Effective Technical Training Programs   53

2.2   Do You Believe Your Management Supports Training?   54

2.3   Do You Believe Your Company Provides Good Technical Training?   55

2.4   Assessing the Perceived Effectiveness of Your Organization's Technical Training   59

2.5   Job Description of a Technical Training Coordinator   61

2.6   Job Description of a Technical Training Instructor   61

2.7   Competencies Essential for Technical Trainers   63

2.8   Who Develops Technical Training in Your Organization?   64

2.9   Is Technical Training a Separate Department in Your
       Organization?   65

  3   Part II Within the Scheme of the Book   71

3.1   An Interview Guide to Examine Strategic Issues in Technical
       Training   92

3.2   Benchmarking Data Guide   96

3.3   A Guide in Gathering Necessary Competitive Information of Value
       for Planning Technical Training   101

3.4   A Worksheet to Organize Information for Formulating Strategic
       Planning for Technical Training   102

3.5   A Worksheet to Assess the Quality of the Strategic Plan for
       Technical Training in an Organization   103

4.1   A Worksheet to Formulate a Vision for the Technical Training
       Function   109

4.2   Worksheet for Clarifying the Role of the Manager of Technical
       Training   110

4.3   A Model to Depict the Key Responsibilities of a Leader/Manager
       of Technical Training   112

4.4   Worksheet to Brainstorm Activities to Support the Responsibilities
       of a Technical Training Manager or Leader   113

4.5   Examples of Standards for Technical Training   115

4.6   Worksheet to Structure Your Thinking on Groups with Whom You
       Come Into Contact   119

  4   Part III Within the Scheme of the Book   122

5.1   The ADDIE Model   125

5.2   Types of Analysis   126

5.3   Worksheet for Conducting Performance Analysis   128

5.4   Worksheet for Conducting Learner Analysis   129

5.5   Worksheet for Conducting Work Setting Analysis   130

5.6   Worksheet for Conducting Instructional Setting Analysis   132

5.7   Worksheet for Conducting Job Analysis   134

5.8   Worksheet for Conducting Task Analysis   135

5.9 Template for a Lesson Plan for a Classroom-Based Technical Training Course   139

5.10 Template for a Lesson Plan for a Web-Based Technical Training Course   140

6.1 Training Curriculum Matrix   148

6.2 Course Descriptions Linked to the Training Curriculum   149

6.3 Understanding a Training Need   153

6.4 General Methods to Assess Training Needs   154

6.5 Sample DACUM Chart of an Entry-Level Trainer in China   161

6.6 Questionnaire to Assess Training Needs Based on a Dacum Chart   166

6.7 The Skilbase Chart Concept   169

6.8 How a Skilbase Chart Is Used for Employee Recordkeeping   172

7.1 Principles of Procedures Mapping   182

7.2 Layout of a Job Chart   183

7.3 Creating a Job Aid Cover Sheet   184

7.4 Sample Cover Page   185

7.5 How to Write Decision Tables   186

8.1 Delivery Methods Used in Technical Training   194

8.2 Worksheet to Structure Your Thinking on Delivery Methods   196

8.3 Sample Checksheet Format to Guide On-the-Job Training   203

8.4 Worksheet to Structure Your Thinking on Self-Directed Learning Activities   211

5 Part IV Within the Scheme of the Book   228

10.1 Procedures for Planning Training for Equipment Installation   234

11.1 Sample Safety Matrix   257

12.1 Thinking About the Root Cause(s) of Human Performance Problems   270

12.2 Worksheet for Considering Interventions   271

6 Part V Within the Scheme of the Book   279

ACKNOWLEDGMENTS

No book is written by one or two people alone. We would like to extend our most profound thanks to the people who helped us craft this book. They are

Karen Benkowski for her editing of Joe's writing for this book and for providing him with sound feedback, and especially for her support in helping Joe reach this goal.

Kelli Dammen, Joe Benkowski's assistant, for her help in sending out the surveys that yielded useful information for part of this book.

Xuejun Qiao, William J. Rothwell's able graduate student, who helped track down the copyright permissions for this manuscript.

Kathy Swan, instructor of workforce education and development at The Pennsylvania State University, for her excellent feedback offered from a union perspective.

However, the responsibility for what is contained in the book is ultimately ours. We share accountability for the outcome.

William J. Rothwell
State College, PA
Joseph A. Benkowski
Menomonie, WI

PREFACE

If you consider the phrase *technical training* to mean *instructing people how to conduct the unique aspects of a special kind of work and apply the special tools, equipment, and processes of that work,* then technical training has been around about as long as the human race. Early cave drawings may have been schematic diagrams to train people how to hunt. And it is difficult to imagine that the builders of the pyramids of Egypt or Stonehenge in England could have built those strange, massive edifices without offering some rudimentary training to the laborers. The history of technical training is a long one (Swanson and Torraco, 1995). Its focus is not just on providing knowledge but also on building *skill*, which means the know-how to do work.

In the early stages of human history, technical training was conducted by telling and showing learners how to perform and then watching as learners demonstrated what they could do and how well they could do it. If that sounds familiar, it should: Training, as a process, has not really changed that much over the last several thousand years. But what has changed are the means and media by which training is carried out. Just as each phase of the industrial revolution was punctuated by changes in manufacturing methods, processes to improve quality, and the costs of manufacturing, technical training has also shifted its emphasis correspondingly over time. Demands to improve technical training have coincided with the wrenching demands placed on businesses at each stage of industrial development. In today's business world, a key problem is finding and keeping people with the know-how to do the work and meet or exceed customer expectations. And technical training can help to solve that problem.

Dramatic changes have taken place in business operations over the last hundred years. The technologies used today would have been mind-boggling to those who worked in the early 20th Century. As technology has advanced, so too has the need for technical training to help people apply that technology and keep their knowledge and skills current in the face of the rapid changes resulting from technological advancement.

This book is intended to provide practical information for technical trainers, especially those who are new to the job and are promoted from within their organizations. At this point it is worth noting that some confusion currently exists over what groups or organizations are the targets for technical training. Some people think of technical training as focused on engineers and other workers who must apply special knowledge in manufacturing settings. Other people think technical training is focused on management information systems (MIS) professionals and other workers who must apply special knowledge in high-technology companies. And still other people think of technical training as focused on any worker who must apply devices such as personal computers and the software that governs them to their work. But, as defined in this book, technical training is really geared to all three groups—and to other groups that must use specialized methods or technology to achieve work results. The basic principles of good technical training are the same regardless of the targeted participants. This book should prove to be useful to anyone who helps workers use new and emerging work processes and technology. The overall schematic diagram representing the organization of the book is presented in Exhibit 1.

Part I lays the foundation for the book. Chapter 1 defines technical training, distinguishes it from other categories of training, emphasizes its importance, and summarizes key trends likely to shape the future and affect technical training. Chapter 1 introduces the results of a small-scale survey of technical trainers undertaken by the authors of this book in year 2000 and lists key reasons why organizations support technical training. Chapter 2 opens with three case studies that dramatize the characteristics of effective technical training. The chapter also catalogs unique competencies that effective technical trainers should possess.

Part II focuses on planning and managing the technical training function. Chapter 3 opens with a case study about the means by which a real, albeit disguised, organization carried out strategic planning for technical training. It then reviews key issues that should be addressed in strategic planning for technical training. Chapter 4 examines the unique role and

EXHIBIT 1. THE ORGANIZATION OF THE BOOK

Chapter 1: **What Is Technical Training?**	**Part I:** **Foundations of** **Effective** **Technical** **Training**
Chapter 2: **What Are the Characteristics of Effective Technical Training?**	
Chapter 3: **Establishing an Organizational Plan for Technical Training**	**Part II:** **Planning and** **Managing the** **Technical** **Training** **Function**
Chapter 4: **Leading and Managing the Technical Training Department**	
Chapter 5: **Basic Principles of Instructional Systems Design**	**Part III:** **Key Issues** **in** **Training** **Course** **Design**
Chapter 6: **Identifying Technical Training Needs**	
Chapter 7: **Preparing Technical Training Programs**	
Chapter 8: **Determining and Using Delivery Methods**	
Chapter 9: **Evaluating Technical Training**	
Chapter 10: **Using Vendors and Managing Original** **Equipment Manufacturers**	**Part IV:** **Special Issues** **in Technical** **Training**
Chapter 11: **Operating Apprenticeship and Safety** **Training Programs and Working with Unions**	
Chapter 12: **Achieving Results with Alternatives to Technical Training**	
Afterword	**Part V:** **Concluding** **Thoughts**

responsibilities facing those who manage technical training programs inside organizational settings.

Part III turns to key issues in technical training course design. Chapter 5 provides an overview of the instructional systems design (ISD) process, which is a big-picture roadmap for building effective technical training. Chapter 6 reviews ways to identify technical training needs but emphasizes the Developing a Curriculum (DACUM) method as especially useful. Chapter 7 offers detailed information about how to prepare technical training programs, including the important issue of how to prepare technical manuals. Chapter 8 examines how to select and use delivery methods, ranging from on-the-job training to sophisticated multimedia-based delivery modes. Chapter 9 offers thoughts on how to evaluate technical training.

Part IV examines special issues in technical training. Chapter 10 describes how to use vendors and original equipment manufacturers (OEMs) to design, develop, deliver, and evaluate technical training. Chapter 11 takes a look at establishing and operating apprenticeship and safety training programs. It also examines how to work with unions. Chapter 12 challenges you, the reader, to find alternatives to technical training, such as job aids and consultative approaches to improve human performance.

The book concludes with an Afterword. It shares the authors' insights on lessons learned from experience in technical training. Following the Afterword appear four Appendices. Appendix I provides instruments to permit you to assess and build your competencies as a technical trainer. The second Appendix is a manual of guidelines for technical training and development that can be adapted and used in many organizations. The third Appendix illustrates products that represent the work of an organization's strategic planning for technical training committee. The fourth and final Appendix provides a questionnaire that can be useful in assessing technical training needs.

William J. Rothwell
State College, PA
Joseph A. Benkowski
Menomonie, WI

BUILDING EFFECTIVE TECHNICAL TRAINING

PART I

FOUNDATIONS OF EFFECTIVE TECHNICAL TRAINING

Part I provides the layout for the book. It

- Defines the term technical training
- Distinguishes technical training from soft skills training and management training
- Explains why technical training is important
- Describes key factors influencing the role of technical training in organizations
- Lists key reasons why organizations support technical training
- Lists important trends influencing the future of technical training
- Identifies characteristics of effective technical training programs
- Catalogs unique competencies that effective technical trainers should possess

Exhibit 2 is the blueprint for Part I within a schematic diagram of the total book.

EXHIBIT 2. PART I WITHIN THE SCHEME OF THE BOOK

Chapter 1: **What Is Technical Training?**	**Part I: Foundations of Effective Technical Training**
Chapter 2: **What Are the Characteristics of Effective Technical Training?**	
Chapter 3: **Establishing an Organizational Plan for Technical Training**	**Part II: Planning and Managing the Technical Training Function**
Chapter 4: **Leading and Managing the Technical Training Department**	
Chapter 5: **Basic Principles of Instructional Systems Design**	
Chapter 6: **Identifying Technical Training Needs**	**Part III: Key Issues in Training Course Design**
Chapter 7: **Preparing Technical Training Programs**	
Chapter 8: **Determining and Using Delivery Methods**	
Chapter 9: **Evaluating Technical Training**	
Chapter 10: **Using Vendors and Managing Original Equipment Manufacturers**	
Chapter 11: **Operating Apprenticeship and Safety Training Programs and Working with Unions**	**Part IV: Special Issues in Technical Training**
Chapter 12: **Achieving Results with Alternatives to Technical Training**	
Afterword	**Part V: Concluding Thoughts**

CHAPTER ONE

WHAT IS TECHNICAL TRAINING?

How does your organization manage technical training? Read the following vignettes and, on a separate sheet of paper, describe how *your* organization would most likely manage each situation. When you finish, be prepared to explain how each vignette may illustrate a need for technical training.

Vignette One

The company has acquired a new technology for a work process. Workers must be trained to use the new technology.

Vignette Two

New software has been purchased for use by the company's secretaries and other workers. Training on the software is essential if the full benefits are to be realized.

Vignette Three

An industrial plant is switching over to a new product line. Workers, accustomed to manufacturing an older product line, must be familiarized with a new manufacturing process and a new product.

Vignette Four

An organization is experiencing difficulty in finding trained machinists. Company management decides to tackle this business problem by taking several steps. One step is to work with a local vocational school. Another step is to participate in a union-managed apprenticeship program. A third step is to contribute funds to a local proprietary school that trains machinists.

Vignette Five

The managers of one company want to comply with government-required safety training requirements for workers. However, company managers want to do more than just run people through required training. Instead, they wish to use the training to improve job performance and workplace safety as part of a holistic wellness and work life balance program.

Vignette Six

Managers in one organization believe it will be cost-effective to train information technology (IT) professionals to meet company-specific needs. But the managers are not sure where or how to start such a program.

Defining Technical Training

As the vignettes above illustrate, people in organizations need help in learning how to do work that is uniquely specific to an organization, occupation, or job category. But different ways exist to think about technical training.

One way is to think of it in terms of practically focused training given to job categories that are usually considered to be technical. Another way is to think of technical training as its meaning is implied by the words *technician, technical,* and *technology.*

Technical Training: Its Meaning Based on Work

One way to think about technical training is to link it to practical training geared to job categories that are commonly regarded as technical. For example, the U.S. Bureau of Labor Statistics has a specific definition for *technical occupations.* They are "occupations involved in carrying out technical and technological functions in health, engineering, science, and other disciplines. These occupations may perform research, development, testing, and related activities. These occupations may operate technical equipment and systems." Such occupations as laboratory technicians, pilots, hydrographers, and radar operators are included (www.bls.gov/ncs/ocs/ocsm/commogadef.htm). Even more specifically, the Bureau of Labor Statistics lists examples of technical occupations (www.bls.gov/ocsm/commoga.htm):

Health Technologists and Technicians

A203 Clinical Laboratory Technologists and Technicians

A204 Dental Hygienists

A205 Health Record Technologists and Technicians

A206 Radiologic Technicians

A207 Licensed Practical Nurses

A208 Health Technologists and Technicians, N.E.C.

Engineering and Related Technologists and Technicians

A213 Electrical and Electronic Technicians

A214 Industrial Engineering Technicians

A215 Mechanical Engineering Technicians

A216 Engineering Technicians, N.E.C.

A217 Drafters

A218 Surveying and Mapping Technicians

Science Technicians

A223 Biological Technicians

A224 Chemical Technicians

A225 Science Technicians, N.E.C.

Miscellaneous Technicians

A226 Airplane Pilots and Navigators

A227 Air Traffic Controllers

A228 Broadcast Equipment Operators

A229 Computer Programmers

A233 Tool Programmers, Numerical Control

A234 Legal Assistants

A235 Technical and Related Occupations, N.E.C.

Hence, in one narrow sense, technical training means training focused on any or all of the job categories or occupational groups identified above.

Four occupational groups projected to be the fastest-growing in the U.S. labor force between 1998 and 2008 are technical in nature. They are, with numbers in the thousands of jobs, as follows (www.bls.gov/news. release/ecopro.t06.htm):

			Employment Change	
Occupational Category	*1998*	*2008*	*Number*	*Percent*
Computer engineers	299	622	323	108
Computer support specialists	429	869	439	102
Systems analysts	617	1,194	577	94
Database administrators	87	155	67	77

Two of ten occupations with the largest expected job growth between 1998 and 2008 are also technical in nature. They also overlap with the four occupational groups projected to be the fastest-growing. They are, with numbers in the thousands of jobs, as follows (www.bls.gov/news.release/ecopro.t07.htm):

Occupational Category	Employment Change			
	1998	*2008*	*Number*	*Percent*
Systems analysts	617	1,194	577	94
Computer support specialists	429	869	439	102

Demand for these technical jobs is increasing, and that puts pressure on educational institutions and employers alike to find ways to prepare people to meet the labor demand.

Technical Training: Its Meaning Based on Definitions

Another way to think of technical training is to link it to words commonly associated with the word *technical*. The word *technical* is defined by the *Oxford English Dictionary* as "[*a person*] skilled in or practically conversant with some particular art or subject" and also "[*an object*] belonging or relating to an art or arts; appropriate or peculiar to, or characteristic of, a particular art, science, profession, or occupation" (1971, II, p. 137). The word *technician* is defined as "a person conversant with the technicalities of a particular subject" (1971, II, p. 136). And the word *technology* is defined, in one sense, to mean "the terminology of a particular art or subject" (1971, II, p. 137).

Hence, *technical training* may be understood to mean *instruction intended to help people perform the unique aspects of a special kind of work and apply the special tools, equipment, and processes of that work, usually in one organizational setting.* Technical training is sometimes called *hard skills training.* It can thus be distinguished from so-called *soft skills training,* which is *training to help people learn how to interact with other people,* and from *basic skills training,* which provides foundational skills on which other skills are built. Basic skills training is often a prerequisite to technical training, considering that as much as 20 percent of the U.S. workforce may be functionally illiterate but only 2.2 percent of U.S. employers offer basic skills training (Hays, 1999).

Technical training can also be distinguished from *executive, management, or supervisory training,* which is focused on *training people how to oversee the work of others and (especially in the case of executive and management training) gain competitive advantage for the organization.* As Swanson and Torraco (1995, p. 3) explain, technical skills training is "focused on people-system, people-thing work behavior." It thus differs from management training, which is "focused on people-idea, people-people work behavior," and from motivational training, which is "focused on people-beliefs, people-values work behavior." That is a definition that has been echoed by at least one other writer who undertook the task of defining technical training (Mitchell, 1997).

As Zemke (1986, p. 18) has noted: "What qualifies as a technical or technological skill to one person is simply rote procedure or something else altogether to another. An informal survey of 160 *Training* readers indicated that most technical skills training was conducted in the areas of computers and/or microprocessors, mechanics, maintenance fundamentals, and electrical." According to Jerome J. Peloquin of Performance Control Corporation, "in its loosest sense, technical training involves teaching people how to do things and fix things."

All the vignettes described in the opening section of this chapter are occasions when technical training is warranted. After all, each vignette describes a situation in which people must be trained to do the unique aspects of a special kind of work, apply the special tools and equipment of that work, and perform that work in a unique corporate culture.

Technical training is not limited to meaning, but includes, *training people how to use technology.* Instead, technical training means *training people how to perform under unique conditions for which special expertise is necessary.* To the extent that training how to use technology requires knowledge of how to perform under unique conditions, they conceptually coincide. Any training process that captures the knowledge of genuine technical experts is thus a form of what one clever observer has called "tecknowledgy" (Whitmore, 1992).

Some confusion exists about the relationship between technical training for heavy industry and technical training for the information technology (IT) industry or for information technology skills in all industries. But they are related. The results of one research study on training for IT called it "one of the fastest growing segments of the technical training field" ("Information Technology Training," 1998, www.astd.org/virtual_ community/research/nhrd_executive_survey_98it.html). Key findings of that study revealed:

- Nearly all organizations provide some type of IT training.
- Expenditures on IT training were headed up in 1998 for most organizations.
- The primary obstacle to IT training is keeping up with the pace of technological change.
- Less than 40 percent of IT courses are taught by in-house employees in the typical company.
- Even courses on IT are largely taught in an instructor-led classroom setting.

Most trainers see IT training as an area of growing importance. In 1997, the most recent date for which information is available, the firms in the study spent about 5 percent of their total training budgets on IT-related training, and many spent more than 25 percent of their total training budgets on IT training (Information Technology Training, 1998, www.astd.org/ virtual_community/research/nhrd_executive_survey_98it.html). Administrative workers are most likely to receive such training, and executives are least likely to receive it. The most common training offered in this area focuses on desktop uses of the personal computer.

Why Is Technical Training Important?

Technical training is important for three key reasons. First, research has shown that technical training has a significant economic impact on employers. Second, technical training accounts for a sizable percentage of all training offered in the United States. Third, its importance is growing as organizations scramble to find, keep, and leverage talent (Ruber, 1996).

Research Supporting the Value of Technical Training

Throughout history, wealth has been measured as being the strength of a nation. According to Johnston:

> In previous centuries, the wealth of a nation was thought to consist of gold in the national treasury and jewels in the emperor's crown. In more recent years, wealth has been equated with factories, mines, and production machinery within a nation's borders. As the miraculous rebirth of Europe and Japan after World War II has proven, however, the foundation of national wealth is really people—the human capital represented by their knowledge, skills, organization, and motivations. (1987, p. 15)

As Johnston (1987, p. 15) goes on to explain, "Education and training are the primary systems by which the human capital of a nation is preserved and increased. How fast people are able to learn is the key that governs the rate at which human capital can be developed. Human capital formation also plays a direct role in how fast an economy grows, more so than other such indicators as the rate of investment in plant and equipment."

Many recent research studies have cited the critically important issues of worker skills and job training as key elements in economic competitiveness. These studies support the view that a broadly trained workforce is essential to an effective national competitive strategy, a view supported for economic development in some foreign nations as well as in the United States (Cellich, 1992). They also support the view that cultivating such a workforce requires widespread changes in worker training practices, the organization of work, and institutional arrangements surrounding the employment relationship.

Various studies have focused attention on how well U.S. corporations measure up to world-class standards in worker training. Parker (1994), in summarizing those studies, concluded that training investments by U.S. corporations fall dramatically short of world-class standards. Despite some variations by industry sector, U.S. corporations invest *less than half as much* as their leading international rivals. Worse yet, U.S. corporations concentrate training on the managerial and professional workforce (Rothwell and Kazanas, 1999)—instead of on other worker groups that actually perform the work, serve the customers, or produce the goods, and get results on the firing line. One consequence of this lopsided approach to human development in organizations is perhaps best summarized in the conclusion of a survey in *Productivity*, which indicated that "top management in 221 major firms cited poor management, weak capital spending, and poor training as the major causes of depressed productivity—not the workers themselves" (Bluestone and Harrison, 1982, p. 16).

Early studies of workplace quality and learning found that educational attainment accounts for sizeable shares of economic growth. A seminal economic analysis concluded that as much as 60 percent of competitive improvements since 1929 can be attributed to advances in knowledge and education (U.S. Department of Labor, 1993). More recent studies have found a significant connection between training and productivity. A survey of 3,420 employers revealed that an increase in training activities from zero to 100 hours raised productivity by 13 to 15 percent (U.S. Department of Labor, 1993).

Bartel (1989) found a significant connection between training and production. Unlike previous research, which relied heavily on data on individual employees, this study relied on data from human resource policies and the economic characteristics of manufacturers. The major finding: *Businesses operating below their expected labor productivity levels in 1983 that implemented new employee training programs realized labor productivity increases at least 17 percent higher than those that did not between 1983 and 1986.* Of the four variables examined in the study, only training showed a positive impact on productivity growth. Technical training figured prominently in these studies as a crucial factor contributing to productivity increases.

Technical training also has implications for individuals' earning power and subsequent career opportunities. Hight (1998, p. 16) found that:

The very low participation rate in computer software training among young adult workers without a high school diploma—1.6 percent—may be particularly harmful to their earnings potential, given the evidence that using a computer on the job significantly affects earnings. And while their rate of participation in technical or skilled-worker training is higher, it still is only about a third of the rate for those with a high school diploma.

Hence, individuals may have a stake in seeking out opportunities for technical training.

Training has emerged as one of several key issues of importance to employers in the first decade of the new millennium. The key business challenges organizations face today include attracting and retaining skilled and talented workers and helping workers keep their skills current in the face of daunting, dynamic business conditions and rapidly changing technology (Oleson, 1999; Stamps, 1998). Training has also been shown to be correlated positively with employee retention. And that makes sense: When employers demonstrate that they are willing to invest money in workers, workers respond with an increased sense of loyalty to that employer.

Technical Training Accounts for a Sizable Percentage of All Training Offered in the U.S.

Technical training is also a common focus of attention among employers. According to Van Buren (2001, p. 13), "The largest share of the typical Benchmarking Service firm's training expenditures for 1999 went to training in technical processes and procedures, and in professional skills. These categories claimed 13 percent and 11 percent, respectively, of the average organization's training expenditures for the year. Coming in next among the course types benefiting from a relatively high level of investment in 1999 were information technology (IT) skills, new employee orientation, and interpersonal communications skills, all around 9 percent of expenditures." Consequently, given the sheer size of employer expenditures on technical training, it warrants attention. In a survey of CEOs of technology firms conducted in the summer of year 2000, training ranked as the number one business concern (Gittlen, 2000).

Employers in the United States face a shortage of talent. Evidence of that can be seen by the action of Congress in 2000 to approve a record-setting 195,000 work-related visas so that immigrants could make up for a shortfall of U.S. talent and technical training (Bloch, 2000). One industry group estimated that more than 840,000 jobs in the technically oriented information technology (IT) field would go unfilled in year 2001 (Glister, 2000; Stone, 2001).

Nor is the United States alone in facing a talent shortage of technical skills, particularly in information technology. "A report for Microsoft by consultants IDC forecasts that the shortage of IT skills in Europe will widen from 460,000 unfilled posts last year to 1.7 million by 2003, or from 5 to 13 percent of total demand. IDC predicts that the IT skills shortage in Europe will become more acute unless urgent action is taken" (Filling the Skills Gap, 2000, p. 6).

What Key Factors Influence Technical and Skill Training in an Organization?

Key factors influencing the role played by technical training in any organization include: (1) the level of management support; (2) the type of organization (manufacturing, health, financial, and so forth); (3) the size of the organization; (4) the reporting relationship of technical training on the organization chart; (5) the collective bargaining status of the organization; and (6) the source of technical trainers.

Level of Management Support

Managers at different levels provide varying degrees of support for technical training. Taken together, the amount of support provided by an organization's management exerts major influence on how much and what kind of technical training the company offers.

Consider the following questions to determine how much the organization's management supports technical training:

- How much are executives, managers, and supervisors willing to invest in technical training?

- What is the organization's current level of financial support for technical training projects?
- How much are competitors spending on technical training, and how does an organization compare to its competitors?
- When new products, services, or technology have been purchased by the organization, how often do executives, managers, and supervisors routinely ask about the training provided to support the application of those products, services, or technology?
- When the organization is about to change its work processes—such as changing an assembly line or switching to an innovation such as lean manufacturing—how often do executives, managers, and supervisors routinely ask about the training provided to support the switchover?

Use the worksheet given in Exhibit 1.1 to structure your thinking about these issues. Use the results to reflect on how much support exists for technical training in your organization.

Type of Company

While some people might think that technical training is only something given in manufacturing firms, that is not true. Recall that the definition of technical training provided earlier was this: *Training people how to do the unique aspects of a special kind of work and apply the special tools, equipment, and processes of that work.* Consequently, technical training can—and is—given in all organizations, including government agencies, nonprofit organizations, retail establishments, and others. Wherever the work requires specialized knowledge, workers require technical training.

But the reality is that manufacturing firms do tend to invest more in technical training than other employers. One reason is that it may be easier for manufacturers to see the tangible results of that training. That may not be true in such service-oriented organizations as government agencies, charitable organizations, or retail firms.

EXHIBIT 1.1. WORKSHEET TO ASSESS LEVEL OF MANAGEMENT SUPPORT FOR TECHNICAL TRAINING

Directions: Use this worksheet to structure your thinking about the organization's commitment and level of support for technical training. For each question appearing below, provide your answers. Then circulate this worksheet and compare notes with others in the organization.

1. How much are executives, managers, and supervisors willing to invest in technical training?

2. What is the organization's current level of financial support for technical training projects?

3. How much are competitors spending on technical training, and how does the organization compare with its competitors?

4. When new products, services, or technology have been purchased by the organization, how often do executives, managers, and supervisors routinely ask about the training provided to support the application of those products, services, or technology?

5. When the organization is about to change its work processes, such as changing an assembly line or switching to an innovation such as lean manufacturing, how often do executives, managers, and supervisors routinely ask about the training provided to support the switchover?

The Size of the Organization

Generally speaking, the larger the organization, the more specialized its technical training tends to be. In small employers, trainers assume many responsibilities. Technical training may be just one item in their overall duties, and they may also be expected to handle other issues as well. On the other hand, in a larger employer, trainers specialize. There may be trainers reporting to line managers in production or operations. There may also be trainers reporting to other groups—such as management information systems (MIS), human resources (HR), marketing and sales, and other groups.

There are many pros and cons for technical training functions in small versus large organizations. The purpose of this book is not to debate the differences but to discuss what you should do as a technical trainer to leverage your impact. If you are employed as a technical trainer in a small business, you will find that training must usually be important if it is to garner management support. Small companies usually do not hire full-time technical trainers unless someone in the organization sees a compelling need. Whether the person is hired from outside or promoted from inside, a technical trainer's responsibility is to ensure that the organization achieves its operational goals. Some companies promote or transfer employees from inside the organization to serve as technical trainers. They may (or may not) have had any previous experience in technical training. Usually those hired with no training experience have demonstrated some outstanding qualities that attracted management attention. Those qualities might include specialized knowledge of work processes, outstanding interpersonal skills, good attitudes about the company, excellent working relationships with all levels in the organization, and good communication skills—to name but a few desirable traits.

Technical trainers lacking training experience should consider attending seminars or taking courses to build their training skills. Local technical or community colleges usually offer train-the-trainer experiences, and that is one way to build training skills quickly. This training should cover how to assess training needs, as well as how to design, develop, deliver, and evaluate training. Reading books like this is also an excellent place to start (see American Society for Training and Development, 1994a, 1994b; Clark, 1994; Dent and Weber, 1999; Kemp, and Cochern, 1994; Sharpe, 1998).

Organizational awareness is essential for you as a technical trainer. You should be familiar with the work processes as well as with organizational reporting relationships. Veteran employees of an organization, however, will find it more important to learn about the training process itself. One way to do that is to join local training organizations, such as the American Society for Training and Development (ASTD). Local chapters of this organization hold periodic meetings in which practical training topics are discussed, and the organization maintains a website (www.astd.org) where trainers meet to trade queries and information. ASTD can also assist in finding organizations that provide training seminars and in finding first-rate self-study material geared to building competence in the training process. If you are a trainer in a small organization, you can usually spot training problems more easily than if you are in a large organization because the structure is not so complex. That means you can act to solve problems faster. Besides having an understanding of the organizational structure and the theory of training, you should find ways to make yourself visible to both employees and management. By that we mean you should spend time with the workers to show that you care about them, the work they do, and the problems they face. Establishing good interpersonal relations with workers makes it easier to spot problems that training can solve.

If you are a technical trainer in a large organization, you will most likely face different challenges. Larger organizations tend to hire technical trainers possessing specialized skills in training, sometimes obtained from formal educational preparation. In this situation the main hurdle for you as a technical trainer is to become knowledgeable about the organization, its people, and its business. Having expert training skills is no guarantee of success. Trainers must also be able to communicate with others, deliver the training, and talk the business. One way to build this credibility is to spend time working different shifts and finding out what is going on by walking around the workplace.

Reporting Relationship

There is an old saying that "what you see depends on where you sit." That saying is as true for you as a technical trainer as it is for other people. If you report to the VP of manufacturing, you will naturally focus your attention on manufacturing issues. If you report to the director of MIS, you will naturally focus on MIS issues. If you report to HR, you will naturally focus on HR issues.

Of course, your position on the organization chart affects your ability to command attention—and gain, or sustain, credibility. When you are positioned closest to where the action is, and the group(s) you serve, you will naturally be best positioned to deal with operational problems as they arise. Conversely, if you are placed in reporting relationships that remove you from daily action, you may be less responsive to pressures felt on the firing line.

Collective Bargaining Status

Is the organization unionized? If it is unionized, then the union can either greatly assist technical training or pose a barrier to it. Not all unions share the same perspectives on training. Some unions regard training as a wise investment—so long as workers are paid in ways commensurate with their increased productivity. In other cases, unions actually supply the training for their members. That is one way to restrict entry to the union and control the quality of those who subsequently become union members.

Source for Technical Trainers

Where do technical trainers come from? How are they sourced? Generally speaking, technical trainers may be part-time, full-time, or contractual (Segall, 1995). Part-time technical trainers perform training as an additional work activity, something above and beyond their normal work. Full-time technical trainers devote all of their time to training but are employees of the organization. Contractual technical trainers are employed by vendors, consulting firms, community colleges, vocational schools, or other such providers.

Part-Time Technical Trainers. Workers can serve as part-time technical trainers. They may be asked to give a course to their less-knowledgeable peers, provide on-the-job training or one-on-one coaching. In some situations, relying on part-time technical trainers can be a highly successful approach.

Part-time technical trainers enjoy advantages. First, they know the work better than others who are removed from daily work activities. Second, they are knowledgeable about ways to improve the work process. Third, they possess the credibility with their peers that comes from having performed the work.

At the same time, however, part-time technical trainers may have disadvantages. First, although they know the work, they may not be able to communicate what they know to others. Knowing the work and conducting training on it are two different things. In fact, sometimes those who know the work are contemptuous of those who do not—or, worse, assume that novices know (or should know) more than they actually do. Second, they may not have sufficient time to devote to their training chores, having to deal with work crises and fight daily fires instead. Third and finally, part-time trainers may not get respect from their co-workers and thus face a credibility problem as an authoritative, reliable source of information.

Full-Time Technical Trainers. In a large organization, technical trainers devote their time to technical training only. In these situations, technical trainers can focus on meeting training needs. Since their sole purpose is technical training, trainers are visible to managers and workers alike and are not distracted, as part-time technical trainers may be, with getting the work out. In these situations, technical trainers can establish working relationships with those whose training needs they strive to meet. When this happens, the technical trainers can use the input of the workforce to pinpoint and address training needs.

There are several advantages to using full-time technical trainers. First, they can devote full-time to meeting training needs and can develop professional training skills in ways that make them superlative trainers. Second, they may also have the time to learn time-consuming training delivery methods—such as the intricacies of web-based training or delivery by CD-ROM or videoconference—that would most likely be beyond the time-commitment capabilities of part-time technical trainers. And third, they have the time to follow up with learners, ensuring that they master what they learn and apply it.

But there can also be disadvantages to using full-time technical trainers. They may become overly self-confident in their ability to design training and select training methods. They may not be as knowledgeable—or as credible—about the intricacies of the daily work as those part-time technical trainers who are actually doing the work every day.

However, good technical trainers avoid falling into this trap. They ask for input. They listen carefully to what the workers are saying. They get out and watch people as they work, and they talk to them. They are not prone to the "ivory tower" problem of providing training without first-hand experience with daily problems.

Contractual Technical Trainers. Since having part-time or full-time trainers may not always be the answer for an organization, another way to design and deliver technical training is to rely on outside experts possessing the necessary expertise. Many companies elect to take this route. They rely on trainers supplied by community colleges, four-year universities, or private vendors.

An advantage of using contractual trainers is that they can be chosen carefully for their knowledge of the technical work and for their training delivery skill. Their references can be checked, and their credentials can be verified. They may also be selected to address specific problems for which the organization has no ready supply of talent or expertise. Additionally, they may have gained insights from other organizations that they can share.

The chief drawback of using contractual technical trainers is the cost, since the out-of-pocket expense of employing a contractor can be substantially higher over a short time than relying on full-time or part-time workers. Another drawback is that contractual technical trainers may not be familiar with the unique corporate culture of the organization in which they work and may not be familiar with exactly how the work process is carried out in one organization. To solve this problem, organizations take care to give contractors an orientation to the organization and one key contact to keep the contractors' relationship with the vendor targeted.

Why Should an Organization Support Technical Training?

Why should an organization support technical training? To answer that question and others related to it, the authors sent out a survey in October 2000 to 150 technical trainers chosen at random from three hundred past participants in a Technical Instructor Institute held at the University of Wisconsin-Stout. Ten surveys were returned as undeliverable. Ninety-five trainers responded for a response rate of 65 percent, and the survey results were compiled and analyzed in February 2001. While the results of this small-scale survey are not intended to be representative of all technical trainers in the United States—or elsewhere—they are instructive and do provide useful information.

Of the respondents, a majority (51.6 percent) held the title of technical trainer. Most (50.6 percent) came from organizations employing between five hundred and 1,999 people. Most (64.2 percent) came from manufacturing. Exhibit 1.2 presents information about the industry categories of respondents' organizations; Exhibit 1.3 presents information about the sizes of the respondents' organizations; Exhibit 1.4 presents information about the job categories of respondents; and Exhibit 1.5 summarizes the respondents' perceptions about the chief reasons why their organizations sponsor technical training.

The top four reasons for supporting technical training, as indicated by survey respondents, were tied. The first reason cited was to help organizations "remain competitive." Technical training is a means of giving workers the skills they need to improve production and to meet or exceed customer expectations. Technical training is perhaps the easiest form of training to justify, since it is tied directly to the work that people do.

The second reason cited was to "reduce downtime." Training may make workers more productive and thus less prone to lose valuable time on their jobs.

The third reason cited was to "increase the skills of workers." That is an obvious reason to support technical training. When based on the work that people do, technical training does serve to build individual skills, where *skills* mean *know-how*.

EXHIBIT 1.2.   DISTRIBUTION OF RESPONDENTS BY INDUSTRY

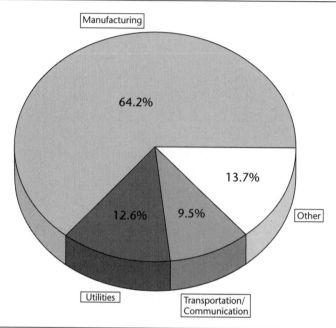

Source: J. Benkowski and W. Rothwell. (2001). *Successful Technical Training Practices.* Unpublished survey results. Stout, WI: The University of Wisconsin.

The fourth reason cited was to "improve productivity." Not surprisingly, managers and other training stakeholders expect training to provide an ample, and often measurable, return on investment. It is intended to help workers increase their work output.

Other reasons also ranked high among the reasons to support technical training. Those included "reducing waste," "increasing the performance of workers," and "multi-skilling." Training builds awareness of the importance of using an organization's resources productively. It can also help to create a pool of workers who can function interchangeably as people go on sick leave or on vacation.

Ranked lower among reasons to support technical training were to "meet safety regulations," "tie to advancement," "improve employees' ability to respond to changing environmental demands," "provide increased opportunities for high potential workers," and "contribute to implementing the organization's strategic plan." From those results, it appears that

EXHIBIT 1.3. DISTRIBUTION OF RESPONDENTS BY SIZE OF ORGANIZATION

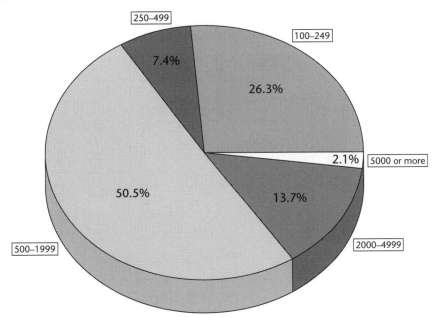

Source: J. Benkowski and W. Rothwell. (2001). *Successful Technical Training Practices.* Unpublished survey results. Stout, WI: The University of Wisconsin.

reasons linked more to the general betterment of the organization ranked lower than those clearly linked to individual productivity improvement.

Ranked lowest of all was to "replace retired workers." While the U.S. workforce is aging and that is creating unique problems (Rothwell, 2000a), the survey respondents in our study did not indicate that technical training is conducted primarily to prepare replacements for retiring workers.

Trends Influencing Technical Training

For more than fifty years, training has not played a dominant role in American life. Indeed, events in training (generally) and in technical training (specifically) have tended to follow the lead established by the U.S. military and by U.S. business.

EXHIBIT 1.4. DISTRIBUTION OF RESPONDENTS BY JOB FUNCTON

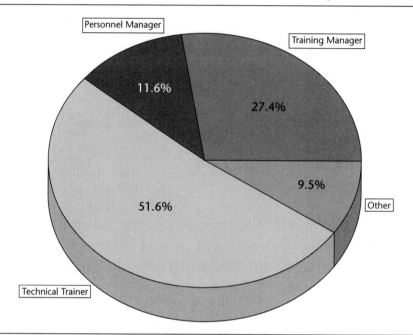

Source: J. Benkowski and W. Rothwell. (2001). *Successful Technical Training Practices.* Unpublished survey results. Stout, WI: The University of Wisconsin.

The most important events surrounding technical training date from World War I and World War II. During wartime, defense contractors found themselves needing to gear up quickly—and get their workers geared up quickly—to handle defense production. It was during that time that government encouraged contractors to improve the quality of their on-the-job training and their supervision. Wartime focused attention on training.

But the future points toward faster change and even more dynamic business conditions (Carnevale, 1995). One survey of training trends between years 2000 and 2005 pointed toward more focus on consumers for information technology training, more interest in "trainer certification" (Eline, 1999b; Miller, 1999), and the effects of an aging labor force (Training Trends 2000–2005, 2000). Other attempts have been made to examine trends affecting training (generally) or technical training (specifically). In an important 1997 study, the American Society for Training and Development

EXHIBIT 1.5. PERCEIVED REASONS WHY ORGANIZATIONS SPONSOR TECHNICAL TRAINING

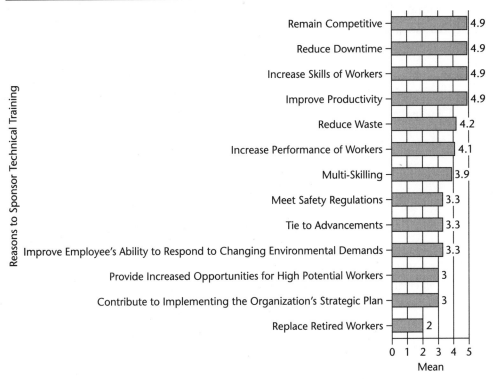

Source: J. Benkowski and W. Rothwell. (2001). *Successful Technical Training Practices.* Unpublished survey results. Stout, WI: The University of Wisconsin.

pinpointed seven key trends that would influence HRD in the future. These trends focus on (Bassi, Buchanan, and Cheney, 1997):

- Training
- Globalization
- Changes in organizational structure
- The way work gets done
- The impact of technology
- The role of the HRD professional
- More attention to the workers

It does not require much of a stretch of the imagination to assert that these trends will also influence technical training in the future. Although these trends are directed to the broader field of workplace learning and performance (WLP) (Rothwell, Sanders, and Soper, 1999), they also influence the direction of technical training and therefore warrant review.

Trend 1: Training

Generally speaking, employers should shift from thinking about training people to improving performance and to cultivating learning organizations where employees are given the opportunity and tools they need to learn new skills. Technical trainers must likewise change from thinking that training is the solution to every problem to thinking about what causes a human performance problem and how that problem may be solved or even how its causes can be averted (Rothwell, Hohne, and King, 2000). Technology will continue to lead the way in which technical training can meet the needs of the rapid changes taking place in business and will make learning tools and information available to workers, often in real time (Van Buren, 1998).

Trainers today are hearing more about the so-called *learning organization*. In a traditional organization, training is usually developed, implemented, and evaluated by the training department staff. Others within the organization may provide some input into the training, but trainers have final say. Courses are designed, developed, and delivered to people in the organization as need arises. The organization may even develop a course catalog. These courses may be offered as needed or on a yearly schedule. Some companies even establish a minimum number of training hours to be completed by employees each year.

The traditional organization thus leaves little discretion for employees to decide what their training needs are or how those needs should be met. But, as organizations have sought to empower workers, build team spirit, and encourage employee involvement, many have begun to experiment with ways of making individuals responsible for their own learning (Rothwell and Sensenig, 1999). The employer makes learning resources available online and in organization-provided learning centers where workers can stop by at their leisure (or during downtime) and participate in instruction as time permits and as individual needs dictate. Individuals may establish individual development plans (IDPs) annually (Dubois and Rothwell, 2000). A learning organization is "an organization skilled at creating, acquiring, and transferring knowledge, and at modifying its behavior to reflect new knowledge and insights" (Garvin, 1993, p. 80).

The learning organization concept thus provides an alternative to a traditional approach to training. The traditional approach may emphasize classroom attendance, night classes at local technical colleges, and similar planned group events. But, as part of the learning organization, employees are encouraged to assume more responsibility for their own learning, which is viewed as a continuous improvement process rather than as one-time learning events. At the same time, technical training is moving away from specific skill content, which can date quickly, and toward more conceptual approaches (Herschbach, 1998). When an organization adopts a learning organization approach, technical trainers find that they must become more creative. No longer will group events dominate technical training. Much can be done through apprenticeships, on-the-job training, coaching, mentoring, online instruction, and other learning technologies. Of course, workers must be equipped with basic skills on which to build other knowledge (O'Roark, 1998).

Trend 2: Globalization

Many organizations today are doing business globally. In fact, global business has been on the rise for some time, spurred by e-commerce and by the increasing ease of international travel.

The implications of global business on technical trainers have been profound. American trainers must promote European standards such as ISO certification (Eline, 1998b; Russo, 1998), and European counterparts pursue the American Malcolm Baldrige National Quality Award. The North American Free Trade Agreement (NAFTA) has made it easier for U.S., Canadian, and Mexican companies to do business with each other in ways comparable to the ease with which commerce flows across the European union.

Technical trainers find themselves challenged to respond to the growing globalization of business. They must often ensure that training materials are culturally adapted for international use (Russell and Driscoll, 1998). They must also oversee the design, development, delivery, and evaluation of technical training materials in multiple languages (Reynolds, 1993).

Trend 3: Changes in Organizational Structure

Companies will continue to reshape themselves to become more customer-oriented, productive, and profitable. These changes are taking place in the ways that companies are restructuring, reengineering, or redesigning their organizations. Each change in structure for an organization often carries with it new challenges for how the work is done, which is a topic of key importance to technical trainers. For that reason, it is likely that technical trainers will need to become more involved in strategic planning and poised to adapt to a dynamically changing environment if technical training is to be supportive of the changes facing organizations.

Trend 4: The Impact of Technology

Two technology-related trends will most likely have the greatest impact in the future.

The first trend is that changing technology will increase workers' skill requirements. Technical trainers will often be tasked to help workers in their companies keep pace with changing technology, upgrading both their basic skills and their technical skills. That is particularly true as organizations begin installing enterprise resource programs (ERPs) that call for a whole host of new skills in reinventing work processes.

The second trend is that training will increasingly be delivered through technologically based or technologically assisted methods. Training will move from the classroom to the web, to e-mail, to video, and to other technology-assisted delivery media. Knowing what media to choose to maximize a return on investment while encouraging worker learning most effectively will be a key to success for future technical trainers.

Looking back over more than twenty years, the training field was facing many of the same challenges it faces today. Perhaps the biggest challenge is to discover methods that keep trainees engaged in the learning process so that there is no need for retraining on the same topics. Many methods have been tried. None are fail-safe, as the secret is really centered in what engages, involves, and motivates adult learners. Historically, much training has been dependent on printed material. That material does not always engage learners, so if learners need help they have to wait on instructors to give it to them.

E-learning, which is associated with technologically based training, when used effectively, has the ability to involve learners. It is not the medium nor the message, but the interactivity that is the key to success. If e-learning can do that better than classroom instruction can, then it will be successful.

Trend 5: The Way Work Gets Done

Increasing amounts of work will be done virtually—that is, by computer from home. While that is not practical for many manufacturing processes, it is practical for many areas in which technical trainers may perform—including IT-related businesses, such as computer programming. To make that even more complicated, much of that virtual work will be done across borders, intensifying the need for cultural sensitivity, language instruction, and translation services.

Another trend beginning to take shape is that workers will become more involved in the training process. Just as they are becoming more involved in the daily operations of their employers, they expect similar empowerment when it comes to their training. Technical trainers will find themselves functioning as facilitators, coaches, and mentors in addition to their traditional role as instructors. It is also likely that technical trainers will serve on action learning teams, some of those international and some of those virtual, to help workers learn in real time by attacking genuine business problems (Rothwell, 1999). Technical trainers will find themselves tasked to develop better methods of identifying and evaluating workers with requisite skills and competencies for their jobs, upgrading workers in line with national and international skill standards, and evaluating the cost-effectiveness of training itself.

Trend 6: More Attention to Workers

Attracting, retaining, and motivating talented workers in the future will likely remain as important as it is today. That is particularly true as an aging Baby Boom generation moves toward retirement, creating a huge shortfall of experienced talent (Rothwell, 2000a). Technical trainers serve an important role in linking employers and employees. They serve as an additional source of information to normal supervisory channels, and their role in attracting, retaining, and motivating workers is just now being explored.

Part of this challenge will center around changing demographics. The U.S. workforce will not remain like it is today. More women, minorities, and older workers will be employed in the foreseeable future. The Hudson Institute published a study entitled *Workforce 2000: Work and Workers for the 21st Century* (Johnston, 1987). The report predicted that women and minorities would represent approximately 85 percent of all new workers entering the workforce. More immigrant workers, many needing English language instruction, will also be employed. Technical trainers will play a key role in helping to attract, retain, and motivate a workforce that will not look the same in the future as it does today.

Summary

In this chapter we defined *technical training* as *instruction to help people conduct the unique aspects of a special kind of work and apply the special tools, equipment, and processes of that work, usually in one organizational setting.* Technical training differs from so-called *soft skills training,* which means *training to help people learn how to interact interpersonally with others.* It also differs from *executive, management, or supervisory training,* which is focused on *training people how to oversee the work of others and (especially in the case of executive and management training) gain competitive advantage for the organization.*

Research supports the view that technical training leads to improved organizational productivity. But technical training's role in any organization hinges on such crucial factors as the level of management support, the type of organization, the size of the organization, the reporting relationship of technical training, the collective bargaining status of the organization, and the source of technical trainers.

A small-scale survey conducted by the authors indicated that the top four reasons for supporting technical training were tied. The first reason cited was to help organizations "remain competitive." The second reason cited was to "reduce downtime." The third reason cited was to "increase the skills of workers." The fourth reason cited was to "improve productivity." Not surprisingly, managers and other training stakeholders expect training to provide an ample return on investment. It is intended to help workers increase their output. And many trends identified by the American Society for Training and Development have a bearing on the future of technical training.

The next chapter will turn to examining the characteristics of effective technical training programs and the competencies of effective technical trainers.

CHAPTER TWO

WHAT ARE THE CHARACTERISTICS OF EFFECTIVE TECHNICAL TRAINING?

This chapter opens with three case study descriptions of technical training programs. The chapter then describes the characteristics of effective technical training and catalogs the unique competencies that technical trainers should possess. In this way, the chapter sets the stage for the remainder of the book by describing desirable characteristics of effective technical training in organizations and for technical trainers who carry it out.

Case Study 1

As you read the case study that follows, write down what the organization is doing exceptionally well. When you finish reading the case, continue on to read the next ones.

Case Study: Technical Training in the U.S. Postal Service*

Public sector organizations are being asked to improve service quality, to be more innovative in providing goods and services, and to reduce operating costs. To achieve these purposes, many agencies are implementing structural changes and are adopting new technologies and innovative strategies for delivering goods and services. As a result, most public sector employees, from senior-level executives to street-level or line personnel, are called upon to upgrade their knowledge and skills. Several options are available to public sector employees for acquiring new skills, such as educational institutions' courses, internal training courses, and informal on-site training. Unfortunately, the types of courses and skills required by employees differ very widely, depending in part upon their position within the agency and in part upon their job responsibilities. For example, a senior executive may desire a conceptual understanding of new management techniques in a particular field, whereas a data-entry clerk may seek to learn more about a new database software package.

Most of the academic literature on training and development in the public sector focuses on the needs of management and assesses ways to improve human relations within the organization through training interventions. Almost no attention has been directed toward technical training programs, and little work has been done regarding training methods used in public agencies.

In the late 1950s, research on human resource management began to emerge that depicted organizations as sociotechnical systems. For example, Trist and Bamforth (1951), who studied work changes in a coal-mining operation, found that technical changes in work processes had a substantial impact on social relations within the organization, suggesting that social and technical aspects of work are not mutually exclusive. Adopting new technologies or innovative approaches to work may lead to changes in an individual's job responsibilities and role within the organization. Furthermore, employees may find that they have been displaced from their jobs as computers and machines are used to do tasks that had previously been their responsibility. The triumph of a high performance organization is the result of more than having state-of-the-art technology; it is rather the ability of the organization to integrate technology into its system of personal interactions in such a manner that the technology does not subvert the organization's social subsystem. High performing organizations often use targeted training to integrate new technologies into the workplace. Several scholars have focused generically on characteristics of technical training in business, and some of these findings do indeed have applications in the public sector. The literature on

*Source: S. Seldon, Multiple Approaches for Meeting Workforce Needs: Technical Training in the United States Postal Service. *Review of Public Personnel Administration*, 1996, *16*(3), 59–73. Used by permission.

technical training indicates that, with the passage of time, the nature of technical work has changed greatly in many areas of work and new technologies have been introduced that alter the basic skill requirements and job responsibilities of many technical workers. The workforce is aging and new technological innovations are being introduced. In turn, organizations are continually reevaluating their existing training and development programs and, consequently, are investing more heavily in training and retraining entry-level and current technical employees. Moreover, Carnevale and Goldstein (1990) contend that the emerging ethnically diverse U.S. workforce often is not equipped to handle the new requirements of public sector jobs because new job-seekers come from populations in which our previous human capital investments have been woefully inadequate. As a result, both private and public organizations may find it difficult in the near future to locate enough skilled workers to meet their demands.

Not only do public agencies compete with one another and with other private sector organizations to attract skilled craftsmen, they must be concerned about retaining these workers. For example, the Armed Forces trains the largest number of skilled craftsmen in the public sector, and over time many of these trainees have matriculated to the private sector for higher wages. Although some research has examined military training and other public sector apprenticeship training programs for blue-collar public sector employees, very little is known about how other public agencies train and develop skilled craftsmen to work in environments where technological changes are occurring (Booth and Rohe, 1988; Riccucci, 1991). Several public organizations, such as the Federal Aviation Administration (FAA) and the United States Postal Service (USPS), have adopted comprehensive and innovative curricula designed to provide intensive, innovative technical training to thousands of new and permanent employees each year.

This article provides an overview of a centralized, cutting-edge approach to technical training employed by the United States Postal Service. It begins with a general overview of the role, structure, and organization of technical training in the USPS and identifies various methods used to provide such training. The discussion then moves to a description of the technical training program of the United States Postal Service, emphasizing curriculum development, alternative delivery methods employed, and the role of technical training in the organization. Given the limited scholarly attention to technical training in the public sector, this article is predominantly descriptive in its focus.

The Nature of Technical Training

In order to perform most types of technical work employees must grasp a theoretical understanding of their job as well as develop the physical and mental skills to accomplish the tasks associated with their jobs. Technical training courses range from high physical activity safety training and heavy equipment operations to sedentary word processing, and impart skills directed at increasing an understanding of, and proficiency in, a specific kind of activity, particularly one involving methods, processes, procedures, or technique (Katz, 1955). These activities are often staples of an organization's operation, and frequently are vital in achieving organizational efficiencies (Carnevale, Gainer, and Schulz, 1990; Mitchell, 1992).

Technical Workforce

Three primary groups comprise the technical workforce: *technical professionals,* such as scientists, architects, and engineers; *technicians,* such as medical records technicians and air traffic controllers; and *skilled craft or blue-collar workers,* such as electricians, machinists, and system operators. The primary and secondary mechanisms for providing training and development to these groups can differ widely. For example, technical professionals receive most of their training through formal education supplemented with both formal and informal training in the field. Typically, technicians have some degree of formal education; however, their field training is of primary importance in skill and knowledge development. Technicians' curricula are job-specific, they tend to focus on the principles of new technologies, typically emphasize new uses for existing technologies, and often entail official professional certification or licensing (Carnevale, Gainer, and Schulz, 1990).

Skilled craft workers are unlikely to have formal educational training in their trade and, therefore, are dependent on the type of formal and informal training on the job that is found in apprenticeship programs. As a result, the training opportunities provided by an organization are critical in the current and future skill development of technically competent blue-collar workers.

As mentioned previously, the nature of technical training of blue-collar employees has evolved because of changes in the work processes primarily due to computerization or mechanization of jobs. Some agencies, such as the USPS, have adopted some more technologically advanced approaches to ensure that employees will possess the necessary knowledge and skills to be productive organizational members. In addition, training and development curricula have been expanded to include numerous specialized topics such as safety, environmental regulation, employee assistance, and diversity.

Work Content and Organizational Technical Training Structure

The extent to which technical training has the potential to contribute to the strategic mission and operative objectives of an organization depends in part on how technical training is controlled and where the technical training function is located within the organization (Carnevale, Gainer, and Schulz, 1990). Technical training operations are typically organized using one of the following three structural arrangements: centralized, decentralized, or a combination of both. The following summaries highlight the merits and identify the organizational characteristics most appropriate for each structural arrangement (Carnevale, Gainer, and Schulz, 1990).

A *centralized training structure* is one in which training is controlled or coordinated from a single point within the organization. This structural arrangement is advantageous in that it reduces potential duplication of efforts among different departments and units and should lower training costs as staff, material resources, equipment, and facilities are consolidated into a single entity. Moreover, a centralized program should promote uniformity in focus and quality of training, and ensure that all employees have access to the same training opportunities.

A *decentralized training structure* is one in which control over training responsibilities is delegated to lower organizational levels, and the organization lacks a common point of coordination among different training partners and units. Such an approach works well in organizations that produce multiple goods and services using different processing methods or levels of technology. When organizational units have similar products or processes, a decentralized structure may not be as efficient and may not effectuate a link between training and the overall mission of the organization.

Under a *combined structural arrangement,* certain training responsibilities or programs are controlled or coordinated from a single point within the organization. When appropriate, other phases or types of training, however, are decentralized and implemented by lower levels. This hybrid arrangement incorporates an element of central control and influence, and at the same time allows localities to meet their unique training needs.

As suggested earlier, the structural arrangement of the training function influences the strategies employed by organizations to adapt to changing technologies and work processes. The type of training structure selected by an organization may depend, at least in part, on the extent to which the work can be standardized. With a centralized training function, a single entity is responsible for systematically planning, developing, and delivering a training system. This type of approach is best suited for work that lends itself to standardization. The organization has more control over the development and direction of training and, therefore, should be able to socialize employees to the overall mission and objectives of the organization more easily. Furthermore, a centralized training system should provide continuity and uniformity in training for employees dispersed throughout the organization doing similar jobs. When training responsibilities are decentralized, tasks are delegated to various organizational units and individuals who are typically in direct contact with line personnel. The primary benefit of this approach is that supervisors and/or training specialists assess the performance of individual employees in specific local contexts to determine training needs. Thus, the deficiencies and needs of smaller units and individual employees may be addressed more directly and expediently when training responsibilities are delegated.

Providers of Technical Training

As a whole, technical training has been described as being highly fragmented since multiple entities are typically used to implement specific training courses. In many cases organizations rely on internal trainers, but just as frequently they refer employees to educational providers and negotiate contracts with external entities to provide training.

An organization may depend in part on some or all of the following institutions for its technical training and development requirements:

1. Educational Institutions: Elementary and secondary schools, noncollegiate post-secondary vocational schools, two-year community colleges, technical institutes, four-year colleges and universities
2. Nonschool Training Institutions: Apprenticeships, vendors, professional associations, unions, community organizations, private instructors, correspondence schools, informal nonworkrelated learning

Organizations are still in the best position to conduct internal technical training needs assessments to identify new skills and knowledge required by workers (Carnevale and Goldstein, 1990). However, whether an organization is the most appropriate institution for delivering the training depends on the structure and size of its training staff, the delivery methods used by its instructors, and its organizational resources.

Training Delivery Methods

Some organizations have adopted innovative teaching approaches that have improved the quality and quantity of technical training and, subsequently, have made them less reliant on outside providers for training. Unlike ten years ago, many organizations now have access to high-tech delivery techniques such as satellite networks, interactive video and computers, and audio networks. These methods have been touted as being more cost-effective and time-efficient than traditional methods of training, and they have expanded many organizations' capacities for conducting in-house training (Carnevale, Gainer, and Schulz, 1990). These mechanisms also enable organizations to standardize and to centralize training while delivering courses in a more decentralized set of settings (Carnevale, Gainer, and Schulz, 1990).

The most efficient and effective programs are designed and delivered in response to the work content and specific needs of the organization and its employees. The structure of the organization's training system will affect the manner in which both organizational and employee needs are assessed, and influence the strategy adopted by the organization for meeting these needs. Once overall technical training goals and objectives are established, decisions must be made regarding who will provide the training and with respect to the most effective method of delivering courses. These choices are critical as they ultimately shape the quality of training courses. A well-developed training system provides an infrastructure that allows the organization to adapt quickly to changes in work processes and to build employee competence.

The Nature of Technical Training in the United States Postal Service

With the rapid expansion and growing complexity of postal mechanization, the Postal Service established a centralized training center to strengthen the quality and quantity of training received by technicians and skilled craft persons. The National

Technical Training Center (TTC) was opened in Norman, Oklahoma, in 1969 to provide such training. However, by the early 1980s, the Postal Service judged it needed a cutting-edge, technologically smart central resident facility designed with sufficient flexibility to meet the changing needs of its workforce. The Postal Service opened a new campus training facility in September of 1988 that contained over 40 classrooms and 43 labs designed specifically for USPS technical training. The typical classroom and laboratory has removable walls, allowing the space to be quickly modified as equipment and learning programs change. Each classroom seats fourteen students, contains video players, monitors, projection screens, and connects to an internal studio for video broadcasts. The facility contains the latest in learning technology with complete video tape and audio-visual production studios. A 433,000 square foot, 1,000 room housing complex is located next to the TTC facility, which provides students with easy access to the training facility. Because of the size and sophistication of the TTC, the USPS is able to provide technical training to thousands of employees each year.

Structure, Organization, and Curriculum of the National Technical Training Center

Most phases of the USPS technical training curriculum are centralized. The majority of trainers are located in the TTC where they design, develop, conduct, and evaluate most of the training courses. In 1995, the TTC employed a staff of 249, and of those 107 (42.97 percent) were contract employees. The USPS uses many contract trainers and support staff, who are presently employed through an agreement with the University of Oklahoma. USPS has found that contract staff provide a cost-effective method of supplementing a core of permanent, full-time technical trainers.

The technical training curriculum includes over 120 courses on subjects such as computerized mail processing equipment, building systems, data communications, and information systems, postage vending machines, and postal vehicles. The current curriculum includes apprenticeship training, supervisory training, retraining, and new technology training. A curriculum planning and development team is responsible for evaluating the new and changing training needs of the USPS. This team works closely with field customers and USPS specialized training teams to develop new classes and to evaluate existing training courses.

In total, more than 1,800 course offerings were taught to over 39,000 employees in 1995. The facilities and environmental support team taught the most courses (31.59 percent) and trained the most employees (44.77 percent), averaging three days of training per student. However, the more technologically advanced courses are longer, on the average providing 8 to 10 days of training per student.

The number of students trained by TTC has been increasing generally since 1988. During 1995, 15,400 students received resident training and 23,706 received training in the field, representing a 33.58 percent increase in resident training and a

81.85 percent increase in field training from 1994. These increases reflect an enhancement in training across the postal curriculum, especially in environmental support courses such as waste reduction, recycling, and hazard communications. The significant growth in numbers of trainees between 1994 and 1995 is due in part to the mixture of delivery methods employed by TTC; that is, more students completed distance learning training courses in 1995 than in previous years.

Training Delivery Approaches

Currently, the TTC combines various delivery methods such as resident training, distance learning, self-study, and on-site field training to administer courses to thousands of postal service employees each year. The following discussion focuses on resident training and distance learning because they are TTC's most frequently employed methods.

Resident Training. Resident training is provided at the TTC to employees from across the United States. The TTC often operates resident training sessions up to 20 hours a day. The underlying assumption of resident training is that courses should bridge theoretical concepts and practical application. During a typical course, students spend part of their time attending class lectures and participating in class discussions, and the other part of their training is spent in an adjacent training laboratory practicing the concepts that are learned in the classroom. The average number of students receiving resident training has fluctuated since 1988, due largely to budget constraints and advances in alternative delivery methods.

Distance Learning. The TTC first incorporated distance learning as a delivery technique in the late 1980s to meet the escalating training needs of their employees due to the adoption of new technologies. The TTC operates one of the most versatile distance-learning delivery systems in the nation, incorporating audio, graphics, and live satellite training. Postal-owned networks are used for distance learning, including the Postal Satellite Training Network (PSTN), Postal Audio Training Network (PATN), and audiographics systems that are being upgraded to multimedia capability. The Postal Service has been recognized as an innovative leader in distance learning and teletraining by the U.S. Distance Learning Association (United States Postal Service Technical Training Center, 1995). The use of distance learning enabled the TTC to train nearly twice as many employees in 1995 as it did in 1992 when its faculty was downsized in the reorganization of the USPS. In 1995, 17,595 students (45 percent) of the U.S. Postal Service Technical Training Center's students took courses in five major curriculum areas via the TTC's distance learning networks.

The Postal Satellite Training Network uplinks live satellite broadcasts to over 310 sites throughout the United States. The video is one-way, with two-way telephone interaction between instructors and students. During 1995, over 11,700 students participated in 18 different substantive training courses offered at different times on the

PSTN. For example, using the satellite broadcasting network, the TTC trained over 2,400 employees in one year on the Vending PBSM 624 machine, a task which would have taken over 3.5 years to complete using the resident training approach.

In 1995, over 5,800 students received training in nine courses over the Postal Audio and Audiographics training networks. Over 460 postal facilities are equipped to receive both teletraining and audiographic courses via the PATN. The audio teletraining uses a telephone bridge to link instructors from the Training Center to postal students in their home offices. The network of audiographics adds interactive computer graphics to teletraining lectures. Instructors are responsible for developing and designing computer graphics training materials that are installed on computers located in participating field offices. The instructor leads the course from his or her computer in the TTC and controls the students' progression through the training course. The trainees and instructor are able to interact both verbally and with the computer by using the keyboard and screen. For example, the trainee or trainer can write on their computer screen pad and the data is transferred to the computer screens of all participants.

Additionally, trainers integrate alternative delivery methods when appropriate. For example, in 1995 the TTC offered eight weeks of training for 670 employees on the Remote Bar Coding System. Seven of those eight weeks required that students reside at the TTC and participate in a lab-intensive course. One week, however, was taught using audiographics and resulted in an approximate savings of $800 per student in avoided travel, food, and housing costs (United States Postal Service, 1995).

The TTC has used distance learning programs to achieve some of the same goals as resident training, but only reach larger audiences in shorter periods of time. For example, a typical resident course requires two instructors for 14 students for lecture and lab, while a typical distance learning course uses one centralized instructor to teach up to 56 students at 14 sites. With the necessary equipment installed throughout field offices, the USPS will be able to continue to increase employees' access to technical training courses by adapting existing courses and developing new courses to be taught via the postal training networks.

Changing Work Processes in the USPS

Since 1987, the Postal Service has invested over $2.6 billion for capital equipment to automate mail processing and delivery point sequencing operations. In the past four years, the Postal Service installed over 4,000 optical character readers, delivery bar code sorters, and other pieces of equipment at postal facilities throughout the country. By the end of 1997, about 12,000 pieces of automated sorting equipment will be in place (United States Postal Service, 1994a). Postal automation plans for the 1990s call for additional and dramatic expansion in the use of high-technology equipment to process the nation's mail. This expansion is expected to highlight critical requirements for more advanced technical training. With foresight, the Postal Service created a training infrastructure that will permit them to adapt to technological advances and to address the changing workforce needs of their employees.

The Postal Service has designed a delivery system that has not increased in constant dollar cost during the last 15 years. The 1995 average training cost in 1980 dollars per training day is about 5 percent lower than it was in 1980. Thus, when adjusting for inflation, the TTC is providing technical training at a slightly more efficient rate than in 1980. This trend no doubt reflects the incorporation of alternative and innovative training delivery mechanisms.

USPS' Technical Training Delivery Methods and Knowledge Acquisition

USPS' technical training design provides it opportunities to implement cutting-edge training practices. Several of these approaches can be linked to contemporary theories of knowledge acquisition that extend the scientific paradigm and enhance technical rationality. The following discussion will focus on two aspects of the USPS training system that have direct implications for knowledge acquisition: (1) hands-on training; and (2) distance learning.

The resident technical training courses are designed so that employees learn and acquire skills by using hands-on learning laboratories to supplement traditional classroom instruction. This approach lends itself to resolving learning problems exposed by the epistemological investigations of Schoen (1983), Schmidt (1993), and Zuboff (1988).

Schoen specifically argues that an individual knows differently while at work than before or after work. He draws a distinction between knowing-in-action or knowledge from work and knowledge-in-action or knowledge extracted from work that is theoretically developed and, subsequently, applied to specific work situations. Moreover, Schoen demonstrates that individuals learn while they are engaged in work, an idea which he illustrates to be different from viewing work externally. The primary implication of his research for training is that knowledge obtained outside of the context of work must then be translated into a sense for the work while working. According to Schoen (1983), it seems right to say that our knowing is in our action. As mentioned previously, the TTC structures most classes to incorporate both traditional classroom lectures and exercises and hands-on lab sessions. Trainees are typically introduced to new diagnostic principles and theories in the classroom that they later apply in a hands-on lab setting. This approach enables employees to compare, contrast, and synthesize what they learned in both settings.

This approach also corresponds with the strategy used by Schmidt, a student of Schoen's, to explain discrepancies in analyses of major disasters (using the 1975 failure of the Teton Dam in Idaho as an example). Schmidt (1993) demonstrates that technical-rational and organizational explanations alone are insufficient, and that attention must be directed toward the testimony of those who have developed a "feel" for the work to capture the subtleties of the situation.

The second aspect of the technical training system of the USPS that will be highlighted in terms of knowledge acquisition is distance learning. The TTC's use of distance learning to deliver lectures fits with Zuboff's work on the impact of computers on the workplace. In a pathbreaking study, Zuboff focuses on the way the computer interrupts the direct linkage between judgment and sensory observation of physical work.

As the medium of knowing was transformed by computerization, the placid unit of experience and knowledge was disturbed. Accomplishing work depended upon the ability to manipulate symbolic, electronically presented data. Instead of using their bodies as instruments of acting on equipment and materials, the task relationship became mediated by the information system (Zuboff, 1988).

Because courses taught via the distance learning networks also incorporate hands-on segments, the USPS increases the diagnostic capabilities of technicians being trained in increasingly computer-mediated systems. The Technical Training Center's combination of symbolic instruction and applied learning offers considerable opportunity for future study and evaluation similar to the approaches used by Schoen (1983), Schmidt (1993), and Zuboff (1988).

Conclusion

The USPS has a state-of-the-art resident technical training facility and faculty that have the capability of training over 39,000 technical workers a year. Training among the various types of technical jobs is closely coordinated because USPS has a centralized technical training center. Furthermore, using advances in delivery techniques, the TTC has significantly increased student access to training and improved the overall cost-effectiveness of technical training. The technical training infrastructure of the USPS serves as a model to other public agencies. Most significantly, this training system directly supports the agency's strategic goals by ensuring that all employees are provided with the best technical training available in either the public or private sector.

This article should stimulate more consideration and discussion among practitioners and academicians about the future role of technical training in the public service, the organizational and delivery options available to agencies, and the impact of these decisions on employees' knowledge acquisition. Moreover, it offers an example of an existing program that may be used as a prototype for updating and improving other public sector technical training systems. Future research should be directed toward understanding the process of developing technical training curricula, the potential uses of technical training in the public sector, and the advantages and disadvantages of different structural arrangements of training systems, alternative training providers, and innovative delivery methods. Finally, this article has sought to promote the argument that the attention of public personnel administration academics and professionals should be directed toward understanding the impact of technical training on the social and interpersonal aspects of public organizations.

References

Booth, W. S. and C. A. Rohe (1988). Recruiting for Women and Minorities in the Fire Service: Solution for Today's Challenges. *Public Personnel Management, 17,* 53–61.

Carnevale, A. and L. J. Gainer (1989). *The Learning Enterprise.* Washington, DC: American Society for Training and Development.

Carnevale, A. and H. Goldstein (1990). Schooling and Training for Work in America: An Overview, pp. 25–54 in L. A. Ferman, M. Hoyman, J. Cutcher Gershenfeld, and E. J. Savoie (eds.) *New Developments in Worker Training: A Legacy for the 1990s.* Madison, WI: Industrial Relations Research Association.

Carnevale, A., L. J. Gainer, and E. R. Schulz. (1990). *Training the Technical Workforce.* San Francisco, CA: Jossey-Bass Publishers.

Carnevale, A., L. J. Gainer, and A. S. Meltzer (1990). *Workplace Basics: The Essential Skills Employers Want.* San Francisco, CA: Jossey-Bass Publishers.

Katz, R. (1955). Skills of an Effective Administrator. *Harvard Business Review, 33,* 33–42.

Riccucci, N. M. (1991). Apprenticeship Training in the Public Sector: Its Use and Operation for Meeting Skilled Craft Needs. *Public Personnel Management, 20,* 181–193.

Schmidt, M. R. (1993). Alternative Kinds of Knowledge and Why They Are Ignored. *Public Administration Review, 53,* 525–530.

Schoen, D. A. (1983). *The Reflective Practitioner: How Professionals Think in Action.* New York: Basic Books.

Trist, E. L. and K. W. Bamforth (1951). Some Social and Psychological Consequences of the Longwall Method of Coal Getting. *Human Relations, 4,* 3–38.

United States Postal Service, Technical Training. (1995a). *Distance Learning.* Norman, OK: Technical Training Center.
  (1990). *FY1990 Annual Report.* Norman, OK: Technical Training Center.
  (1991). *FY1991 Annual Report.* Norman, OK: Technical Training Center.
  (1992). *FY1992 Annual Report.* Norman, OK: Technical Training Center.
  (1993). *FY1993 Annual Report.* Norman, OK: Technical Training Center.
  (1994a). *FY1994 Annual Report.* Norman, OK: Technical Training Center.
  (1994b). *FY1994 Annual Report.* Norman, OK: Technical Training Center.
  (1995). *FY1995 Annual Report.* Norman, OK: Technical Training Center.

White, J. D. and G. B. Adams, (eds.) (1994). *Research in Public Administration: Reflections on Theory and Practice.* Thousand Oaks: SAGE Publications.

Whitehill, B. V. and B. A. McDonald (1993). Improving Learning Persistence of Military Personnel by Enhancing Motivation in a Technical Training Program. *Simulation and Gaming, 24,* 294–313.

Zuboff, S. (1988). *In the Age of the Smart Machine: The Future of Work and Power.* New York: Basic Books.

Case Study 2

As you read the next case study, continue to make notes about what the organization is doing exceptionally well. When you finish reading the case, continue to read about the characteristics of effective technical training in organizations and the competencies of effective technical trainers.

Case Study: Southwestern Power's In-House Technical Training Program*

In 1988, the Southwestern Power Administration (Southwestern) acquired the services of Black and Veatch for technical support both on- and off-site. The small, recently resurrected engineering department of Southwestern, one of five power marketing administrations under the Department of Energy, found itself with a large backlog of work on its hands. This work, which had accumulated during the years that Southwestern was without an engineering staff, was needed to maintain and upgrade the utility's three-state transmission system.

Due to the lack of sufficient experienced personnel, Southwestern engineers, some recent college graduates, were required to manage multiple engineering projects with very short-time requirements. Although the new staff was making progress, the backlog of work continued to grow. Southwestern decided to acquire help in the form of a technical support contractor. After an open, competitive process, Southwestern selected the firm of Black and Veatch to provide on-site support through a team of experienced engineers located at Southwestern's Tulsa headquarters. Additional off-site support was provided from other B and V offices throughout the U.S. Three years later, in the fall of 1991, with the workload finally under control, Southwestern found itself with another impending problem: The B and V contract was due to expire in 1993, at which time Southwestern would lose all of the on-site contractor staff together with their accumulated experience.

Constructing Support-Engineering Infrastructure

Much of Southwestern's engineering staff still had less than 5 years experience, having had little actual hands-on design, since the primary duties of Southwestern engineers were as project managers, not as designers. B and V had provided assistance in many areas. There was a need to capture and perpetuate their expertise at Southwestern prior

---

*Source: Durham, J. Southwestern Power Administration's In-House Technical Training Program. *Transmission and Distribution,* 1992, 44(13), 28–32. Used by permission.

to the expiration of their contract. After meetings with B and V, Southwestern engineers drew up a plan to develop and sustain an infrastructure for their future branch of engineering. This plan included several key elements. Southwestern engineers would gain hands-on design experience on a small number of projects with B and V providing guidance and support. B and V would assist Southwestern in the development and refinement of standards for design and drafting. Southwestern would utilize automation to the maximum extent feasible, including the acquisition or development of computerized tools to assist in planning and design. A computer engineer would be hired to oversee the overall automation process. B and V would act as consultants to this effort.

In coordination with Southwestern's Division of Maintenance, the engineering branch would improve the project management process. Since Southwestern's small engineering staff was responsible for a wide variety of technical areas, the agency could not afford a great deal of specialization. Cross training was one way to minimize the creation of islands of expertise. Southwestern would develop a comprehensive, sustainable training program for present and future Southwestern engineering and maintenance personnel. This program would include core courses in power system planning design and project management. Courses that met specific, ongoing needs for Southwestern would have standard manuals and would be videotaped for future use. B and V would develop and conduct training courses in power-systems design and related areas.

Design Courses Needed

Substation and transmission line design are usually not found as courses in the engineering curriculum in engineering schools. Design personnel for these systems typically learn their craft on the job or through supplemental formal training at seminars, professional association meetings, and other specialized courses. B and V had recognized the need for a more formal training program for their own personnel to close some experience gaps and bring all design personnel up to a common base level of design knowledge and skills. After surveying their design personnel, B and V created a set of courses for in-house training.

Southwestern's engineering personnel became aware of these training courses, and after reviewing the contents of these courses, Southwestern decided that, with some modifications, several of these courses could form part of the core courses for Southwestern engineering personnel. The decision was made to have B and V hold these courses at Southwestern's headquarters at Tulsa. Since there were only a few engineers in Southwestern's Engineering and Planning branch, personnel who might benefit from these courses from other organizational elements with Southwestern were invited. These elements included operations, maintenance, customer service, plus environmental, health and safety. Personnel from the hydropower branch of the Tulsa District Corps of Engineers were also invited to attend. Since many of the course attendees were not engineers, it would be somewhat of an experience to see how useful these courses might be.

The decision was made to videotape the classes to allow those who could not attend the first course offerings to view the courses at a later date. The tapes would also be available for newly hired personnel when they came on board. Copies of the videotaped courses and manuals would also be made available to Southwestern's customers for the price of duplication. The original videotapes would be in 8mm Hi-8 format with copies made to standard 1 and 2-inch VHS. Taping the original in standard VHS was deemed to be of too low resolution to display material on the overheads and markerboard. The camera was manned to permit zooming and panning but no editing of the tapes was performed. Speakers wore a clip-on microphone to assure a consistent level of sound both for the live audience and the videotape.

Description of Training

The courses began in November of 1991 and were completed in April of 1992. Class time was about 6 hours per day with individual courses ranging from one to three days. B and V professional personnel, with considerable hands-on experience in each of the areas covered, taught the courses using a variety of audio-visual equipment—transparencies on overhead projectors, slide presentations, drawing board, and projected computer displays. Previous knowledge required of students included algebra, some trigonometry, and basic physics. The emphasis of these courses was on practical applications rather than theory. A brief description of the courses follows.

Substation Design I: An Introduction to Substation Layout and Design. Emphasis is placed upon the systems approach design with constraints such as space, geography, and utility standards. Insulation coordination, bus design and arrangement, lighting protection, and equipment selection are covered in-depth.

Substation Design II: A Continuation of Substation Design I. Emphasis is placed upon system specifics and equipment such as construction specifications and methods, repair and replacement, SF6-insulated substations, rigid and strain bus, ground-grid design, control-building design, and special problems related to high-voltage and space considerations.

Control and Protection: An Overview of Protective Relaying Philosophy and Design Techniques. The course participants are introduced to fundamentals of electronics, protective relaying philosophy, transformer and reactor protection, bus and distribution protection, line protection and control-panel layout, schematics, wiring, and related drawings. Zones of protection and various types of equipment are covered.

Transmission Line Design I: Introduces Overhead Transmission Line Design. Basic principles of electricity and magnetism, fundamentals of mechanical loading, insulator clearance and spacing, national Electric Safety Code Standards, sag-tension data, structure selection, and layout design are covered.

Transmission Line Design II: A Continuation of Transmission Line Design I.
Emphasis is placed on design criteria development, insulation coordination, design of
structures and foundations, and right-of-way planning.

*Electric and Magnetic Fields (EMF): A Presentation on the Physics and Regu-
lations Related to Electric and Magnetic Fields.* This course is a presentation of
factual information on the nature of electric and magnetic fields. It includes a method
of determining the strength of fields near electric lines and substations and summarizes studies and reps completed by others on health-related issues. Existing laws
and regulations are reviewed, along with current utility practices addressing public
concerns.

Participants rated courses from GOOD to EXCELLENT on course evaluations. Class
sizes ranged from 20 to 35 people. Most of the comments from both field and office
personnel were favorable. Some of the comments on the courses were:

- "The depth of knowledge of the instructors was a strong point. These seminars will
  enable us to be more informed with the public."
- "Excellent marshalling of physical aspects and general issues of EMF."
- "A strong point was the hands-on section on plans and profile."
- "Very good speakers; they were able to speak to the attendees at their level of
  comprehension."
- "One of the highlights of the transmission line design course included a contest to
  design the best transmission line between two substations. The class divided up
  into teams of 3 to 5 people for this competition. There were benefits from simultaneously teaching the courses to personnel from both headquarters and the field.
  The field personnel gained some knowledge of the process of design, while office
  personnel benefited from the many observations which the field provided based
  on their practical experience. Field personnel attending the courses included a
  mix of supervisory, engineering, electrical craftsmen, and line maintenance personnel. Other attendees included dispatchers from Southwestern's control center,
  a public utilities specialist and an environmental specialist."

The Future for Technical Training at Southwestern

Southwestern considers the training courses a success, but would make the following changes for future courses:

- "Provide more group activities like the transmission-line competition."
- "Use computer-generated slides where possible."
- "Lengthen classes to allow more hands-on workshops."

Other courses still planned for engineering planning personnel include:

- TQM for the engineering environment
- Project management: One to two week comprehensive overview of
    1. Power system operations.
    2. Power system supervisory and control.
    3. Power system communications.
    4. Power system analysis.
    5. Power system planning.
    6. Hydropower integration.
    7. Short circuit relaying courses.

These overview courses would probably be taught in-house by Southwestern personnel. In addition to videotaping, Southwestern is also investigating the possibility of developing computerized instruction tutorials.

Personnel in the Division of Administration and Rates at Southwestern have requested that courses be prepared for non-technical personnel. These courses would provide an overview of engineering and planning activities at Southwestern. Several Southwestern people who have attended the Western Area Power Administration's (WAPA) Introduction to Power Systems Operation course were impressed by the ability of WAPA's staff to teach complex material in a way that non-technical people could understand. Southwestern is presently evaluating plans to develop one or two overview courses for non-technical people to be taught by Southwestern engineering personnel. It may also be possible for Southwestern to include its customers in future courses. One subject that is always of considerable interest is EMF.

Case Study 3: Training at Rockwell Collins*

Rockwell Collins' new learning strategy will allow the company to expand its training offerings by 40 percent while it saves $14 million over three years—and that's a conservative estimate.

Did that get your attention? It should. During the next three years, training at the communication and aviation electronics giant will evolve from a fragmented classroom curriculum into a centralized, technology-based approach to learning.

To pull off this feat, Rockwell Collins began by formulating a plan, an 82-page strategic plan, that outlines a move from primarily classroom-based training to "alternative" learning formats—self-paced Web-based training (WST) at the desktop, computer-based

---

*Source: Fister, S. Reinventing Training at Rockwell Collins. *Training*, 2000, *37*(4), 64–70. Used by permission.

training (CST) courses on CD-ROM via kiosks and learning labs, and live training via on-line virtual classrooms. By 2003, year four of the plan, 70 percent of the curriculum will be delivered via technology, and many of the courses that remain in the class-room will have CST or WST components to make them more efficient, says Cliff Purington, manager of learning and development at RC's headquarters in Cedar Rapids, IA.

A key component of Rockwell's transformation is the collaboration it created among training vendors to ensure it could build an efficient training system. But more on that later.

History Lessons

An organization with 50 years of history behind it, Rockwell Collins today manufactures cockpit instruments, in-flight entertainment systems, and ground-communication tools. It has 15 international offices in addition to its 42 domestic locations. How do you change the approach to training?

First you need to find out what you're dealing with. Purington was hired in September '98 to change the way the company delivered training to its 14,000 employees, half of whom are based outside the Cedar Rapids headquarters. He and his team, which included The Performance Engineering Group Inc. (PEG), an organizational effectiveness and change management consultancy in Santa Barbara, CA, began by investigating the training environment and collecting existing training data.

"We needed a thorough understanding of the culture, structure, infrastructure, perceptions of the current training, and any other data that would allow Purington to get a clear picture of the organization," says Chris Butler, president of PEG. "Rockwell Collins has always been committed to training. They've always invested a lot of money and resources on training." Even in hard times, when many companies were cutting back training staffs, Rockwell maintained its training investment, he says.

"The problem was that 100 percent of the investment was going to classroom instruction," says Purington. The training department simply couldn't keep up with the company's changing needs through classroom training alone, he says.

The learning and development team interviewed and surveyed hundreds of employees about their reactions to traditional training and their take on outside-the-classroom alternatives. The team reviewed past training budgets and delivery methods, digging up figures on hours spent in training per employee per year, repeat rates for certain classes, student cancellation rates, no-show rates and class evaluations. They also analyzed Rockwell's "best place to work" attitude surveys, which are conducted every two years to measure job satisfaction.

Seven years' worth of historical data, results from more than 300 employee surveys, interviews with key leaders, and several focus group discussions revealed some startling facts. For example, of the 1,400 courses offered during that time, 72 percent were conducted only once. On average, 28 percent of registered participants were no-shows, and the 7,000 RC employees outside the Cedar Rapids headquarters had very limited access to training. Almost 40 percent of them received 15 or fewer hours of training per year.

Fifty-three percent of those surveyed said work demands had forced them to cancel out of a scheduled training session. Another 48 percent said they had to leave training because of work demands, and 92 percent said they'd been unable to attend scheduled training three or more times.

Surveys also reflected support among RC employees for a new approach to learning: Sixty-two percent wanted to receive training outside of traditional classrooms; 72 percent wanted to be able to start and stop training when they wanted to; and 75 percent wanted to learn at their own pace. In other words, Rockwell employees were ready for the change to computer-based training.

A Map for the Future

With this data in hand, the team developed a plan outlining the future of training at Rockwell Collins. It calls for delivering 70 percent of Rockwell's curricula via computer-based learning methods by the end of 2001. In December of 1999, the company was already at the 30 percent mark.

The new learning system will use a number of elements to create a rich training environment. All business units will have learning councils, made up of RC managers and internal learning consultants, who will oversee training needs analyses and evaluate whether training is the right solution for performance problems. RC will participate in an industry cooperative of large organizations that share specific training needs, creating an extranet of computer-based courses that all co-op members can use, thus reducing the cost of training for all. RC also hopes to offer online graduate courses and possibly degree programs to employees through Kansas State University.

[Says] Cliff Purington: "The problem was that 100 percent of our training investment was going to classroom instruction."

The learning and development (L and D) team tied the strategic training plan to the company's vision and bottom line to ensure upper management buy-in. But the new approach to learning wasn't too tough to sell once the team determined that technology-assisted delivery would reduce Rockwell's training budget by a minimum of 40 percent during the first three years of implementation.

The L and D team eventually calculated that, over the three-year life of the grand plan, the company would save $14 million on labor, travel, and off-site expenses—airfare, hotel costs, and reduction of on-the-job hours lost to off-site training. "We used more than 40 algorithms to show payback, and those numbers were validated by the finance group," says Purington.

The $14 million savings does not reflect the return on investment attributable to improved job performance or better retention rates expected from offering increased just-in-time training. That's why the L and D team feels $14 million is a conservative estimate. Factor in these less quantifiable paybacks, contends Purington, and he'd expect a savings of twice that much.

Even though switching to online and computer-based training required a significant investment in 1999, the L and D team did it with the same training budget it had in 1998—6.6 percent of annual payroll. "We delivered all of the necessary training, bought the hardware and software, and hired four more people with the same budget," says Purington. Most of the savings came from the purchase of a library of information-technology courses from SmartForce (formerly CBT Systems), which saved RC the cost of sending 3,000 people to classroom courses.

Teaming Up Vendors

In January 1999, with management's support and a plan in place, the L and D team started looking for vendors. Rather than interviewing a slew of companies individually, listening to proposals, and handing down his decisions, Purington invited 50 vendors to a group meeting. First he outlined the plan, then he made an announcement: "No one of you can offer me a turnkey solution, and I don't want to manage a whole lot of vendors. I want a team, with everyone on a level playing field."

Gathering the vendors together in this fashion caused a certain, shall we say, apprehension. "They were all fairly uncomfortable," says Steve Junion, an IT specialist at Rockwell and member of the L and D team. This is an uncommon approach, PEG's Butler acknowledges. There's not one contractor and a lot of subcontractors; there's no leader, except Purington and his team. In fact, many of the vendors balked at the idea. After the initial meeting, a few told Purington that it would never work.

But it has. Less than a year later, 12 vendors were on board, sharing secrets and modifying their products to work with competitors' products. Among those vendors are Allen Communications and Gulliver Ritchie, both of whom are customizing specialty courses for RC such as training on the damaging effect of static electricity; Pinnacle Multimedia is providing its Learning Management System to manage all of Rockwell's training online; SmartForce and The Belgard Group are supplying computer-based off-the-shelf IT and soft-skills courses; Centra Software is bringing its virtual-classroom offering to the table; and several others are providing hardware and software.

After their initial hesitation, vendors have overwhelmingly endorsed the team format. "I like this approach because the company has the knowledge and can judge the ability of the people helping them," says Steve Allen, technology chair at Allen Communications in Salt Lake City. "It's the most innovative approach we've seen," says Bill Belgard of the Belgard Group, a leadership training consultancy based in Portland, OR. "All of the vendors are working together like a symphony instead of a bunch of solo acts."

Still, putting a group of vendors in a room and telling them to work together isn't enough to make it happen. In this case it's working because Rockwell Collins has a detailed plan that maps out exactly what it wants and who is going to provide it. "The strategic plan is key to the process," says Jim Kosse, regional account manager for SmartForce. "We can see where we fill a role." For example, the plan lays out the criteria and contributions required to meet its return-on-investment goals for the CST rollout in the first year. "It gives us a target," he says. "They're saying: 'Here are our goals. How can you help us meet them?'"

"Without the plan it would be chaos," says Allen. A comprehensive strategic plan helps vendors to be less competitive because they see their place in the overall strategy and how they will profit from it. "This is what's missing from most organizations," he says.

A Meeting of the Minds

In November, Purington invited all the vendors who made the cut to Cedar Rapids to celebrate what they'd accomplished so far and to discuss the future. Thirty representatives from 15 vendors spent the morning sharing ideas.

The occasion marked the fact that in five months almost all of the Year One goals had been met, including delivering 30 percent of the curriculum via computer, establishing a common design process, creating learning labs for employees without computer access, and launching the first virtual classroom.

Meanwhile, employees got their first taste of the new and improved Rockwell Collins learning system last summer. The system went up in July '99, but with little fanfare, says Purington. And that was by design. Employees quietly discovered the 230 courses, allowing the L and D staff time to gauge responses and iron out any bugs.

In November, Rockwell Collins officially rolled out the new system with posters, articles, corporatewide e-mail announcements, and a demo CD-ROM featuring highlights from the new training for all 14,000 employees. "We've had excellent responses," says Junion. "Lots of people outside headquarters had been neglected in the past, and they are very excited about Web-based training."

Characteristics of Effective Technical Training

The three preceding cases described many characteristics of effective technical training programs in organizations. It is worthwhile to consider what those are. They are summarized in the following sections. As you read what we have written, compare our notes to those we asked you to prepare as you began reading the cases.

For additional information, consider the results of the authors' year 2000 survey of technical trainers, which was first described in Chapter One. According to the respondents to that survey, effective technical training programs share common characteristics. (See Exhibit 2.1.)

EXHIBIT 2.1. PERCEIVED CHARACTERISTICS OF EFFECTIVE TECHNICAL TRAINING PROGRAMS

Source: J. Benkowski and W. Rothwell. (2001). *Successful Technical Training Practices.* Unpublished survey results. Stout, WI: The University of Wisconsin.

Management Supports Technical Training

The single most important characteristic for effective technical training, as identified by respondents to the survey, was that "management supports technical training." That means management supplies the time, money, people, and resources to carry it out. Lack of resources is one indicator that management support is lacking. According to the respondents to our survey of technical trainers, 84.2 percent indicated that they believed management supported technical training, while a discomforting minority of 15.8 percent did not believe that technical training in their organizations enjoyed support. (See Exhibit 2.2.) Fewer respondents (81.1 percent)

EXHIBIT 2.2.   DO YOU BELIEVE YOUR MANAGEMENT SUPPORTS TRAINING?

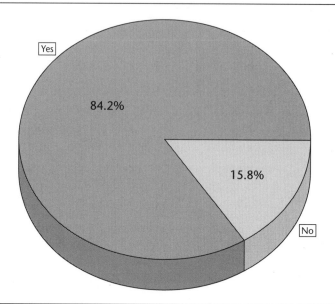

Source: J. Benkowski and W. Rothwell. (2001). *Successful Technical Training Practices.* Unpublished survey results. Stout, WI: The University of Wisconsin.

indicated that the technical training sponsored by their organizations was good, while 18.9 percent did not rate as good the technical training provided by their organization (see Exhibit 2.3).

Other Characteristics of Effective Technical Training

Other characteristics of effective technical training were also ranked high by survey respondents. Among those were that technical training "has good procedural sheets to follow," "has good trainers," "has specific training objectives," and is "tied to company strategic plans." The key message here seems to be that the organization's decision makers are clear about what organizational results they want and use technical training as a means to achieve company ends.

Lowest ranked among the characteristics of effective technical training programs were "meets the short-term needs of the organization,"

EXHIBIT 2.3.   DO YOU BELIEVE YOUR COMPANY PROVIDES GOOD TECHNICAL TRAINING?

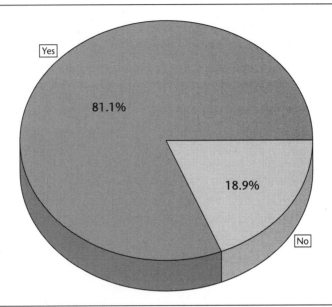

Source: J. Benkowski and W. Rothwell. (2001). *Successful Technical Training Practices.* Unpublished survey results. Stout, WI: The University of Wisconsin.

"structures on-the-job training," "employees are involved with the training plans," and "has an employee/management training committee." Perhaps the reason that these characteristics ranked lower is that they are all not directly tied to technical training but are instead linked to the organization's use of technical training.

Characteristics of Effective Technical Training Derived from the Cases

By reading the case studies presented at the opening of this chapter, you should be able to pinpoint several other characteristics of effective technical training in addition to those identified by the survey. A summary of these characteristics is described below.

Technical Training Clearly Supports the Organization's Needs. Note from reading the cases that technical training clearly supports the needs of each organization. The goals to be achieved by technical training are clear, and the value of those goals to the organization is obvious. Technical training not only supports the organization's strategic business plans but—perhaps more to the point—is immediately useful in making workers more productive.

The Targeted Groups for Technical Training Are Clear. As pointed out in Chapter One, the meaning of the term "technical" in "technical training" may have various meanings. But in organizations where technical training is effective, the targeted participants are clearly identified. In fact, note that in the U.S. Postal Service case, the exact groups targeted for participation are listed by name.

The Organizational Structure for Technical Training Is Based on Organizational Goals. In the U.S. Postal Service and Rockwell Collins cases, technical training is an enormous, ambitious effort. But the organizational structure to support it has been clearly identified and based on clear thinking about the organizational scheme best-suited to support the role of technical training in the organization. That is important.

Vendors Are Managed Effectively. Technical training may be designed, delivered, and evaluated by many groups from inside or outside an organization (Allum and Hofstader, 1998; Jasinowski, 1998; Sheets, 1995). Large organizations—such as the U.S. Postal Service, Southwestern Power, and Rockwell Collins—have carefully delineated the role vendors play in technical training. The Postal Service has even created a catalog of different kinds of vendors, which is useful, since it can spark thinking about which groups may possess specialized expertise to handle specific technical training issues particularly well.

Training Delivery Methods Are Selected Based on Considerations of Cost, Time, and Learning Effectiveness. Considerable attention in recent years has focused on web-based training and other media-based or media-assisted training delivery methods. But effective technical training is not biased in favor of one delivery method to the exclusion of others. Instead, the focus is on how to balance cost, time, and learning effectiveness. Deliberate attention is paid to these issues.

There Is an Organized Technical Training Curriculum. The word *curriculum* comes from a Latin word meaning "to run a race" (Rothwell and Sredl, 2000). A *curriculum* means an *instructional plan.* Two considerations should be borne in mind during the planning of technical training: (1) *long-term needs,* which are predictable and are based on relatively enduring work responsibilities for targeted learners; and (2) *short-term needs,* which stem from dynamically changing business conditions, technology, and work processes (Rothwell and Sredl, 2000).

Long-term needs can be predicted. For instance, if an individual is to be promoted to supervisor of a technical unit, he or she will need preparation and/or orientation to the supervisory role. A supervisor's work requirements are, after all, different from an individual contributor's work requirements. Long-term needs can be predicted by examining job descriptions, competency models, reports from experienced workers, and other sources. When long-term needs are met, individuals are equipped with what they need to know, do, or feel to perform their work effectively. A curriculum is thus, in a sense, a relatively enduring training plan that is intended to help individuals meet or exceed the work requirements for the positions into which they are hired, transferred, or promoted. Organizations can establish a technical training curriculum to manage the cultivation of essential technical competencies and skills among workers over time (Dowding, 1993).

Short-term needs may vary over time. If the organization plans to adopt new technology or modify its work processes, short-term training may be needed to help individuals understand what to do, how to do it, why it is worth doing, and how success can be measured.

Note from the cases that both the U.S. Postal Service and Southwestern Power have established training requirements. Other organizations have benefited from thinking long-term about their training requirements and using that as a means for transitioning from onsite to online courses (see, for instance, Fister, 2000).

Rate Technical Training in Your Organization

Use the assessment instrument provided in Exhibit 2.4 to assess the characteristics of technical training in your organization. Then circulate that assessment instrument to others in your organization to prompt them to clarify desirable characteristics for effective technical training. Use this assessment as a starting point for getting clear what goals technical training should strive to achieve and pinpoint any conflicting expectations affecting the organization's technical training.

The Unique Competencies of Technical Trainers

There is a growing trend to use subject-matter experts (SMEs) as technical trainers (Clark, 1994; Williams, 2001). A *subject-matter expert* is an individual who knows the work intimately, often from having done it personally. He or she is an expert in the content (Sugar and Schwen, 1994; Williams, 2001). A subject-matter expert stands in contrast to an *instructional design expert* (IDE), who is tapped for his or her special knowledge, skill, and ability in designing, developing, delivering, or evaluating training.

Unfortunately, subject-matter expertise is not the only characteristic necessary to design, deliver, and evaluate effective technical training. Other competencies are also essential (Chance, 1995). A *competency* is anything that leads to successful job performance (Dubois and Rothwell, 2000). Competencies therefore go beyond mere knowledge, skill, or attitude. They may include levels of motivation, personality traits, and awareness of bodies of knowledge that are necessary to achieve desired work results and meet or exceed customer expectations. To meet the job requirements of a technical training coordinator or a technical training instructor (see Exhibits 2.5 and 2.6), then, technical trainers require unique competencies. They also require special training and coaching to assume this new role (King-Taylor, 1999).

EXHIBIT 2.4. ASSESSING THE PERCEIVED EFFECTIVENESS OF YOUR ORGANIZATION'S TECHNICAL TRAINING

Directions: Use this worksheet to assess how well you believe your organization is managing technical training. For each item listed in the left column below, rate what your organization is doing in the right column below. Use the following scale: **6 = strongly agree; 5 = agree; 4 = somewhat agree; 3 = somewhat disagree; 2 = disagree;** and **1 = strongly disagree.** When you finish, add up the scores in the right column. Then read how to score your instrument below.

Characteristics	*Your Ratings of Your Organization*					
In my organization:	Strongly Agree 6	Agree 5	Somewhat Agree 4	Somewhat Disagree 3	Disagree 2	Strongly Disagree 1
1. Technical training clearly supports the organization's needs.	6	5	4	3	2	1
2. The targeted groups for technical training are clear.	6	5	4	3	2	1
3. The organizational structure for technical training is based on organizational goals.	6	5	4	3	2	1
4. Vendors are managed effectively.	6	5	4	3	2	1
5. Training delivery methods are selected based on considerations of cost, time, and learning effectiveness.	6	5	4	3	2	1
6. There is an organized technical training curriculum.	6	5	4	3	2	1
7. Management supports technical training in the organization.	6	5	·4	3	2	1
8. There are good procedural sheets in the organization for trainers to follow.	6	5	4	3	2	1

(Continued)

EXHIBIT 2.4.   ASSESSING THE PERCEIVED EFFECTIVENESS OF YOUR ORGANIZATION'S TECHNICAL TRAINING (*Continued*)

Characteristics	Your Ratings of Your Organization					
In my organization:	**Strongly Agree** **6**	**Agree** **5**	**Somewhat Agree** **4**	**Somewhat Disagree** **3**	**Disagree** **2**	**Strongly Disagree** **1**
9. The organization has good technical trainers.	6	5	4	3	2	1
10. Each training experience has specific training objectives.	6	5	4	3	2	1
11. Technical training is tied to company strategic plans.	6	5	4	3	2	1

Total (Add up the scores from the right column above and place in the box at right)

Scoring

Directions: Consult your score. Then examine the range of scores appearing in the left column below. Find where the score of your organization falls. Then read the information opposite that score to gain deeper understanding of the status of technical training in your organization.

If your score falls between:	Then:
66 to 56	Grade your organization an "A" on its technical training. Your organization has a well-managed, effective technical training function. Congratulations. You should work on enhancing an already effective program.
55 to 45	Grade your organization a "B" on its technical training. Your organization is making some efforts in technical training. However, some improvements could be made.
44 to 34	Grade your organization a "C" on its technical training. Your organization is devoting about an "average" amount to technical training, but is not doing all it could. Technical training in your organization needs work.
33 to 23	Grade your organization a "D" on its technical training. Your organization is devoting less than an "average" amount to its technical training and is falling short of what it could be doing. Much work needs to be done to improve technical training in your organization.
22 to 12	Grade your organization an "F" on its technical training. Your organization is devoting far less than an "average" amount to its technical training. Take immediate steps to improve technical training in your organization.
1 to 11	Grade your organization worse than an "F." Your organization is nowhere near adequate in managing technical training. Take immediate steps to improve technical training in your organization.

EXHIBIT 2.5. JOB DESCRIPTION OF A TECHNICAL TRAINING COORDINATOR

A technical training coordinator:

Coordinates activities of instructors engaged in training employees or customers of industrial or commercial establishment. Confers with managers, instructors, or customer's representative to determine training needs. Assigns instructors to conduct training. Schedules classes, based on availability of classrooms, equipment, and instructors. Evaluates training packages, including outline, text, and handouts written by instructors. Assigns instructors to in-service or out-service training classes to learn new skills as needed. Monitors budget to ensure that training costs do not exceed allocated funds. Writes budget report listing training costs, such as instructors' wages and equipment costs, to justify expenditures. Attends meetings and seminars to obtain information useful to training staff and to inform management of training programs and goals. Monitors instructors during lectures and laboratory demonstrations to evaluate performance. May perform other duties as described under Supervisor [any industry] Master Title. May develop and conduct training programs for employees or customers of industrial or commercial establishment [Instructor, Technical Training (education) 166.221-010]. GOE: 11.07.03 STRENGTH: L GED: R5 M3 L5 SVP: 8 DLU: 87

Source: www.stepfour.com/jobs/155157054.htm

EXHIBIT 2.6. JOB DESCRIPTION OF A TECHNICAL TRAINING INSTRUCTOR

A technical training instructor, sometimes called a technical training specialist, performs the following work activities:

Develops and conducts programs to train employees or customers of industrial or commercial establishment in installation, programming, safety, maintenance, and repair of machinery and equipment, such as robots, programmable controllers, and robot controllers, following manuals, specifications, blueprints, and schematics, and using hand tools, measuring instruments, and testing equipment. Confers with management and staff or Technical Training Coordinator (education) 166.167-054 to determine training objectives. Writes training program, including outline, text, handouts, and tests, and designs laboratory exercises, applying knowledge of electronics, mechanics, hydraulics, pneumatics, and programming, and following machine, equipment, and tooling manuals. Schedules classes based on classroom and equipment availability. Lectures class on safety, installation, programming, maintenance, and repair of machinery and equipment, following outline, handouts, and texts, and using visual aids, such as graphs, charts, videotape, and slides. Demonstrates procedures being taught, such as programming and repair, applying knowledge of electrical wire color coding, programming, electronics, mechanics, hydraulics, and pneumatics, using hand tools, measuring instruments, and testing equipment, and following course outline. Observes trainees in laboratory and answers trainees' questions. Administers written and practical exams and writes performance reports to evaluate trainees' performance. Participates in meetings, seminars, and training sessions to obtain information useful to training facility and integrates information into training program. May repair electrical and electronic components of robots in industrial establishments. May install, program, maintain, and repair robots in customer's establishment [Field Service Technician (machinery mfg.) 638.261-026]. May be designated according to subject taught as Instructor, Programmable Controllers (education); Instructor, Robotics (education). GOE: 11.02.02 STRENGTH: L GED: R5 M4 L5 SVP: 8 DLU: 86

Source: www.stepfour.com/jobs/166221010.htm

Since the 1960s, much research has centered around the competencies necessary for success as a trainer (Rothwell, Sanders, and Soper, 1999; Rothwell and Sredl, 2000). The earliest research focused only on what trainers should know, do, and feel. More recent research has centered less on the knowledge, skills, and attitudes for trainers than on what is necessary to achieve improved productivity. Training is only one way to achieve improved performance. There are at least fifty other ways to improve employee productivity—including improving the job aids given to performers, improving the match between incentives/rewards and desired results, ensuring ergonomic design of the work, grouping together related tasks into coherent jobs, and providing effective reporting structures—to name but a few (Langdon, Whiteside, and McKenna, 1999).

According to the respondents to our survey of technical instructors, some competencies are particularly important for job success. Highest ranked in the survey were such competencies as "working well with workers," "understanding adult learning," and "applying good interpersonal skills" (see Exhibit 2.7). Ranked lowest or least important in the survey was "being involved at the start" in technical training.

The survey also revealed that most technical training in organizations, at least among respondents to the authors' survey, is developed by the training department or by trainers. (See Exhibit 2.8.) That is important, since it gives credence to trainers' opinions about the most important competencies necessary for success. About half of the respondents in our survey were positioned in their own department. (See Exhibit 2.9.) Trainers in our responding organizations were positioned to know what was required for success.

Generally speaking, effective technical trainers must be willing to get involved in the daily work problems encountered by the workers. In that respect they play an important role, since managers may seem isolated from daily operational problems to hourly workers. Effective technical trainers can build rapport with workers and managers alike and sustain effective interpersonal relationships.

Learning to manage time is particularly important to full-time technical trainers. Of course, no matter what work you do, finding the time to do everything can be difficult. The average professional attends more

EXHIBIT 2.7. COMPETENCIES ESSENTIAL FOR TECHNICAL TRAINERS

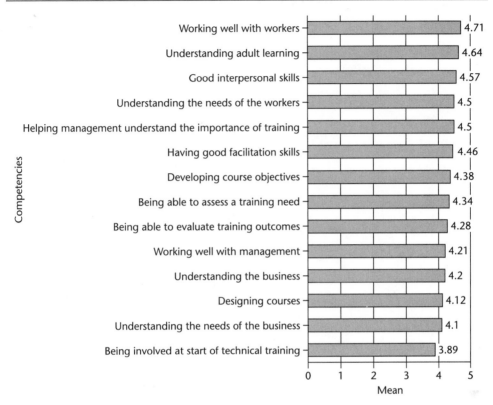

Source: J. Benkowski and W. Rothwell. (2001). *Successful Technical Training Practices.* Unpublished survey results. Stout, WI: The University of Wisconsin.

than sixty meetings per month (Bersani, 1999). Workplace demands are increasing on all workers, and that includes technical trainers. To be effective at time management, take care to follow these tips: (1) keep your commitments; (2) save the time needed to be creative; (3) avoid the endless meetings trap; (4) keep your enthusiasm for your work; and (5) always think about how you can leverage what you do, getting more than one thing done at the same time and juggling multiple tasks simultaneously.

One way you can manage your time is to develop a personal time management strategy. Companies and departments have long used strategies as a guide for meeting organizational goals and maintaining focus amid

**EXHIBIT 2.8.   WHO DEVELOPS TECHNICAL TRAINING
IN YOUR ORGANIZATION?**

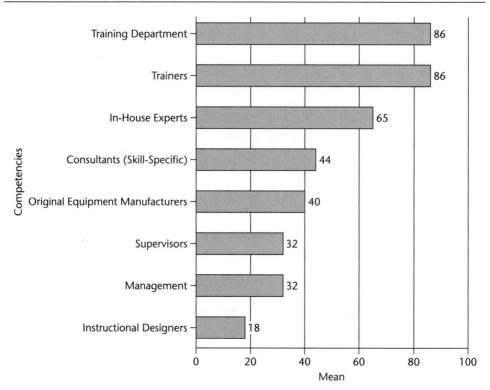

Source: J. Benkowski and W. Rothwell. (2001). *Successful Technical Training Practices.* Unpublished survey results. Stout, WI: The University of Wisconsin.

competing priorities. A well-planned personal time management strategy can reduce the frustrations caused by trying to do too much in too little time. Developing a personal time management strategy may seem like an unnecessary effort, but effective technical trainers take care to set priorities and ensure that they link time use to the priorities. They avoid getting side-tracked on low-priority issues.

Effective technical trainers establish a plan for every key project in which they are involved (Doyle, 1999). While many good software programs

EXHIBIT 2.9.   IS TECHNICAL TRAINING A SEPARATE DEPARTMENT IN YOUR ORGANIZATION?

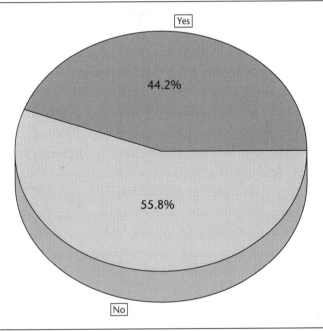

Source: J. Benkowski and W. Rothwell. (2001). *Successful Technical Training Practices.* Unpublished survey results. Stout, WI: The University of Wisconsin.

exist to help manage projects, technical trainers do not need them if they take care to

- Choose projects that will have an impact by contributing to the achievement of business needs
- Identify the steps necessary to complete each project and the results desired from each step
- Clarify the project milestones, both in terms of what must be done and how its relative success will be measured
- Clarify who is responsible for what, and by when, on each project step

Savvy technical trainers will display a project sheet in their offices to give others the impression that they are organized, focused, and goal-oriented.

Managers will note these organizational skills and will be more likely to be flexible when they make unexpected requests for technical training services.

Technical trainers should also possess a grasp of adult learning theory and practice (Knowles and Hartl, 1995). The theoretical foundations of training are based in the psychology of adult learning. Although training has been evolving since the earliest times, the awareness of what makes adult learners unique is relatively new. Actually, it was not until Eduard C. Lindeman wrote *The Meaning of the Adult Learner* (1926) that adult learning principles were clearly differentiated from those appropriate for children. And it was not until the 1950s that the differences between children as learners and adults as learners was seriously considered.

Studies conducted by Houle (1961), Tough (1971; 1979), and Knowles (1980) have helped to shape modern thinking about adult learners. Tough found that adults expend considerable time and energy exploring individually oriented learning projects to solve life- or work-related problems.

Houle identified a key need of the adult learner—*they need to know why they should learn something.* People are what they are, not what someone else wants them to be. Similarly, people learn what they want to learn, not what someone else wants them to learn. If, for instance, managers need to increase production or reduce machine downtime, then they must motivate interest in that problem among employees. Motivation is thus the critical driver for learning (Clinton, 1998). Lacking motivation, adults simply will not learn or will not remember what they learned.

Houle also showed that *adults have a desire to learn only if they can see the benefits to themselves.* Adult learning experiences are successful only when they prompt learners to discover things for themselves, when the learners actively participate in the learning process, when they see the benefits to learning, when the learning relates to what the learners find familiar, and when learners receive positive reinforcement during the learning process.

Technical trainers should apply these principles of adult learning by structuring active discovery rather than passive lecturing. Only when they do will technical training be most effective.

Use the assessment instrument appearing in Appendix I to assess your own competencies against those required for success as a technical trainer. Then plan for how you can build your technical training competencies.

One way is to continue reading this book. You should also give some thought to your career—whether it will be in technical training (Carnevale, 1993) or in some other field.

Summary

This chapter summarized characteristics of effective technical training and the competencies needed for success as a technical trainer. The next chapter explains how to establish an organizational plan and strategy for technical training.

PART II

PLANNING AND MANAGING THE TECHNICAL TRAINING FUNCTION

Part II focuses on planning and managing technical training. It

- Discusses what is needed to establish a company strategic plan for technical training
- Reviews key roles and responsibilities of those who manage technical training in organizational settings
- Explains why an organization should develop a strategic plan to guide technical training
- Clarifies what is (and should be) the role of the technical trainer in formulating and implementing such a plan
- Emphasizes the importance of a champion (or champions) necessary for such a plan to be successful
- Enumerates how a strategic plan for technical training can be formulated in a way that builds support
- Supplies reasons to explain why an external consultant should usually be used in the strategy formulation process and the role played by the consultant

- Clarifies why a steering committee should be used and the role of such a committee
- Clarifies why a strategic planning committee should be used and the role that should be played by such a committee
- Describes how meetings for a strategic planning committee should be planned and managed
- Explains briefly how the budget process should be handled
- Defines environmental scanning for the strategic planning process and reviews what should be examined when formulating a strategic plan for technical training
- Defines benchmarking and describes how it can be effectively carried out in the strategic planning process
- Reviews what role should be played by communication in the strategic planning process
- Offers advice on how a union or unions should be involved in the strategic planning process
- Defines competitive analysis and explains when and how it should be conducted
- Lists the steps by which a strategic plan for technical training should be developed
- Reviews how a strategic plan for technical training should be implemented
- Lists other important issues that should be considered as an organization formulates and implements a strategic plan for technical training

Exhibit 3 is the blueprint for Part II within a schematic diagram representing the book's total scheme.

EXHIBIT 3.   PART II WITHIN THE SCHEME OF THE BOOK

Chapter 1: **What Is Technical Training?**	**Part I:** **Foundations of** **Effective** **Technical** **Training**
Chapter 2: **What Are the Characteristics of Effective Technical Training?**	
Chapter 3: **Establishing an Organizational Plan for Technical Training**	**Part II:** **Planning and** **Managing the** **Technical** **Training** **Function**
Chapter 4: **Leading and Managing the Technical Training Department**	
Chapter 5: **Basic Principles of Instructional Systems Design**	**Part III:** **Key Issues** **in** **Training** **Course** **Design**
Chapter 6: **Identifying Technical Training Needs**	
Chapter 7: **Preparing Technical Training Programs**	
Chapter 8: **Determining and Using Delivery Methods**	
Chapter 9: **Evaluating Technical Training**	
Chapter 10: **Using Vendors and Managing Original** **Equipment Manufacturers**	**Part IV:** **Special Issues** **in Technical** **Training**
Chapter 11: **Operating Apprenticeship and Safety** **Training Programs and Working with Unions**	
Chapter 12: **Achieving Results with Alternatives to Technical Training**	
Afterword	**Part V:** **Concluding** **Thoughts**

CHAPTER THREE

ESTABLISHING AN ORGANIZATIONAL PLAN FOR TECHNICAL TRAINING

If an organization lacks a plan for technical training, the training is unlikely to be effective. Like any organizational effort, technical training must be planned and managed. Top managers, union leaders, workers, and others having a stake in technical training must be clear about what results they want from it, why they want it, when they want it, and how they will know if they got it. Technical trainers play an important role in clarifying these issues and in making the case for technical training (Meyer, 1993).

While much has been written on linking corporate training to strategic business planning (see, for instance, Gilley and Maycunich, 1998; Rothwell and Kazanas, 1994), less research has focused specifically on strategic planning for technical training. And yet, having a plan for technical training is essential to having a big-picture, long-term view of how technical training will contribute to achieving organizational results. That is particularly important for organizations poised for making such major changes as implementation of an enterprise resource planning (ERP) system (Eline, 1999c; Elsenheimer, 1999), implementation of employee skills standards (Barron, 1999c), the introduction of new products

(Caiazza, 1999; Newman, Pallesen, and Visk, 1999), the building and launching of a new industrial plant (Ekkebus, 1996), or the delivery of customer product training (Gottlieb, 1999).

This chapter opens with a case study that describes how a real but disguised organization established a company strategic plan for technical training. Following the case study, we distill the key lessons learned from this real-world example and review the steps in establishing an organizational strategic plan for technical training.

Case Study: Formulating and Implementing an Organizational Strategic Plan for Technical Training

This case study describes one technical training manager's experience in developing a strategic plan for technical training. In this context, a *strategic plan for technical training* means a long-term plan for training technically oriented workers. It is worth emphasizing that *strategic objectives articulate the measurable, long-term results to be achieved,* while a *strategic plan or strategy is the means by which to achieve those objectives.*

The Background

Over the years, a large, diversified corporation managed technical training for its industrial plants from the corporate headquarters. Many training programs were developed to meet the needs of plant managers, operations managers, directors of various corporate departments, and division vice presidents. The organization's strategic objectives were the drivers behind the decisions made about what training would be developed and what departments would be served by the training.

In developing the list of training needs, the technical training manager would arrange a meeting with directors or vice presidents of the organization's divisions to discuss their technical training needs as the budget for the next year was being prepared (see Treinen and Douglas, 1995). As a result of these meetings, training needs were identified and priorities were set. Most technical training needs stemmed directly from the goals of the organization and were explicitly justified on that basis.

The technical training manager took initiative to learn how each department operated and successfully established rapport with people at all organizational levels. By maintaining good interpersonal relationships, the technical training manager gained keen insight into training needs. Technical training seemed to be effective in meeting the organization's needs.

But as the technical training manager became more knowledgeable about the organization, he saw the need to form closer ties with those he served. That was a starting point for his search to find ways to avert human performance problems rather than merely react to them once they were identified. As a result, the director of human resources gave permission to the technical training manager to develop a strategic plan for technical training.

As a first step in developing the strategic plan, the technical training manager reviewed all technical training that had been carried out in the organization over the preceding four years to determine what had been successful and what could have been improved. Additionally, the technical training manager held meetings with people from all levels of the organization to solicit their input about what issues should be addressed by the organization's technical training strategy. He also benchmarked several well-known companies that were renowned for the high quality of their technical training.

The technical training manager devoted about three months to gathering information and preparing a written strategic plan to guide the organization's technical training. Once the strategic plan for technical training was written, it was presented individually to all division heads whose operations would be affected by it. The technical training manager also traveled to each company plant to give a presentation about the strategic plan, since he believed that local involvement was key to the plan's success. He also wanted to receive feedback to determine what changes should be made to the plan and how much agreement he had with the stakeholders about their identified roles in the strategic implementation.

For the most part, the strategic plan was well-received. The plan spoke to the concerns of many managers. But six months after the plan was adopted, the technical training manager began to feel that he was losing the support he had initially seen for the plan. The evidence of that eroding support was apparent, since diminishing time, resources, and attention were devoted to the plan. After just nine months, the strategic plan was not being fully used to guide operations. Its full impact was never felt.

What benefits that were derived from the plan stemmed from what parts of the original strategic plan were implemented. That included the implementation of a structured train-the-trainer program, enhancements to training program design, and line management involvement in the training design process.

Revisiting the Training Strategy

Three years passed before the technical training manager mounted a new effort to formulate and implement a strategic plan for technical training. A company reorganization prompted a renewed effort to plan for technical training. Before the reorganization, all training functions reported to one HRD director, and each training function worked with divisions it supported in the organization. But the reorganization carved up the training function and placed each training unit into the departments or divisions they served. Technical training was placed in the HR division focused on operations, and that same division included safety, labor relations, and organization development. This division was responsible for serving the HR needs of all departments associated with corporate and plant operations.

The new director of this division almost immediately asked the question, "Is there need for technical training?" The technical training manager replied, "Yes, but a strategic plan for technical training should be developed." The new director responded, "I thought you developed one several years ago." The training manager replied, "Yes, but we never enjoyed sufficient buy-in to harvest the benefits from it." The director then asked, "How will the process of developing the technical training be different this time?" The technical training manager replied, "This time personnel will be involved in every step of the planning process."

A second factor giving impetus for change was the appointment of a new vice president of plant operations. He took a proactive role in technical training. A third factor supporting the need for a new technical training strategy was the formulation of strategic plans for purchasing, manufacturing, engineering, and plant operations. In each strategic plan, technical training emerged as a key focal point for action. Political infighting between departments ceased, since technical training had already been identified as key to future success.

Planning the Process

Unlike the first (and failed) attempt to develop a strategic plan for technical training, the new approach called for substantial and continuing input from different hierarchical levels. Those to be involved in formulating and implementing the plan included personnel from each corporate department that supported business operations and plant personnel. It is worth noting that personnel were selected so that each plant location had a representative participate in establishing the strategic plan for technical training. That created a line of communication to each plant. Another criterion for selecting personnel was their relationship to training. Key stakeholders from all hierarchical levels were to be represented—including plant managers, HR managers, engineering workers, safety personnel, maintenance workers, operators, technical trainers, supervisors, and information systems professionals. This large group provided a way to secure input from all organizational levels.

A consultant was hired to facilitate the strategy formulation process. Three consultants were invited to interview, and they were selected by the technical training manager. The selection decision was made based on feedback from organizations that had been previously benchmarked for their excellence in technical training. Each consultant was sent, in advance of the interview, a list of questions. Each consultant was also advised to bring to the interviews a list of references to support his or her experience in strategic planning. The interviews were conducted by the director of HR operations, engineering director, director of operations, plant technical trainer, and the technical training manager. An evaluation sheet was developed so the interviewers could list the strengths and weaknesses of each consultant. The interviewing process and evaluation sheets worked well, and they led to a unanimous decision about which consultant to select.

The consultant's first step was to hold a one-day meeting with technical trainers and managers from engineering, operations, and HR. The purpose of the meeting was to develop agendas for subsequent meetings and the goals of each meeting. This process also helped to establish tentative meeting dates so all members of the strategic planning committee could schedule their activities accordingly. This process gave senior management an idea of the time, resources, and approach that would be taken in the project. To ensure that members of the strategic planning committees appreciated the importance of their assignments, three vice presidents and two directors opened the first meeting.

A steering committee of senior managers was also established. The purpose of the committee was to guide the development process. After each planning meeting, the technical training manager and consultant would update the steering committee on the progress made and the concerns voiced by the strategic planning committee. This feedback also helped the steering committee make decisions on financial and other resource issues demanding action with sufficient lead time that decisions could be made in time for the next strategic planning meeting. Since all plants were unionized, the human resource manager's duty was to meet with appropriate union officials and explain the purpose of the strategic plan for technical training. Several union members served on the strategic planning committee.

Planning Schedule

The strategy planning committee met for five two-day sessions over a five-month period. Between meetings, members were assigned work. These assignments included visiting best-practice companies to benchmark their technical training, scanning conditions in the internal and external environment that would affect technical training, and researching information on such topics as training standards that could guide all phases of technical training design. The teams made presentations on the information they had gleaned from their trips or from sources they had consulted at the opening of each meeting. Also at each meeting strategic planning committee members received feedback from the steering committee.

At the end of this process, the organization had successfully formulated an effective strategic plan for technical training. The involvement of a steering committee gave the process, and its product, ownership at the highest levels. The involvement of the strategic planning committee gave the strategic planning process, and its resultant strategic plan, broad support among such varied locations as corporate headquarters and plants and among union and management alike. The goal of this effort was to ensure ownership based on commitment at every step from strategy formulation through implementation. The strategic planning committee grounded the process in meeting workers' needs, and the steering committee aligned the process with the organization's strategic objectives. Additionally, since many people were involved, the strategy formulation process was widely communicated.

While this case does not provide all the details of the strategy formulation and implementation process, it does serve to underscore key issues to be considered when formulating and implementing a strategic plan for technical training.

The Nuts and Bolts of Strategic Planning for Technical Training

As we begin to discuss strategic planning for technical training, consider some important questions that need to be addressed:

- Why should an organization develop a strategic plan to guide technical training?
- What is (and should be) the role of technical trainers in formulating and implementing such a plan?
- Why is a champion (or champions) necessary for such a plan to be successful?
- How can a strategic plan for technical training be formulated in a way that builds support for its implementation?
- Why should an external consultant be used in the strategy formulation process, and what role should a consultant play?
- Why should a steering committee be used, and what should be the role of such a committee?
- Why should a strategic planning committee be used, and what should be the role of such a committee?
- How should meetings for a strategic planning committee be planned and managed?
- How should the budget process be handled?
- What is environmental scanning for the strategic planning process, and what should be examined when formulating a strategic plan for technical training?
- What is benchmarking, and how can it be effectively carried out in the strategic planning process?
- What role should communication play in the strategic planning process?

- How should organized labor be involved in the strategic planning process?
- What is competitive analysis, and when and how should it be conducted?
- How should the strategic plan for technical training be developed?
- How should the strategic plan for technical training be implemented?
- What other important issues should be considered as an organization formulates and implements a strategic plan for technical training?

This section of the chapter addresses these important, and fundamental, questions.

Why Should an Organization Develop a Strategic Plan for Technical Training?

Each year U.S. organizations spend billions of dollars on training. Unfortunately, that money is not always wisely spent. Training is not the solution to every human performance problem. However, many managers grasp at training as a quick fix for many problems that they face. One reason is that they are at their wit's end in looking for a solution to a problem, and they seize on training as a way to solve problems.

A strategic plan for technical training is important to focus and unify efforts. Like most plans, a strategic plan for technical training should make clear what technical training is meant to do—and what it is not meant to do. It should make the goals of the effort explicit and show how they align to the organization's goals and help to meet business needs.

A common saying in many organizations is that "training is the first thing to go in lean times." That may be true in some settings. But it is less often true when training is specifically targeted to improving production, customer satisfaction, or service delivery. Technical training should not be managed as a firefighting operation (Gilley and Maycunich, 1998), since firefighting can be handed off to others in lean times (Carnevale, Gainer, and Villet, 1990). A better approach is to target technical training to achieve a specific purpose and meet specific objectives. When that is the case, cutting training makes no sense, since it results in production or operational problems.

What Is (and Should Be) the Technical Trainer's Role in Formulating and Implementing a Strategic Plan for Technical Training?

To be successful in developing a strategic plan for technical training, technical training managers need to possess two key competencies.

First, they must see the need and be committed to that cause. A lack of vision is a common cause of failure. A strategic plan for technical training cannot be formulated if the person in charge of technical training fails to take a leadership role.

Second, technical training managers must build strong partnerships with key stakeholders in the organization. A *stakeholder* is a person or group having a stake in technical training and standing to gain (or lose) from it. There are many stakeholders for technical training, and strategic alliances must be established. Stakeholders must be persuaded, based on how they can benefit, that a strategic plan for technical training will be advantageous to them. Developing partnerships takes time. Key stakeholders must view technical training—and the person running it—as proactive and regard training as a means by which to achieve business ends.

Why Is a Champion (or Champions) Necessary?

A *champion* is someone who is usually positioned at the senior management level who leads the charge for change. To formulate and implement a strategic plan for technical training, a champion is necessary. That champion must be committed to the effort because he or she believes that it will lead to results of benefit to the organization.

Of particular importance in finding and keeping a champion is the way that technical trainers talk about their work. If they talk about the need for training as if that were important in itself, managers will turn a deaf ear to what they say. But if technical trainers talk about training as a means to the end of achieving improved individual and organizational performance, managers will usually sit up and take notice.

Consider a simple example. Suppose that the technical trainer has discovered the need to develop a training program for *quick changeover,* the shift on an assembly line from making one product to another. (If handled poorly, assembly line changeovers can lead to long and costly shutdowns.) If the technical trainer (on the one hand) describes the need for such a program and then focuses the discussion on how the training will be designed and delivered, managers may regard it as "just more training that will take time away from making the products." But if (on the other hand) the technical trainer describes the need for such a program by showing how much time changeovers are currently taking and how long they could take if training were given, managers can easily see the business need for the training. It is thus positioned as an investment of time and money that will quickly pay off rather than sounding like knowledge in pursuit of an application.

There is an important lesson to be learned from this example. Managers do not see the need for training as an end in itself. But technical trainers, who work with training every day, are so close to it that they often see training as warranted in its own right. The moral to the story? Trainers should take steps to translate what they think from "trainerspeak" into "managementspeak." The key is to start with the business problem, showing how much it is costing, and then show how that cost can be reduced if workers receive training. When technical trainers do that, they relate what they do to the problems managers face.

Demonstrating the need for a strategic plan for technical training should be handled in much the same way. The technical training manager should cite the cost of not having such a strategy. That can usually be done by describing training that was given that probably should not have been. Or it can be done by dramatizing the wasteful use of resources that have resulted from not formulating and implementing a strategic plan for technical training.

Case in point: A multinational corporation (which shall remain unnamed here) was leaving technical training plans to each plant manager. Company executives believed that plant managers were best-positioned to decide what training was needed for their plants. But when a consultant was called in—one author of this book—he discovered by doing some research that the company's fifty-eight plants were actually doing business with over eighty-five different training consultants. Many services offered by these consultants were duplicative and could have easily benefited other plants. But, since no strategic plan for technical training existed and there was no method to examine technical training across the organization, documented waste resulting from duplicative services amounted to at least $10 million in this company per year. The cause of this problem? It was clearly a case in which the organization had not formulated a strategic plan for technical training, and the result was unnecessary and costly duplication of efforts.

How Can a Strategic Plan for Technical Training Be Formulated in a Way That Builds a Partnership?

Building partnerships in organizations is no easy task. Even today, when decision makers emphasize how important it is to "build team spirit," managers of each department often continue to act like feudal lords who want to protect their turf. If managers regard collaboration with the training department in this way, everyone loses.

Too often, managers want to call trainers for help after the managers have already decided what to do. Training is considered, for instance, only after a work process is changed or when new equipment is selected. But it should be considered instead at the outset of the decision-making process so that the training is completed when the new work process is ready to go online or the new equipment has already been installed. Ask yourself: What is the consequence of not managing the training? Answer: Costly delays and expensive mistakes as workers figure out on their own what to do because they did not receive just-in-time training (Rothwell, 1996a and 1996b).

As Gilley and Maycunich (1998) write:

Many HRD programs are perceived to be outside the mainstream of the organization because they are viewed as merely the main internal training houses for employees. Because of this, training is not considered critical to the success of the organization nor are the HRD professionals taken seriously. Moreover, little attention is given to the outcomes of training or the impact it has on an employee's performance. Another perceptual problem is that HRD professionals are not viewed as credible because they don't live in the real world, facing the problems other organizational members face. Because of these perceptions, HRD programs are often treated with a lack of respect. (p. 25)

In contrast, an effective strategic plan for technical training is established with a partnership in mind. Technical trainers should take the lead to show the need for such a strategy, develop a track record of being proactive, and seize the initiative to dramatize the need for training department involvement as operational decisions of strategic importance are made. It also helps to show management that delays in requesting training lead to problems that could have been avoided easily if trainers had been involved from the outset.

Why Should an External Consultant Be Used in the Strategy Formulation Process, and What Role Should a Consultant Play?

External consultants are usually hired on the basis of their experience. For this reason, using an external consultant is often important in formulating a technical training plan and strategy. Indeed, selecting a consultant is one of the most critical steps in developing a strategic plan for technical training.

Finding a consultant takes time. It is usually a three-step process: (1) sourcing qualified consultants; (2) interviewing the consultants; and (3) selecting a consultant and contracting for service.

Sourcing Qualified Consultants. Use several ways to source a qualified consultant. One way is to contact organizations such as the American Society for Training and Development or the Society for Human Resources Management and ask for recommendations. These organizations can provide lists of consultants. A second way is to network with business acquaintances and other companies. A third way is to surf the web to see if possible consultants are listed there.

As the sourcing process begins, clarify the interview questions you want to ask prospective consultants. Know the role you want the consultant to play and what experience he or she should possess. Examples of issues to explore might include what results the consultant has achieved from past work with organizations in establishing strategic plans for technical training; what experience he or she has had in building coalitions from groups across large organizations; what final results were achieved from the consultant's efforts; how he or she developed a work plan and communicated it; and what products or services the consultant delivered to their clients.

Begin contacting consultants only after you are clear what you are looking for and have a list of about six to eight possible consultants from which to choose.

There are essentially three ways to work with consultants. One approach is to devise a list of basic facts about the organization, called a "Fact Sheet," and a list of questions on a "Question Sheet." On the fact sheet you should include relevant information about the organization and the project. Also add information on organizational policies about travel reimbursement, voucher submission, and the estimated time from voucher submission to payment. (Explain any procedure for vendor pre-qualification if appropriate.) On the question sheet you should ask about the consultant's previous experience in helping an organization formulate a strategic plan for technical training, kinds of organizations and industries with which the consultant has worked, and any other important questions that occur to you. Be sure to spell out who will pay for the travel to and from the interview and who will bear the cost of such other travel-related expenses as lodging and food.

A second approach is more formal. Write a *request for a proposal* (RFP). An RFP is a detailed description of the problem, the organization's choice of solution, the justification for that solution, the expected project steps, and required timeline. Then provide a deadline and, if possible, the estimated authorized funding available. Submit the RFP to identified consultants and solicit written proposals from them.

A third approach is less formal. Simply phone hand-picked consultants and discuss the project with them. Explain how you got their names. Explain the background of the project and then let them take initiative to ferret out the information they will need to prepare a written proposal that describes what the problem is, what the solution should be, how the solution can be justified, what steps a project should take, how long it will take, what it will cost, and who should be involved in the project.

Interviewing Consultants. Assemble a committee from the organization to help select the appropriate consultant. Try to choose people who will give broad representation within the organization. After all, the organization's buy-in to the consultant will be affected by who decides to select him or her and how many people are involved.

When all information is received from the consultants, narrow down the possibilities to three possible finalists. Use a selection committee consisting of the same personnel who will be involved with the face-to-face interviews. That may include hourly and management personnel who are the key receivers ("customers") of technical training. A total of five or six people on the committee is recommended.

Scheduling interviews is an early challenge. Recognize that good consultants are in demand and probably must juggle the needs of multiple clients. Also realize that it may not be possible to have all committee members present for every interview. Do not allow scheduling problems to delay the process. Instead, work with the committee to agree on a list of questions that can be posed to all applicants to ensure some consistency across interviews. Each member of the selection committee should be involved in the questioning process for each interview so as to gain ownership and support. Help that along by rotating the questions around the panel. A rating scale should also be considered for each question, since that may help them to arrive at a selection decision. After each interview, committee members should hold a meeting to discuss how well the consultant answered the interview questions.

Selecting a Consultant and Contracting for Service. Consultant applicants should be ranked based on how well they answered the questions and described their previous experience. Ranking helps the committee members focus on reaching agreement on a choice. But remember at the same time that the consultant applicants are also interviewing the committee, so a ranking is also important in case the best-qualified consultant decides not to work with the organization.

When the selection has been made, develop a contract with the consultant that spells out the agreement. Finalize a work plan and develop an estimate of the timeline and the project expenses.

Why Should a Steering Committee Be Used, and What Should Be the Role of Such a Committee?

A *steering committee* should consist of senior managers. The role of such a committee is to serve in an advisory capacity to members of a strategic planning for technical training committee. Since senior managers control the resources of an organization, their role is crucial. Without the support of senior managers, the strategic plan can never be implemented.

The appropriate people to place on a steering committee is a management decision. However, several issues should be considered in making that decision. Those issues include:

- Which senior managers are interested in technical training because their employees participate in it frequently or because its role is key to meet the strategic objectives of their own departments?
- Which members of senior management possess skills relevant to technical training and are also willing to serve on such a committee?
- Which members of senior management can exert sufficient influence on others in the senior ranks so that their decisions and actions on the committee will have credibility?

The champion of the strategic plan for technical training should clearly serve on this committee. That person's input is critical to success and to ensure continuing attention from his or her peers.

An ideal size for a steering committee is between seven and twelve people. Members should commit to attend meetings and provide active feedback. They should be told in advance how much time and effort they can expect to commit to committee participation. Another good idea is that committee members, once appointed, should agree on how many times people can miss committee meetings and still remain in good standing on committee assignments.

Why Should a Strategic Planning Committee Be Used, and What Should Be the Role of Such a Committee?

Technical training will never achieve its full impact on training programs unless it enjoys the full ownership of its customers and stakeholders. Without their input, technical trainers will usually play a reactive, rather than a proactive, role. A *strategic planning committee for technical training* is meant to be one way to gain support from key stakeholders. The committee should represent different locations, hierarchical levels, and organizational parts. Its role is to do more than simply advise. Instead, members should work with the consultant and technical trainers to formulate a detailed strategic plan to guide the long-term direction of technical training in the organization. They should also work to communicate that plan, persuade senior managers to support it financially and personally, implement it, and evaluate it. To emphasize a key point: This is a working committee and does not just watch others work.

The committee size will usually be determined by identifying and selecting representatives from each major department that technical training supports. At least three different groups may be "supported by" technical training. One group consists of those who use technical training to improve employee performance. A second group consists of those in the organization who purchase new equipment or change work processes and then request help in training equipment users or workers affected by new processes. A third group consists of management personnel, who are always key customers and stakeholders of technical training—and should be regarded as such. All three groups should be represented on a strategic planning committee.

Committee members should take a hands-on approach to investigating the need for technical training. Members represent a microcosm of the organization. Particularly good people to choose for such a committee consist of those having interest, those having a stake in outcomes, those having a good attitude to contribute to the long-term improvement of technical training in the organization, and those possessing exemplary work records.

How Should Meetings for a Strategic Planning Committee Be Planned and Managed?

Another important task is to develop a schedule of meetings for the strategic planning committee. That can usually be done at the launch meeting when all members should be present. If managers need an estimate of how much time will be devoted to meetings and what will be the schedule, the external consultant can usually develop an estimate. One way to hold meetings to a minimum is to take care to plan each meeting carefully and require pre-work. A project management chart is one method that can be used to lay out all activities, the time required for them, and their expected completion dates. Using such a chart can also help keep the committee's work on schedule. Organizing the plan up-front will result in less confusion and produce greater time to formulate and communicate the strategic plan for technical training. Depending on the size of the planning committee, it should be acknowledged at the outset that all members will not be expected to attend every meeting. However, all members will be expected to attend *most* meetings and remain actively involved through e-mail follow-ups.

How Should the Budget Process Be Handled?

It is important to develop a budget, both for the strategy formulation process and for strategy implementation. A tentative budget is needed at the time the committee begins to meet to estimate expenditures for the consultant and the meetings of the strategic planning committee. Consider such issues as these:

- Has the consultant provided a tentative budget for the project? (That is advisable.)
- Has the technical training manager estimated how many meetings will be necessary, where they will be held, how travel expenses will be handled, and any additional expenses (such as benchmarking trips) that may need to be made by committee members?
- Have materials been budgeted for?
- Have phone calls and other necessary and contingent expenses been estimated?
- Can meeting rooms be used in the company, or will it be necessary to pay for room rental off-site?

Many times a tentative budget is requested by top managers before they are willing to approve the development of the strategic plan for technical training.

What Is Environmental Scanning for the Strategic Planning Process, and What Should Be Examined When Formulating a Strategic Plan for Technical Training?

Environmental scanning is a key step in any strategic planning process. In fact, it is environmental scanning that sets strategic planning apart from the more static long-term planning. But what is environmental scanning? What should be examined in an environmental scan? How should the environmental scanning process be conducted?

What Is Environmental Scanning? How is environmental scanning defined? According to Rothwell and Kazanas (1994):

> *Environmental scanning for HRD* is the process of monitoring trends, issues, problems, or events which may create future learning needs as a result of environmental changes. These changes often require new knowledge and skills among people affected by them. Hence, environmental change may affect the learning needs of the general public, an organization's external stakeholder, members of each work group, individuals preparing for career advancement, or incumbents of each job class. (p. 117)

The result of environmental scanning is an *environmental scan* that looks at the future learning needs of people in the organization and how these needs will affect the organization. These future needs will then be used in formulating the strategic plan for technical training.

What Should Be Examined in an Environmental Scan? Environmental scanning can be focused on political, technological, social, market, geographic, and other external conditions as they may change over time. By asking questions about what changes can be expected in these sectors and what consequences those changes are likely to have on the organization and its members, decision makers can formulate their thinking about ways to avert future threats and seize future opportunities. They may even begin to construct *scenarios*—different visions of the future—and plan for how to deal with each of those. The same technique can be used in strategic planning for technical training as well as in corporate strategic planning.

Environmental scanning can take technical training from being reactive to proactive, integrating it with the organization's strategic decision-making process. As strategic planning committee members scan the environment, they can choose from among a dizzying array of options on what to look at. The choice of what external environmental issues and sectors to consider will depend on the organization and what sectors are most critical for its long-term competitive success. The following external environmental factors may be examined:

Political Sector

- Government regulation/deregulation of industry
- Government regulation of safety, environmental pollution
- Government purchases of goods and service
- Trade policy

Technological Sector

- Some jobs will just disappear
- Increased pressure on people to become computer literate
- Artificial intelligence
- Automated office systems

Social Sector

- Corporate social responsibilities
- Company responsibilities to consumers
- Company responsibilities to investors
- Work, what do people think about work?
- Leisure
- Family

Market Sector

- Customers
  - Demographics
  - Newly developed
  - Long-standing
  - Future product line

- Competitors
  - Identifying key competitors in the current business
  - Different business they contemplate entering
  - Change in a competitor's product
  - Advertising methods
  - Pricing methods
  - Key suppliers
  - Consumer groups
  - Customer loyalty
  - Costs
  - Strategies
  - Experience
  - Financial matters

Geographic Sector

- Future movements of consumers
- Competitors
- Suppliers
- Distributors

How Should the Environmental Scanning Process Be Conducted?

Once the strategic planning committee identifies what external environmental sectors to examine, the next step is to gather information. One method is to conduct interviews with experts in each sector who can provide current information, likely future changes, and predictions about the likely impact or consequences of those changes in that sector.

Exhibit 3.1 provides a guide that can be used during the interviewing process. It requests information on current requirements, projected future requirements, and ideal ways to address the requirements.

As a simple example of how the guide might be used, consider this: In one sector identified as political (government regulation of safety), environmental pollution was a major factor due to the nature of the business. To address this sector, an interview was conducted with a plant safety engineer. Under the *current requirements*, the plant has to conduct forklift training and two hours of classroom theory ever year. Under the *projected future requirements*,

EXHIBIT 3.1. AN INTERVIEW GUIDE TO EXAMINE STRATEGIC ISSUES IN TECHNICAL TRAINING

Directions to the user: Use this Interview Guide during environmental scanning for technical training. Select an individual with expertise on cutting-edge issues affecting the organization's work. Then pose the questions appearing below.

Name of Respondent	**Name of Interviewer**	**Today's Date**

1. What are the most important issues affecting the organization in the future?

2. What are the current requirements for technical training in organizations related to these important issues?

3. What future requirements are projected (or expected) in the future related to these important issues?

4. What are the ideal ways to address these requirements?

5. What is the likely impact or implications of the issue?

the safety engineers have become aware that the new regulation will require three hours of training each year and that the company will have to show evidence that participants are competent in the information presented. What is the *ideal way to address the new requirements*? For this example, each participant would be required to take a test, new training materials would need to be developed, and a test would also have to be written and validated. In the case of a unionized plant, the union would also have to be notified and address issues that are written in the contract concerning testing. This information would then be used in formulating the strategic plan for technical training.

Not all information gathered in the environmental scanning process will apply to technical training. It will be reviewed by the strategic planning committee to determine whether it is relevant. If it is, then it will be identified in the final plan. From the example above, you can see that gathering this information will take time and that more than one department and/or person should probably be interviewed for each sector. When the environmental scan has been completed, the strategic planning committee will review the interview results and distill key issues for consideration in formulating the strategic plan for technical training.

What Is Benchmarking, and How Can it Be Effectively Carried Out in the Strategic Planning Process?

Benchmarking looks at companies possessing best-in-class practices. This information helps to build a new understanding of approaches to solve old problems. It can also build an impetus for change to grapple with future problems or issues among those stakeholders involved in conducting the benchmarking process.

Widely used in total quality management, benchmarking may also be applied during strategic planning for technical training. As part of developing a strategic plan for technical training, benchmarking other organizations can help to identify areas in which your organization possesses strategic strengths and weaknesses. Benchmarking is valuable not only to your organization but also to the organization being benchmarked. Decision makers in each organization can take away new ideas and apply them to solving organizational problems.

Prerequisites and Guiding Principles for Benchmarking. There are three key prerequisites to effective benchmarking. First, decision makers should recognize that other organizations are better at certain disciplines, processes, and practices. Second, it is not always worthwhile to invent things from scratch. Third, benchmarking can help to slash the time needed for the diffusion of innovation and ideas.

Five principles should guide the benchmarking process. First, successful benchmarking requires a commitment from management. Second, other companies are often more willing to share than might be expected. (But do not ask others for any information that you are not willing to share about your own organization's processes and practices, since that will not lead to a productive and mutually beneficial relationship between the organizations.) Third, successful benchmarking depends on how well you know the way in which your organization's work is accomplished. Fourth, realize that your best-in-practice company is also constantly improving as customer requirements become more demanding. Fifth and finally, no organization can afford the luxury of thinking it is good enough.

Determining What Is to Be Benchmarked. What to benchmark should be determined by what has been identified as key objectives to be addressed by the strategic plan. As one example, consider the following list of four key issues that were taken from a real-world case in which the organization conducted benchmarking as a stage in formulating a strategic plan for technical training: (1) to standardize the approach to technical training for the company; (2) to provide high quality training, training materials, procedures, and other performance support media to employees; (3) to effectively and efficiently provide training to all manufacturing facilities in a short time frame; (4) to effectively and efficiently incorporate electronic document control, training documentation, and performance management tools. These four major objectives for the strategic plan for technical training would be the focal points for investigation in benchmarking.

Most benchmarking visits are usually scheduled for the duration of one-half to one full day. Time is of the essence. Therefore, if you find yourself leading a group on a benchmarking trip, do not deviate from the objectives of the benchmarking project once they have been established. It is easy to get sidetracked with other questions—especially if members of the benchmarking team represent other departments in the organization. There is a temptation to ask questions relating to their department needs. It is important to devise, in advance of a visit, a list of questions to ask during the benchmarking trip. That will help to keep a group focused. The list of questions should be developed as part of the strategic planning committee assignments before benchmarking visits begin. It is important to maintain this consistency, especially if several companies are being benchmarked by different task force team members. The questions will ensure consistency across benchmarking visits. Exhibit 3.2 provides a list of questions developed for a technical training benchmarking visit.

Selecting the Companies to Benchmark. Benchmarking does not mean visiting company competitors. In any case, they are not usually willing to permit such visits. The purpose of benchmarking is to visit best-practice companies. Therefore, you should remember that the goal is to find organizations with best practices—not the same products as your organization.

There are several ways to find companies that would be valuable to benchmark. One approach is to look for articles on companies that are showcased in magazines like *Training* or *Training and Development*. Innovative companies often want publicity for their efforts, so finding them may not be too difficult. Another approach is to network with professional colleagues in training-related organizations—such as the Technical Skills Professional Practice Area of the American Society for Training and Development or the national members of the International Society for Performance Improvement. Once you have a list of potential companies, contact, by phone or e-mail, the relevant department (such as technical training) that is to be the focus of your visit. You can tell from your phone conversation or the e-mail response you receive how receptive company representatives might be. In cases where they cannot accommodate a request, they may be willing to supply information over the phone or arrange a meeting with someone from their technical training department. This contact is also another source of useful information but is no substitute for in-depth benchmarking.

Reporting Benchmarking Data. Since human memory is notoriously fallible, take time to schedule a debriefing with the benchmarking team a day or two after a benchmarking visit. To do otherwise risks losing the

EXHIBIT 3.2. BENCHMARKING DATA GUIDE

Directions to users: Use this Data Guide to help you structure your benchmarking interviews. Send the questions below to the company to be benchmarked before the date of the visit. This will allow the company to review and plan their response and in some cases explain why certain questions will not be answered. Having the questions sent prior to the visit will also help the visiting company arrange to have the right people available for the discussion.

Company	**Location**
Key Contact Persons and Others Present	**Title**
Interviewer	**Today's Date**

Basic Company Information

1. Industry
2. Products/Services
3. Size (Number of employees)
4. Demographics
5. Geographic Scope (including number of sites)
6. Sales
7. Organizational Structure (request copy of organizational chart)
8. Team-based, self-managed work groups, or other type of organization
9. Statement of company values, vision, mission (request copies)
10. Union status (request copies of labor agreement)

Technical Training Mission

1. What is the company's technical training mission and vision?
2. How is technical training linked to the company's annual business objectives?
3. What is the scope of technical training?
4. How are the demands of safety, quality, productivity, and training prioritized?
5. What process is used to address conflicting priorities?
6. Do you have a one- to five-year plan for training and development?
7. Did you identify any "best practices" in organizing your five-year plan?
8. Did the union have any involvement in the formulation of the plan?

EXHIBIT 3.2.   (*Continued*)

Management of Technical Training

1. Where does technical training report and why?

2. How are technical training needs and priorities established?

3. What kind(s) of recordkeeping system(s) are used to track technical training? Who is responsible?

4. How much use is made of external resources (i.e., outside courses, consultants, subcontractors, outside vendors, etc.)? Why do you use them? Who are the primary technical training consultants?

5. To what extent does the company use non-training professionals in support of technical training?

6. How are communications about technical training managed (i.e., who, how, when, revision, etc.)? (Request copies of any communications, newsletters, measurements, etc.)

7. What are the desired outcomes of technical training in the facility or company? How are they measured? How are training measurements identified or selected?

8. What is different about technical training in the facility or company today from five or ten years ago?

9. Where does the facility or company see training going in the next three to five years?

10. How is technical training performance continuously improved?

11. How is technical training "supported"? Upper management's role?

12. What is the role of the union? What are the roles of hourly technicians/employees?

13. Does the facility or company have employee and management technical training committees? How are they selected? Are committee members permanent or do they rotate?

Technical Training and Education

1. Who designs technical training? (corporate/plant/outside resource)

2. Are technical training programs standardized? (between departments/sites)

3. As part of new temporary employee orientations, what technical training is included?

4. How are literacy and multi-language skill issues for technical training and communications addressed?

5. Are basic skills tied into your technical training process?

   If yes:

   A. What is your definition of basic skills?

   B. Is basic skill training mandatory?

   C. What methods are used to improve basic skills?

   D. How is basic skill training accepted by the employees?

(*Continued*)

EXHIBIT 3.2.   BENCHMARKING DATA GUIDE (*Continued*)

Technical Training Resources and Staff Support

1. What is the size and background of the technical training staff (plant and corporate)?

2. Is this staffing an increase or decrease over the past three to five years?

3. How are technical training dollars allocated? Accounted for?

4. What is the technical training department budget? Where is it budgeted? Technical training department or operating budgets?

5. What are the training dollars per person on average?

Multi-skilling

1. What is your company philosophy with regard to multi-skilling?

2. How would you define multi-skilling?

3. Do you still maintain specialists/experts?

4. What is the role of technical training in the development/implementation of multi-skilling?

5. What role do specialists play in technical training of other employees?

Business Objectives

1. Do your employees understand the overall business objectives and their impact on company success?

value—and information—secured on the visit. The same danger also exists if multiple teams from your organization met with multiple groups from a benchmarked firm. To cite an actual example: One benchmarking team met with hourly personnel and another team met with supervisors. The two teams heard different viewpoints and descriptions! In this case, if the two teams had taken time to compare notes, they could have followed up to clarify areas that were otherwise confusing.

A final report should be written following each benchmarking visit. That report should then be presented to all members of the strategic planning committee and the steering committee. This report can also be used in formulating the organization's strategic plan for technical training.

What Role Should Communication Play in the Strategic Planning Process?

An early step in the strategic planning process is to communicate the organization's commitment to developing a strategic plan for technical training. The organization's executives should make some announcement about the effort even before the members of a steering committee or a strategic planning committee are selected and announced. If the members are selected before an announcement is made, distrustful people may question the purpose of the strategy and the individuals chosen to participate. For this reason, an announcement should be made beforehand to set the stage and explain how the strategic plan for technical training will contribute to meeting business needs.

At the same time, it is important to devise a communication plan and strategy to match each step in the strategic planning process. As each project step is pursued, members of the strategic planning committee and the steering committee should be asked what should be communicated, to whom, when, and how. In that way, key stakeholders are kept apprised of events as they unfold. Most importantly, that should help to retain support from many groups in the organization.

How information is communicated depends on the organization's corporate culture. In some organizations, a "town hall meeting" approach is excellent. In other organizations, information may be placed on company websites, discussed in staff meetings, placed on company bulletin boards, or described in company newsletters.

What is important, however, is to have the first announcement come from senior managers. That dramatizes its importance. Such an announcement should at least explain the purpose of the strategic planning process, how personnel will be involved, and how the process will help the organization meet its business needs. The duration or timeline of the project may also be described.

How Should the Union Be Involved in the Strategic Planning Process?

If the organization is unionized, the business agent should be informed before senior managers make the announcement that the strategic planning process is about to begin. The technical training manager may find it helpful to involve the business agent in selecting the consultant and taking other key steps in laying the groundwork for the effort. The union business agent may be an excellent choice to serve on the strategic planning committee—or recommend someone, such as a shop steward, to serve on the committee. Unions are often strong supporters of training because it helps to keep union members employable. Having the union involved in the process adds to the credibility of the effort and also helps to build union ownership.

What Is Competitive Analysis, and When and How Should It Be Conducted?

Competitive analysis, the systematic process of gathering and analyzing information about what competitors are doing, is the last phase of the strategic planning process. It might seem to be a daunting task to discover the secrets of competitors. But it is important to remember that competitive analysis for technical training is not a cloak-and-dagger effort. It is relatively easy to uncover competitors' directions by attending trade shows, talking to vendors, talking to department heads in your own organization, participating in training conferences, and reading competitors' annual reports.

The purpose of competitive analysis in strategic planning for technical training is to determine what skills will be required if new equipment and work processes are widely adopted in your industry. This information can be helpful in planning and addressing a strategic plan for technical training. Exhibit 3.3 provides a chart that can be used as a guide in gathering necessary competitive information of value for planning technical training.

How Should the Strategic Plan for Technical Training Be Developed?

An organization is prepared to develop the strategic plan for technical training once the environmental scan, benchmarking, and competitive analysis have been completed. It is at this point that consultants earn their money. The consultant's role is to work with the strategic planning committee to facilitate a process of capturing, distilling, and synthesizing the information needed to create a unified, coherent technical training strategic plan that enjoys widespread ownership. Exhibit 3.4 illustrates a worksheet to use in distilling and reporting the information that has been collected.

EXHIBIT 3.3.   A GUIDE IN GATHERING NECESSARY COMPETITIVE INFORMATION OF VALUE FOR PLANNING TECHNICAL TRAINING

Directions to the user: Use this chart to organize your research on competitors as they influence technical training. List the names of the competitors in the left column below. Then, below the column labelled "current products and services," list what products are made or services are delivered by your organization's key competitor. Then, under "projected future products and services," list what products are likely to be made in the future or services are likely to be delivered in the future by your organization's key competitor. Then, finally, under the column labeled "impact or implications," list what technical training issues may be implied by the competitor's projected future products and services. Be sure to use all available sources to compile the competitive information. Add paper as needed.

Competitive Analysis Chart

	Current Products and Services	Projected Future Products and Services	Impact or Implications
Competitor 1			
Competitor 2			
Competitor 3			

How Should the Strategic Plan for Technical Training Be Implemented?

Appendix III provides charts illustrating the products from the work of one company's strategic planning committee as it worked through the steps of the strategic planning process for technical training. Consult those examples to help you as you undertake the process in your own organization. Then use the worksheet in Exhibit 3.5 to assess the quality of the strategic planning process for technical training in your organization.

EXHIBIT 3.4. A WORKSHEET TO ORGANIZE INFORMATION FOR FORMULATING STRATEGIC PLANNING FOR TECHNICAL TRAINING

Directions to the user: Use this worksheet to organize the information you have gathered to help formulate the organization's strategic plan for technical training. Describe the strategy for technical training in the space below. Support it by summarizing the *key information* you have obtained from the strategic planning process.

Strategy for Technical Training (*Describe*):

Competitive Analysis	Environmental Scan	Benchmarking	Focus Groups
What is the analysis of the competition's current state and future direction and the impact of those issues on technical training?	What is the analysis of the elements that affect the technical training strategy? Describe customers and stakeholders.	What companies were benchmarked, and how do practices in those organizations differ from those in this organization?	What were the results of focus groups held at each plant or organizational location to determine the current state of technical training and the likely future needs of internal customers and stakeholders in each location?

1.

2.

3.

4.

5.

EXHIBIT 3.5.   A WORKSHEET TO ASSESS THE QUALITY OF THE STRATEGIC PLAN FOR TECHNICAL TRAINING IN AN ORGANIZATION

Directions: Use this worksheet to assess the quality of the strategic plan and the strategic planning process for technical training in your organization. For each question posed in the left column below, rate the level of agreement you believe to be appropriate for your organization. Circle the number in the right column to indicate your level of agreement that the question has been effectively and fully addressed in the organization. Use the following scale: 6 = strongly agree; 5 = agree; 4 = somewhat agree; 3 = somewhat disagree; 2 = disagree; 1 = strongly disagree.

Has your organization effectively and fully addressed each of the following questions?	Level of Agreement that the Question Has Been Effectively and Fully Addressed in Your Organization					
	Strongly Agree 6	Agree 5	Somewhat Agree 4	Somewhat Disagree 3	Disagree 2	Strongly Disagree 1
1. Why should an organization develop a strategic plan for technical training?	6	5	4	3	2	1
2. What is (and should be) the role of the technical trainer in formulating and implementing such a plan?	6	5	4	3	2	1
3. Why is a champion (or champions) necessary for such a plan to be successful?	6	5	4	3	2	1
4. How can a technical training strategy be formulated in a way that builds a partnership?	6	5	4	3	2	1
5. Why should an external consultant be used in the strategy formulation process, and what should be sought from such a consultant?	6	5	4	3	2	1
6. Why should a steering committee be used, and what should be the role of such a committee?	6	5	4	3	2	1

(Continued)

EXHIBIT 3.5. A WORKSHEET TO ASSESS THE QUALITY OF THE STRATEGIC PLAN FOR TECHNICAL TRAINING IN AN ORGANIZATION (*Continued*)

Has your organization effectively and fully addressed each of the following questions?	Level of Agreement that the Question Has Been Effectively and Fully Addressed in Your Organization					
	Strongly Agree 6	Agree 5	Somewhat Agree 4	Somewhat Disagree 3	Disagree 2	Strongly Disagree 1
7. Why should a strategic planning committee be used, and what should be the role of such a committee?	6	5	4	3	2	1
8. How should meetings be planned and managed?	6	5	4	3	2	1
9. How should the budget process be handled?	6	5	4	3	2	1
10. What is environmental scanning for the strategic planning process, and what should be examined when formulating technical training strategy?	6	5	4	3	2	1
11. What is benchmarking, and how can it be effectively carried out in the strategic planning process?	6	5	4	3	2	1
12. What role should be played by communication in the strategic planning process?	6	5	4	3	2	1
13. How should the union be involved in the strategic planning process?	6	5	4	3	2	1

EXHIBIT 3.5. (*Continued*)

Has your organization effectively and fully addressed each of the following questions?	Level of Agreement that the Question Has Been Effectively and Fully Addressed in Your Organization					
	Strongly Agree 6	Agree 5	Somewhat Agree 4	Somewhat Disagree 3	Disagree 2	Strongly Disagree 1
14. What is competitive analysis, and when and how should it be conducted?	6	5	4	3	2	1
15. How should the strategy for technical training be developed?	6	5	4	3	2	1
16. How should the strategy for technical training be implemented?	6	5	4	3	2	1

Summary

This chapter opened with a case study that described one company's efforts to formulate a strategic plan to guide technical training. The chapter then addressed the following key questions that should be addressed when an organization formulates and implements a strategic plan for technical training: (1)Why should an organization develop a strategic plan to guide technical training? (2) What is (and should be) the role of technical trainers in formulating and implementing such a plan? (3) Why is a champion (or champions) necessary for such a plan to be successful? (4) How can a strategic plan for technical training be formulated in a way that builds support for its implementation? (5) Why should an external consultant be used in the strategy formulation process, and what role should a consultant play? (6) Why should a steering committee be used, and what should be the role of such a committee? (7) Why should a strategic planning committee be used, and what should be the role of such a committee? (8) How should meetings for a strategic planning committee be planned and managed? (9) How should the budget process be handled? (10) What is environmental scanning for the strategic planning process, and what should be examined when formulating a strategic plan for technical training? (11) What is benchmarking, and how can it be effectively carried out in the strategic planning process? (12) What role should communication play in the strategic planning process? (13) How should organized labor be involved in the strategic planning process? (14) What is competitive analysis, and when and how should it be conducted? (15) How should the strategic plan for technical training be developed? (16) How should the strategic plan for technical training be implemented? and (17) What other important issues should be considered as an organization formulates and implements a strategic plan for technical training?

The next chapter will examine the important role of managing a technical training function or department. That topic is a natural next step beyond establishing a strategic plan to govern the long-term direction of all technical training efforts in an organization.

CHAPTER FOUR

LEADING AND MANAGING
THE TECHNICAL TRAINING DEPARTMENT

Leading and managing a technical training department, function, or unit is an important responsibility (Nathan, Santi, and Chisholm, 1995; Rothwell, 2000). While not all technical trainers bear leadership or management responsibility, those who do are (or should be) involved on a daily basis with implementing the strategic plan for technical training described in Chapter Three. Both leadership and management are essential to implementing the strategic plan for technical training.

It is not unusual for people to confuse leadership and management. However, *leadership* is a function of interpersonal influence. It can be divorced from position. In other words, people can exercise leadership if they can influence others. But *management* carries with it the authority tied to organizational rank and position. Not all leaders are managers, but one hopes that most managers are leaders.

Much has been written about the differences between leadership and management (Rothwell and Kazanas, 1999). The goal of this chapter is to focus attention on the unique aspects of leadership and management that should be exercised by those charged with responsibility for technical training in an organization. More specifically, what is the role of leader and manager of technical training? What key responsibilities should the leader/manager carry out, and how should those responsibilities be carried out? This chapter addresses these important questions.

What Is the Role of Leader and Manager of Technical Training?

The leader and the manager of technical training share related, but slightly different, roles.

The Leader's Role in Technical Training

The most important role of the leader of technical training is to establish a vision of how technical training can contribute to meeting organizational needs. A *vision* is an idealized view of what the future should look like. Leaders are especially good at creating a compelling vision and then persuading others to embrace it enthusiastically. Use the worksheet in Exhibit 4.1 to structure your thinking about the vision for technical training in your organization.

The Role of the Manager of Technical Training

Leaders inspire, and managers implement. Managers follow through, ensuring that the people and resources needed to achieve identified strategic objectives are in place at the right times. In short, managers help transform a vision into a reality. They are intimately familiar with the organization's corporate culture, values, and geographic location (Devarics, 1995).

The most recent competency study sponsored by the American Society for Training and Development may be useful to consider here. According to Rothwell, Sanders, and Soper (1999, p. 43), the manager's role is to "plan, organize, schedule, monitor, and lead the work of

EXHIBIT 4.1.   A WORKSHEET TO FORMULATE A VISION FOR THE TECHNICAL TRAINING FUNCTION

Directions: Use this worksheet to organize your thinking about what the technical training function should look like under ideal conditions (not what it looks like now). Answer each question appearing below. Use the blank space to take notes. Once you have finished writing your answers, ask others to write their answers to the same questions. Then compare notes to see how your visions compare. There are no "right" or "wrong" answers in any absolute sense.

1. How should the technical training function in your organization be aligned with the organization's strategic plan? Its strategic objectives?

2. What would be happening if the technical training function in your organization were achieving the best possible results in your organization? What role would it be playing, and how would it be carrying out that role?

3. What results would the technical training function in your organization be achieving if it were functioning in an ideal way? Describe its outputs or results. How would those be measured?

4. In what ways would stakeholders—such as managers, workers, and other relevant groups—be supporting the technical training function if they were supporting it in ways you believe would be most beneficial to achieving the desired results of the technical training function? In other words, how would they be acting, and what would they be doing to contribute to the success of technical training?

individuals and groups to attain desired results; facilitate the strategic plan; ensure that [technical training] is aligned with organizational needs and plans; and ensure accomplishment of the administrative requirements of the function." The demands on the leaders and managers of technical training may vary somewhat by organizational size (Gettle, 1998). Use the worksheet in Exhibit 4.2 to structure your thinking about the most

EXHIBIT 4.2.   WORKSHEET FOR CLARIFYING THE ROLE OF THE MANAGER OF TECHNICAL TRAINING

Directions: According to Rothwell, Sanders, and Soper (1999, p. 43), the manager role "plans, organizes, schedules, monitors, and leads the work of individuals and groups to attain desired results; facilitates the strategic plan; ensures that [technical training] is aligned with organizational needs and plans; and ensures accomplishment of the administrative requirements of the function." Use this worksheet to structure your thinking about the most appropriate ways for a manager of technical training to meet this definition in his or her own organization. Answer the questions below.

1. What should a manager of technical training *do* to "plan, organize, schedule, monitor, and lead the work of individuals and groups to attain desired results; facilitate the strategic plan; ensure that [technical training] is aligned with organizational needs and plans; and ensure accomplishment of the administrative requirements of the function"? (*List specific activities.*)

2. How should the success of a technical training manager be measured?

appropriate ways for a manager of technical training to meet this definition in his or her own organization.

What Key Responsibilities Should the Leader/Manager of Technical Training Carry Out?

There is need for good research to pinpoint the key responsibilities that should be carried out by leaders and managers of technical training. But it is probably not too much of a stretch of the imagination to say that technical training leaders and managers should:

- Clarify the strategic objectives of their organizations
- Align technical training to organizational objectives and business needs
- Work to formulate and implement a strategic plan for technical training in their organizations
- Establish policies, standards, and procedures to support the effective implementation of the strategic plan
- Offer consulting advice to all levels of the organization to improve performance, taking care to distinguish management needs from training needs
- Apply effective instructional design principles when technical training is identified as an appropriate performance improvement strategy
- Organize the technical training function so that it is well-positioned to serve its targeted customers and stakeholders
- Pinpoint what work should be done inside the organization and what work should be outsourced
- Staff the technical training function appropriately and ensure that technical trainers are recruited, selected, developed, and appraised
- Demonstrate effective interpersonal skills and communication skills
- Develop himself or herself on a continuing basis to set a positive example for others

These responsibilities are depicted in the model in Exhibit 4.3. Use the worksheet in Exhibit 4.4 to reflect on how you are or should be meeting these responsibilities.

EXHIBIT 4.3.   A MODEL TO DEPICT THE KEY RESPONSIBILITIES OF A LEADER/MANAGER OF TECHNICAL TRAINING

Technical Training Managers or Leaders Should:

Clarify the Strategic Objectives
of Their Organizations

Align Technical Training to
Organizational Objectives and Business Needs

Work to Formulate and Implement a Strategic Plan
for Technical Training in Their Organizations

Establish Policies, Standards, and Procedures to Support
the Effective Implementation of the Strategic Plan

Offer Consulting Advice to All Levels of the Organization to
Improve Performance

Apply Effective Instructional Design Principles
When Technical Training Is Identified as an Appropriate Strategy

Organize the Technical Training Function So That It Is
Well-Positioned to Serve Its Targeted Customers and Stakeholders

Pinpoint What Work Should Be Done Inside the Organization
and What Work Should Be Outsourced

Staff the Technical Training Function Appropriately and
Ensure That Technical Trainers are Recruited, Selected, Developed, and Appraised

Demonstrate Effective Interpersonal Skills and Communication Skills

Develop Themselves on a Continuing Basis to Set a Positive Example for Others

EXHIBIT 4.4. WORKSHEET TO BRAINSTORM ACTIVITIES TO SUPPORT THE RESPONSIBILITIES OF A TECHNICAL TRAINING MANAGER OR LEADER

Directions: Use this worksheet to reflect on how you are or should be meeting the responsibilities of a manager or leader of technical training. For each responsibility listed in the left column below, brainstorm what you should do in the right column. While there are no absolutely "right" or "wrong" answers in any absolute sense, some answers may be better than others in specific corporate cultures.

Responsibilities of a Technical Training Manager/Leader	What Should You Do to Meet This Responsibility in Your Organization?
1. Clarify the strategic objectives of their organizations	
2. Align technical training to organizational objectives and business needs	
3. Work to formulate and implement a strategic plan for technical training in the organization	
4. Establish policies, standards, and procedures to support the effective implementation of the strategic plan	
5. Offer consulting advice to all levels of the organization to improve performance, taking care to distinguish management needs from training needs	
6. Apply effective instructional design principles when technical training is identified as an appropriate performance improvement strategy	
7. Organize the technical training function so that it is well-positioned to serve its targeted customers and stakeholders	
8. Pinpoint what work should be done inside the organization and what work should be outsourced	
9. Staff the technical training function appropriately and ensure that technical trainers are recruited, selected, developed, and appraised	
10. Demonstrate effective interpersonal skills and communication skills	
11. Develop himself or herself on a continuing basis to set a positive example for others	

How Should the Leader/Manager of Technical Training Carry Out the Key Responsibilities?

The responsibilities described above for leaders/managers of technical training deserve elaboration. The first three were discussed in Chapter Three, and so this section focuses on the remaining responsibilities.

Establishing Policies, Standards, and Procedures to Support the Effective Implementation of the Strategic Plan

A *policy* is simply a guideline. A *standard*, mentioned in the previous chapter, is a description of what should be, and in technical training usually focuses on desirable methods of analyzing training needs, designing and developing training to meet the needs, delivering the training, evaluating training results, and keeping records and otherwise ensuring effective management of technical training. A *procedure* describes, usually in step-by-step format, how to carry out a policy or a standard.

Consistency in technical training is important, and policies, standards, and procedures help ensure that training conducted in one part of the organization or in one location is comparable to training carried out elsewhere in the same organization.

Policies may be written to govern all phases of training, including what training should be offered inside the organization and how other educational experiences—such as external educational tuition reimbursement, conference attendance, and noncredit educational offerings supplied by external vendors—may be integrated with company-provided, in-house technical training.

Standards provide specific guidelines to follow. Exhibit 4.5 gives examples of standards. They may become the basis for evaluating training and guiding offerings across multiple locations.

Procedures are important for compliance with International Standards Organization (ISO) certification. Often, organizations will need to document their procedures for off-the-job and on-the-job training.

EXHIBIT 4.5. EXAMPLES OF STANDARDS FOR TECHNICAL TRAINING

All training in this organization will be:

1. Based on the strategic objectives of the organization
2. Aligned to the strategic plan for technical training
3. In compliance with the policies, standards, and procedures to support the effective implementation of the strategic plan
4. Focused on meeting needs that are appropriately met by training
5. Based on a thorough training needs assessment
6. Based on a thorough analysis of the setting in which the work will be performed
7. Based on a thorough analysis of the work and the tasks performed by the targeted training participants
8. Chosen only after the financial benefits of the training are calculated, based on estimates of the measurable costs of performance problems
9. Focused on meeting training objectives that match up to the technical training needs
10. Prepared so that participants' relative achievement in the training can be tested or measured
11. Selected, developed, or tailored to meet the training objectives
12. Cost-effectively delivered
13. Evaluated for employee reactions, learning, or on-the-job transfer of learning or behavior change

Offering Consulting Advice to All Levels of the Organization to Improve Performance

All problems in the world can be classified into two types. The first kind can be solved by training. It is caused by individual deficiencies between what people need to know, do, or feel to perform successfully and what they actually know, do, or feel. The second kind must be solved by management action and is caused by deficiencies in the work environment—that is, the world surrounding the performer. It is caused by organizational deficiencies between what support the work environment must give to performers and what they are actually given.

Training is a short-term change effort that is intended to equip individuals with the knowledge, skills, and attitudes that they need to perform their jobs effectively. Training is a solution. It is only appropriate when people do not know what to do, when to do it, how to do it, or why it is worth doing.

However, management action is the preferred strategy to solve 90 percent of all problems (Rothwell, Hohne, and King, 2000). It is necessary when conditions in the work environment—that is, the world surrounding individual workers—do not support effective performance. No amount of training will solve performance problems that stem from choosing the wrong person to do the job, for instance. A mistake of this kind is a management problem that can only be solved by management action.

However, leaders and managers of technical training have a responsibility to do more than just point out to others when training is not an appropriate solution to solve a performance problem. Instead, effective technical training managers will establish an effective partnership with managers, giving them information about alternative (and sometimes more effective) approaches to solve performance problems.

Applying Effective Instructional Design Principles

Line (operating) managers do not always understand that rigorously designed training should be carried out in a certain way. That is not surprising, since these managers may never have heard of instructional systems design (ISD), a topic treated in greater depth in the next chapter. ISD is a systematic, proven approach to preparing training that gets results. Technical training managers, however, should be well-versed in the principles of adult learning theory and in the theory and practice of ISD.

Organizing the Technical Training Function

How should a technical training department be organized? How should technical training projects be organized? These key questions should occupy the time and attention of effective technical training managers. If they are not answered correctly and reviewed on a continuing basis, failures can result.

A decade ago, it was common for technical training to be managed out of a central location, such as a corporate headquarters. That positioning sometimes gave technical trainers the aura of authority associated with the corporate headquarters. But it also sometimes meant that they were frozen out, because they were removed from breaking events on the firing line.

More recently, the trend is to decentralize technical training, placing it closer to the operating groups to be served. Instead of reporting to a corporate official, technical trainers end up reporting to the senior manager in charge of the group or location that they are meant to serve. That makes them accountable for results to those who need their help most.

Another recent trend is to use cross-functional teams—composed of those who know the subject matter or the work processes as well as technical trainers (Mueller, 1997; Rothwell, 1999)—to analyze training needs, design and develop the training, deliver it, and evaluate the results. One reason to do that is to ground technical training in the daily realities of work problems. A second reason is to leverage the impact of technical training, ensuring that others in the organization learn by seeing effective approaches to instructional design put into practice. A third reason to do it is that work has become so complex that nobody is thoroughly familiar with all facets of a subject or a problem, and that means that a team approach is usually best-suited to address the complexities of today's workplace.

Pinpointing What Work Should Be Done Inside the Organization and What Work Should Be Outsourced

Outsourcing is often done to minimize how many full-time technical trainers are needed. This helps to reduce operating expenses by minimizing the number of people who must be paid expensive employee benefits. It also has the advantage of giving an organization the ability to tap, on a short-term basis, specialized expertise that may not be available inside.

However, technical training managers must be careful to outsource in effective ways. Outsourcing does not mean abdicating responsibility. Someone must be available from inside the organization to manage the work of contractors, vendors, outside educational providers, and others who may be tapped to meet an organization's technical training needs in whole or part. The challenge facing technical training leaders and managers, then, is to choose what projects or portions of projects will be most cost-effectively handled by external providers, and what projects or portions of projects will be most cost-effectively handled by in-house technical trainers.

Staffing the Technical Training Function Appropriately and Ensuring That Technical Trainers Are Recruited, Selected, Developed, and Appraised

Technical training is rarely outsourced completely, since managers in most organizations want to maintain some control over the training delivered to their workers. Technical training leaders and managers should therefore maintain some competence in recruiting, selecting, developing, and appraising in-house technical trainers. In many respects, the challenge of carrying out these duties is not unique to technical training managers, since the same responsibilities must also be borne by managers in other areas. However, what is unique about these issues for technical training managers is that these duties must be carried out in ways that will be consistent with the organization's requirements for technical training.

Demonstrating Effective Interpersonal Skills and Communication Skills

Technical training leaders and managers must work effectively with others, establishing strategic alliances with many groups inside and outside their organizations. At the same time, they must work to communicate what services they can offer to others—and when their services are not appropriate.

One measure of effective interpersonal skills is the frequency of contact with others in the organization. Another is the nature and focus of such contact. Those are essentially issues also having to do with communication. Use the worksheet in Exhibit 4.6 to structure your thinking on who or what

EXHIBIT 4.6. WORKSHEET TO STRUCTURE YOUR THINKING ON GROUPS WITH WHOM YOU COME INTO CONTACT

Directions: Use Part I of this worksheet to structure or organize your thinking about all the groups with whom you come into contact in your work as a technical training manager. List them in the left column below. Then describe in the center column what that contact is about. In the right column, indicate how you might be able to improve the frequency and quality of your contact with those groups. In Part II, indicate in the left column what groups you should come into contact with. Then indicate in the right column what your contact should be about. Add space as needed.

Part I: Groups with Which You Come into Contact

What Is the Group?	What Is Your Contact About?	How Could You Improve the Frequency and the Quality of Your Contact with This Group?
1.		
2.		
3.		
4.		
5.		
6.		
7.		

Part II: Groups with Which You Should Come into Contact

What Is the Group?	What Should Your Contact Be About?
1.	
2.	
3.	
4.	
5.	
6.	
7.	

groups you most come into contact with and what that contact is about. Then reflect on ways that you may improve that frequency and quality of that contact.

Developing Oneself on a Continuing Basis

Technical training leaders and managers must set the example for personal development if they are to enjoy credibility. It is not realistic to expect others to develop themselves if the technical training leaders and managers are unwilling to do that themselves. Therefore, they must find ways to show how to identify their own development needs and plan to meet them.

Summary

This chapter was intended to stimulate your thinking on the crucially important role to be played by a leader or manager of the technical training function. We have seen that leaders and managers should: (1) clarify the strategic objectives of organizations; (2) align technical training to organizational objectives and business needs; (3) work to formulate and implement a strategic plan for technical training in their organization; (4) establish policies, standards, and procedures to support the effective implementation of the strategic plan; (5) offer consulting advice to all levels of the organization to improve performance; (6) apply effective instructional design principles when appropriate; (7) organize the technical training function; (8) pinpoint what work should be done inside the organization and what work should be outsourced; (9) staff the technical training function appropriately and ensure that technical trainers are recruited, selected, developed, and appraised; (10) demonstrate effective interpersonal and communication skills; and (11) develop themselves on a continuing basis.

The next chapter will focus attention on key principles of instructional design, an item listed in this chapter as a key responsibility for leaders and managers of technical training.

PART III

KEY ISSUES IN TRAINING COURSE DESIGN

Training course design is an important part of the job of most technical trainers. The chapters in this part

- Review the key steps in the systematic design of instruction, using the so-called Instructional Systems Design (ISD) model
- Explain how to identify technical training needs, emphasizing the developing a curriculum (DACUM) process
- List approaches and steps to preparing technical training programs
- Review key issues in determining and using training delivery methods
- Summarize important issues in evaluating technical training programs

Exhibit 4 is the blueprint for Part III within a schematic diagram representing the book's total scheme.

EXHIBIT 4.   PART III WITHIN THE SCHEME OF THE BOOK

Chapter 1: **What Is Technical Training?**	**Part I:** **Foundations of** **Effective** **Technical** **Training**
Chapter 2: **What Are the Characteristics of Effective Technical Training?**	
Chapter 3: **Establishing an Organizational Plan for Technical Training**	**Part II:** **Planning and** **Managing the** **Technical** **Training** **Function**
Chapter 4: **Leading and Managing the Technical Training Department**	
Chapter 5: **Basic Principles of Instructional Systems Design**	**Part III:** **Key Issues** **in** **Training** **Course** **Design**
Chapter 6: **Identifying Technical Training Needs**	
Chapter 7: **Preparing Technical Training Programs**	
Chapter 8: **Determining and Using Delivery Methods**	
Chapter 9: **Evaluating Technical Training**	
Chapter 10: **Using Vendors and Managing Original** **Equipment Manufacturers**	**Part IV:** **Special Issues** **in Technical** **Training**
Chapter 11: **Operating Apprenticeship and Safety** **Training Programs and Working with Unions**	
Chapter 12: **Achieving Results with Alternatives to Technical Training**	
Afterword	**Part V:** **Concluding** **Thoughts**

CHAPTER FIVE

BASIC PRINCIPLES OF INSTRUCTIONAL SYSTEMS DESIGN

Technical training is often required by line managers, workers, and sometimes company suppliers, distributors, or customers. Here is a sample of typical requests that a technical trainer might receive:

- "We need a new company orientation program. The workers we are hiring don't seem to have any appreciation for work ethic."
- "We are planning a switchover on the assembly line. The workers don't know how we will manufacture this new product. It is different from the one we used to make on that line. Why don't you put something together for them?"
- "OSHA is breathing down our necks. Could you put together some safety training that will satisfy the new regulations we expect to be implemented?"

Whether technical trainers manage the technical training function or simply prepare and deliver courses, they must be familiar with the proven steps of the instructional systems design (ISD) process (Beibel, 1995; Clark, 1989; Dent and Weber, 1999; Mancuso, 1995; Stormes, 1997). But what is ISD?

What are the steps in applying ISD to a technical training course? This chapter answers these questions. By doing so, the chapter provides an overview of the essential tasks in planning a technical training course.

What Is Instructional Systems Design (ISD)?

Instructional systems design (ISD) was invented by the U.S. military as an efficient and effective way to train soldiers (Rothwell and Kazanas, 1998). While many different versions of that model have been published, the models share common steps (Rothwell and Cookson, 1997):

- Analyze
- Design
- Develop
- Implement
- Evaluate

These steps, illustrated in Exhibit 5.1, are commonly called the ADDIE model. The word ADDIE is an acronym formed from the first letter of each key word above.

What Are the Steps in Applying ISD to a Technical Training Course?

This section is a review of each step in the ISD process. As you read about these steps, remember that they describe how a technical training course should be designed.

Analyze

Analysis is the first step in applying the ISD model to course design. Analysis should focus on the nature of the problem that may require training,

EXHIBIT 5.1. THE ADDIE MODEL

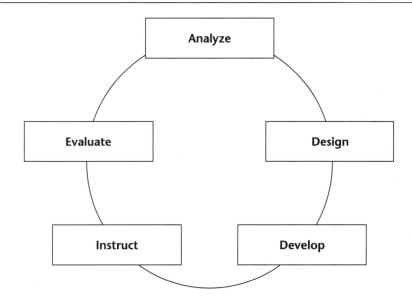

the people targeted to receive training, the work environment in which they will apply what they learn, the training environment in which they will receive instruction, and the work they are expected to perform. Without effective analysis, training cannot be successful. There are many forms of analysis that should be conducted before training design begins. They are depicted in Exhibit 5.2.

Performance Analysis. *Performance analysis* distinguishes problems that can be solved by training from problems that must be solved by management action. As we mentioned in Chapter Four, not all problems can be solved by training. Training is usually a strategy of last resort, since designing effective training can be both time-consuming and expensive. Some organizations have therefore been moving toward training by request only (Eline, 1998d) or to just-in-time training.

Use performance analysis when you are approached by a manager, worker, or other prospective customer with a request for training—or when a prospective customer asks for your help to solve a problem.

EXHIBIT 5.2.   TYPES OF ANALYSIS

Type of Analysis	Description
1. Performance analysis	Distinguish training needs from other needs that must be met by management action.
2. Learner analysis	The process of clarifying the target market for training and pinpointing who they are, what they already know about the topic or issue, and what they feel about the topic or issue.
3. Work setting analysis	The process of clarifying the conditions in which trainees will apply what they have learned after they receive training.
4. Instructional setting analysis	The process of clarifying the conditions in which trainees will receive instruction.
5. Work analysis	The process of examining the job or work that people are expected to do and the procedures they are expected to follow as they perform that work.
6. Job analysis	A form of work analysis that examines the jobs or work that people do.
7. Task analysis	The process of analyzing the specific work duties, responsibilities, or activities performed by people. It is more specific than job analysis and usually answers the question "How do people carry out their duties or conduct, step-by-step, the work they are expected to do?"
8. Training needs analysis	Carried out only after performance analysis has ensured that a performance problem can be solved by training. A training needs analysis identifies what people should know, do, or feel to perform their work effectively. It then pinpoints the gap between what people should know, do, or feel and what they presently know, do, or feel. The result of a training needs analysis should be the identification of specific training needs.

To apply performance analysis, begin by simply asking questions about the problem or the request for training. Find out as much as you can about it. Consider asking at least the following questions (Rothwell, 2000b):

- Who is affected by the problem? How many people are affected?
- What is the nature of the problem?
- When was the problem first noticed?
- Where is the problem most severe?
- Why do you think the problem exists? What causes it? How many possible causes may account for it?
- How much is the problem costing? How can its impact be measured? Is there a way to estimate the cost of the problem to the organization by

assessing metrics associated with quality, quantity, cost, time, or customer service?

Use the worksheet in Exhibit 5.3 to guide your thinking as you apply performance analysis. Add questions as necessary.

Learner Analysis. *Learner analysis* examines the audience targeted to receive training. It focuses on clarifying the characteristics of the people who will receive the training at present or in the future. Consider asking such questions about the learners as these:

- What do they already know about the topic?
- What experience relevant to the topic do they already possess, and how can their experience be assessed?
- What should they know about the topic before they enter the training? Should workers be screened out if they lack specific knowledge, skill, or ability that they should possess in advance?
- What is the attitude of the targeted learners about the training?
- How supportive of the training are the workers' immediate organizational superiors? Will they support the training and hold workers accountable on the job for applying what they learn?

Use the worksheet in Exhibit 5.4 to guide your thinking as you carry out learner analysis.

Work Setting Analysis. *Work setting analysis* focuses on the place in which training is to be applied. The conditions in which people are expected to apply what they learn are critically important. To carry out work analysis, consider such questions as these:

- Under what conditions will workers use what they learn?
- What tools, equipment, and other resources will workers have available when they apply what they have learned?
- What barriers in the workplace may prevent workers from applying what they have been trained to do, and how can those barriers be surmounted?

Use the worksheet in Exhibit 5.5 to guide your thinking as you carry out work setting analysis.

EXHIBIT 5.3.   WORKSHEET FOR CONDUCTING PERFORMANCE ANALYSIS

Directions: Use this worksheet to help you organize your thinking as you conduct a performance analysis. When you are confronted with a situation in which a manager or other stakeholder has requested your services for training, or when the stakeholder is asking for your help to solve a human performance problem of any kind, pose the questions appearing in the left column below. Then write your notes on the answers that you receive in the right column. Remember: The goal of a performance analysis is to distinguish problems that can be solved by training from other problems that may require other actions.

Questions	Notes on the Answers
1. Who is affected by the problem? How many people are affected?	
2. What is the nature of the problem?	
3. When was the problem first noticed?	
4. Where is the problem most severe?	
5. Why do you think the problem exists? What causes it? How many possible causes may account for it?	
6. How much is the problem costing? How can its impact be measured? Is there a way to estimate the cost of the problem to the organization by assessing metrics associated with quality, quantity, cost, time, or customer service?	

EXHIBIT 5.4.   WORKSHEET FOR CONDUCTING LEARNER ANALYSIS

Directions: Use this worksheet to help you organize your thinking as you carry out learner analysis. For each question appearing in the left column below, write your answers in the right column.

Question	Answer
1. What do the targeted participants for the training already know about this topic?	
2. What experience relevant to the topic do the targeted participants already possess, and how can their experience be assessed?	
3. What should the targeted participants know about the topic before they enter the training? Should workers/targeted participants be screened out if they lack specific knowledge, skill, or ability that they should possess in advance?	
4. What is the attitude of the targeted learners about the training?	
5. How supportive of the training are the workers' immediate organizational superiors? Will they support the training and hold workers accountable on the job for applying what they learn?	

EXHIBIT 5.5.   WORKSHEET FOR CONDUCTING WORK SETTING ANALYSIS

Directions: Use this worksheet to help you organize your thinking as you carry out work setting analysis. For each question appearing in the left column below, write your answers in the right column.

Question	Answer
1. Under what conditions will workers use what they learn?	
2. What tools, equipment, and other resources will workers have available when they apply what they have learned?	
3. What barriers in the workplace may prevent workers from applying what they have been trained to do, and how can those barriers be surmounted?	

Instructional Setting Analysis. *Instructional setting analysis* focuses on the place in which training will be conducted. Training may be conducted on the job, near the job, or off the job. Understanding the instructional setting is important in preparing for training, since training is more likely to be applied when conditions in which the training is carried out closely match actual working conditions.

To conduct instructional setting analysis, pose these questions:

- Where will the training be held, and why will it be held there?
- How closely do conditions in the instructional setting match up to the conditions of the actual work setting?
- How can conditions in the instructional setting be made to match up more closely with those in the work setting?

Use the worksheet in Exhibit 5.6 to guide your thinking as you carry out instructional setting analysis.

Work Analysis. *Work analysis* examines the job or work people are expected to do and the procedures they should follow as they perform the work. It is a particularly important form of analysis because many performance problems actually stem from a mismatch between what workers think they are expected to do and what their organizational superiors expect of them. Consequently, work analysis alone—if it increases the match in this understanding—can often be helpful in improving worker performance.

Job analysis is a specialized form of work analysis. It focuses on the jobs that people do—and especially on the work responsibilities they are expected to meet, the job performance standards they are expected to achieve, the frequency with which the work is performed, and the importance of the work duties performed. Ask the following questions to conduct simple job analysis:

- What is the purpose of the job?
- To whom does the job report?
- What kind of people does the job supervise?
- How much discretion do job incumbents exercise in carrying out their work?

EXHIBIT 5.6. WORKSHEET FOR CONDUCTING INSTRUCTIONAL SETTING ANALYSIS

Directions: Use this worksheet to help you organize your thinking as you carry out instructional setting analysis. For each question appearing in the left column below, write your answers in the right column.

Question	Answer
1. Where will the training be held, and why will it be held there?	
2. How closely do conditions in the instructional setting match up to the conditions of the actual work setting?	
3. How can conditions in the instructional setting be made to match up more closely with those in the work setting?	

- What are the primary work responsibilities or activities of the job?
- How much time is, or should be, spent on each activity?
- How critical to work success is each activity?
- What outputs are expected?
- How are outputs assessed for quality? Quantity?
- What qualifications are essential to learn the job?

Use the worksheet in Exhibit 5.7 to guide your thinking as you carry out job analysis.

Task analysis is that part of work analysis that focuses on the minutiae of job activities. It goes a step beyond job analysis (Ruyle, 1999). A simple way to think about it is to ask, for every work responsibility or activity listed on a job description, such questions as these:

- How is that activity carried out step-by-step?
- How does a worker know that this activity is called for?
- How does the worker know that an activity has been successfully completed?

Use the worksheet in Exhibit 5.8 to guide your thinking as you carry out task analysis.

The Results of Analysis. *It is essential that analysis* yield a description of the problem, the number of people affected by it, the specific learning requirements they have, and descriptions of how the instructional and work environments will affect what they learn. Job analysis is essential to clarify what people should know, do, or feel upon training completion.

Design

Design is the second step in applying the ISD model. It specifies exactly what instructional solutions should be used to meet the training needs identified during analysis. While analysis clarifies the problem and specifies its cause, design clarifies the solution and scopes out how it will be applied.

EXHIBIT 5.7.   WORKSHEET FOR CONDUCTING JOB ANALYSIS

Directions: Use this worksheet to help you organize your thinking as you carry out job analysis. For each question appearing in the left column below, write your answers in the right column.

Question	Answer
1. What is the purpose of the job?	
2. To whom does the job report?	
3. What kind of people does the job supervise?	
4. How much discretion do job incumbents exercise in carrying out their work?	
5. What are the primary work responsibilities or activities of the job?	
6. How much time is, or should be, spent on each activity?	
7. How critical to work success is each activity?	
8. What outputs are expected?	
9. How are outputs assessed for quality? Quantity?	
10. What qualifications are essential to learn the job?	

EXHIBIT 5.8.   WORKSHEET FOR CONDUCTING TASK ANALYSIS

Directions: Use this worksheet to help you organize your thinking as you carry out task analysis. For each question appearing in the left column below, write your answers in the right column.

Ask, for every work responsibility or activity listed on a job descriptions, such questions as these:

Question	Answer
1. How is that activity carried out step-by-step?	
2. How does a worker know that this activity is called for?	
3. How does the worker know that an activity has been successfully completed?	

Another way to think of design is to compare it to the process of constructing a building. The architect prepares drawings. Then a building contractor transforms the drawings from paper to reality. In the context of training, design is like the work of the architect. Development and implementation (delivery), taken together, are akin to the work of the building contractor.

During the design phase, technical trainers formulate the training objectives, prepare the testing or evaluation procedures, and create a training course specification.

Formulating Training Objectives. *A training objective,* a term synonymous as we use it with *instructional objective,* describes the results to be achieved from training (Mager, 1997). Think of it this way: A need indicates a problem; an instructional objective describes the solution. Instructional (training) objectives are stated in results-oriented terms, meaning they tell what training participants should know, do, or feel when they complete the training. Objectives are the fundamental foundation for all training (Parry, 1998).

Objectives usually have three parts. *Behavior,* which starts with an action word (verb), indicates what people should do upon training course completion. *Condition* indicates the tools, equipment, or other resources with which learners must be supplied to demonstrate the objective. *Criterion* is the measurable component of the training objective, indicating measures of quality, quantity, cost, time, or customer service.

Consider this example: Upon completing the training, participants will be able to: Type sixty-five words per minute with three errors or fewer when using a word processor. In this example, the word "type" is the behavior. The words "sixty-five words per minute with three errors or fewer" are the criteria, and there are actually three here—one is a measure of quantity, a second is a measure of quality, and a third is a measure of time. The words "when using a word processor" is an example of a condition.

After the objectives for training have been formulated, they should then be sequenced, which means that they should be placed in some order for the learners. While there are many ways by which to sequence training (Rothwell and Kazanas, 1998), technical trainers will usually find that sequencing by procedure or sequencing by problem are the most common ways they will sequence instruction. *Sequencing by procedure* means that training objectives, and subsequently the outline for training itself, will be organized around the order in which work processes are carried out. An example of that might be organizing worker training around the steps in a manufacturing process. *Sequencing by problem* means that the training will be organized around the problems experienced by workers as they attempt to do their work. An example might be organizing worker training around the most common problems that new software users encounter as they begin using a word processing package.

Preparing Testing or Evaluation Procedures. A *test* assesses how much or how well participants met the training objectives. The appropriate test to select is a function of what training objectives were formulated (Bass, 1996; Blair and Giles, 1996).

For instance, if you are merely teaching people facts and figures, then you should use a way to measure their understanding of that information. Knowledge tests may be called for. On the other hand, if you have taught them a skill—such as machine maintenance—you may need to see them perform what they have been taught. Tests of knowledge are usually referred to as *knowledge tests*. Tests of ability are usually called *performance tests*. Trainees who pass tests before training have no need to attend that training, and that can save the organization money by reducing how many people need to participate in it (Schriver and Giles, 1997).

The Results of Design: Preparing a Training Course Specification. The *training course specification* provides essential information such as the purpose of the course, the instructional objectives, the targeted audience, measurement methods and criteria as appropriate, a content outline, the choice of delivery method(s), and any on-the-job follow-up criteria.

A training course specification is particularly important to prepare if the organization plans to outsource the development, delivery, or evaluation of the training. The reason is that the course specification lays out the blueprints for the course. Armed with that information, most vendors should be well-prepared to write a proposal and budget realistically for the course.

Development

Development is the third step in applying the ISD model. In this step technical trainers transform course specifications into lesson plans and other course materials—or else purchase all or part of the material and methods from others. The course is *framed*—meaning that the content needed to make the course complete is prepared. If classroom training is to be used, then it is at this point that trainers write lesson plans, participant guides, instructor guides, tests, video scripts, audiotape scripts, tests, and other material needed. (See Exhibit 5.9 for a template for a sample lesson plan for a classroom-based technical training course.) If on-the-job training is to be used, then trainers prepare lesson plans, checksheets, and other material for coaches or mentors to use at the work site. If web-based or computer-based training is to be used, then trainers prepare the lesson plans and devise online features that will increase interaction with learners—such as virtual blackboards, chat rooms, threaded online discussions, and other relevant ways to increase interaction and contact with learners. (See Exhibit 5.10 for a template for a sample lesson plan for a web-based technical training course.)

Suffice it to say that most of this work requires much writing. For that reason many organizations outsource all or part of this work. It can be labor-intensive to prepare and can, if multimedia delivery methods are chosen, require specialized skills (Salopek, 1998).

During the development step, technical trainers also pilot-test the course. They run a full-scale dress rehearsal of it, just as theater managers

EXHIBIT 5.9. TEMPLATE FOR A LESSON PLAN FOR A CLASSROOM-BASED TECHNICAL TRAINING COURSE

Purpose of the Lesson

Objectives of the Lesson

Organization of the Lesson (Structure)

Targeted Participants

Participant Material

Assessment

Participant Assignment

EXHIBIT 5.10.   TEMPLATE FOR A LESSON PLAN FOR A WEB-BASED TECHNICAL TRAINING COURSE

Purpose of the Lesson

Objectives of the Lesson

Organization of the Lesson

Targeted Participants for the Lesson

Participant Material for the Lesson

Assessment for the Lesson

Participant Assignment

Interactive Elements Used (Threaded Discussions, Chat Rooms, Videoconferencing, and Other media) will run a dress rehearsal to get an acting cast ready to perform on Broadway. The dress rehearsal is called a *formative evaluation*.

There are many "right" ways to run a dress rehearsal. One way is to invite selected members of the targeted audience of participants and run them through the course to see what they think of it. The goal is to find ways to improve the course before it is rolled out. Another way is to invite selected supervisors of the targeted audience. When supervisors attend a rehearsal, they can be asked how to follow up on the training back on the job so as to hold workers accountable for applying what they have learned. Modifications are made to the instructional materials and methods after the dress rehearsal but before the training goes prime time. The final result of the development step, then, is a fully prepared and tested training course.

Implementation

Implementation, meaning delivery, is the fourth step in applying the ISD model. This step is perhaps the most familiar to trainers. It is at this point that trainers implement the plans created during the analysis, design, and development phases. If the course is to be presented in a classroom, then it is delivered there. If the course has been prepared for web-based, video-based, audio-based delivery, then it is prepared in that format. If the course will be translated or otherwise adapted for cross-cultural presentation, then an additional step is usually added for that purpose (Latimer, 1999).

Evaluation

Evaluation is the fifth and final step in applying the ISD model. While the foundation for evaluation is laid in analysis and built in each step following that, it is during after-the-course evaluation that the results of training should become apparent.

Summary

This chapter provided a summary of the essential steps in the instructional systems design (ISD) process: analysis, design, development, implementation, and evaluation. ISD is a rigorous approach to preparing results-oriented technical training. Later chapters will examine these steps in more detail.

The next chapter turns to a more in-depth treatment of analysis and examines how technical trainers analyze training needs.

CHAPTER SIX

IDENTIFYING TECHNICAL TRAINING NEEDS

This chapter focuses in greater depth on identifying technical training needs, a topic raised previously in Chapter Five. Identifying technical training needs requires trainers to take at least two key steps. First, they must distinguish problems that can be solved by training from other problems that cannot. Second, for problems that lend themselves to solution by training, technical trainers must clarify the difference between what people know, do, or feel at present and what they must know, do, or feel to perform effectively.

The chapter opens with a case study that dramatizes the importance of technical training needs assessment and describes a situation faced in a real organization. The chapter then addresses such key questions as these:

- What are technical training needs?
- How are training needs distinguished from other needs?
- What is the DACUM method?
- How can the DACUM method be used as a particularly effective tool in conducting technical training needs assessment?
- What methods can be used to assess technical training needs?
- How is that information then used to build effective training?

The chapter concludes with a continuation of the case study that opened it, providing further information about how the case situation involving training needs assessment was managed in a real organization.

Case Study: Introduction to Technical Training Needs Assessment

Trying to determine the training needs of an organization is a challenge in itself, but trying to do that without having updated job descriptions of the targeted trainees or task analysis results to indicate how they do the work makes training design a daunting issue. That was the situation one trainer faced when he was working for a large manufacturing company. All workers shared the same job title, a practice dating back to the company's origins over one hundred years ago. The only thing that distinguished workers was the department in which they functioned or the equipment they operated. Moreover, each worker could be moved to another department—or to another piece of equipment—on a moment's notice. Seniority was the basis for decisions about who worked where.

Most training was handled informally. Training requests were made by supervisors, who based their perceptions of training needs on performance problems occurring in their work areas or else on changes occurring in work processes. Regularly scheduled training focused on complying with the safety regulations mandated by the Occupational Safety and Health Administration (OSHA).

Workers' Training Records

The company maintained a training database on all workers. Each worker's attendance at mandated training was entered into the computerized recordkeeping system. That provided technical trainers with some information about the training in which individuals had participated. The database was also useful to managers when they were searching for replacements to cover for sick or vacationing workers. Safety training was most closely monitored due to regulatory requirements. The information in the database was not complete, but it was all that technical trainers in the organization had to work with. It was a daunting challenge to identify training needs for individuals, work areas, or plants, due to incomplete information and to the company's practices.

Developing a Technical Training Strategy

The company had several plants located throughout the United States. Each year the technical trainers would meet to discuss common concerns. One meeting focused on the importance of establishing a standardized approach to training.

There were several reasons why this topic commanded such attention. First, all technical trainers in the company shared a common problem: No job descriptions existed to indicate the work performed. Second, each plant developed its own training, which complicated efforts to exchange training programs of common interest. Third, technical trainers were worried that workers would become acclimated to only one mode of training and would therefore resist training delivered in other ways. Fourth, standardization of instructional design approaches could prove beneficial because it could lead to increased consistency in the way training was developed. Fifth and finally, a standardized approach would, the trainers felt, make it easier to train all levels of the organization on a common way of assessing needs, designing and developing training, delivering the training, and evaluating results.

This meeting galvanized support for the development of a corporate-wide technical training strategy. One issue to be addressed was the development of job descriptions. Many ideas were traded on how job descriptions could be prepared. Some favored hiring an external consultant to do this laborious work. Some trainers wanted to do it on their own. And still other trainers wanted some combination of approaches.

One trainer talked about a system he learned about from a graduate student who was pursuing a degree in training and development in which the student used the process to develop a set of trainer competencies. The process was called the DACUM method, and it eventually became the process used to develop over one hundred job descriptions.

Several considerations played a part in selecting the method to be used for developing the job descriptions. Time was an issue when the task involved preparing one hundred job descriptions in a short time. If the process was too time-consuming, it would prove to be difficult to justify it to management. Simplicity was another issue warranting attention. If the approach chosen was too detailed and difficult to understand, employees would grow bored quickly. To justify the cost it would have to be developed by company trainers. The technical trainers for the six plants were therefore identified as the source to develop the job descriptions. Another factor worthy of consideration was whether the job description resulting from a process would be sufficiently detailed to become the basis for assessing training needs. The DACUM method was selected over other methods because it addressed all the issues mentioned above.

A project plan was prepared to conduct DACUM sessions throughout all the plants. Only one or two workers were used instead of the eight to twelve recommended by the creators of DACUM. Since the plants ran three-shift operations, and in an effort to involve all shifts in the process, the number of job descriptions to be developed was divided equally among shifts.

The plan was that, once the job descriptions were developed, content experts from the shifts not involved in the process would review and modify the job descriptions. That would also be done under the guidance of the technical trainers. The final evaluator for each job description would be the supervisor in the area for which the job descriptions were developed.

The process was facilitated by technical trainers. Technical trainers were assigned to different shifts to support the effort. Not all technical trainers were involved at the same time. They rotated every week, returning to their home plants for several weeks before again taking a turn. Usually two technical trainers were assigned weekly to work on the job descriptions. Before the DACUM sessions began, the technical trainers participated in two days of training on the DACUM process. This training focused on how to facilitate a DACUM session. When the DACUM process was discussed during the training session, the technical trainers agreed to use the same major duties for the entire job task—that is, safety, communication, operation, maintenance, reports, materials, and troubleshooting. Miscellaneous was another duty assigned. If the job had some special duty or duties, it would be identified under this point.

Before the DACUM sessions began, the plant manager and human resource manager met with a key union official to discuss the purpose and plan. They emphasized that the sessions would result in better training for employees. That was also of major concern to the union.

To complete a project requiring the preparation of DACUM charts for one hundred jobs required six weeks of work. The project was not continuous. Delays were caused by production and maintenance problems. That was, however, anticipated during the project planning phase. Downtime between DACUM sessions was used by technical trainers to work with management to schedule workers for jobs still requiring analysis.

Completion of the DACUM Charts

When all charts were completed, the next step was to have all employees self-evaluate themselves for their skills for each job they were performing. Over the years workers had actually developed skills in several jobs. Therefore, it was necessary for technical training needs assessment to determine each worker's skill levels. To that end, a job profile sheet was developed. Information on this sheet was gathered from DACUM charts.

There was some concern about the accuracy of *self-reporting*—that is, having employees identify their own skills levels and assess their own training needs. After much discussion, this approach was used. When thirty employees finished their skills sheets, technical trainers met with the employees' supervisors to review and verify the self-assessments. The self-evaluation process proved to be 98 percent accurate when subsequently reviewed by supervisors. Therefore, the remaining skills evaluations were carried out in the same way. When all the job profile sheets were completed, the information was entered into a database to inventory employees' training needs.

What Is a Technical Training Need?

In the most general sense, a *training need* is a difference between what people know, do, or feel and what they should know, do, or feel to perform their work successfully. There are two kinds of training needs: long-term needs and short-term needs. A *long-term training need* is predictable (Rothwell and Sredl, 2000). Whenever people change their jobs or their work, they have predictable training needs. There are only six major actions that can be taken with people in organizations: They can be moved in (hired), moved out (terminated, laid off, or retired), moved up (promoted), moved down (demoted), moved across (transferred), or given more skills where they are (developed in place). Each major action is associated with predictable needs. Whenever people are expected to do something new, they must be given the knowledge, skills, and attitudes to perform the work. That means they have training needs.

One way to address long-term training needs is to establish a training curriculum that shows the training requirements for each department or work group by hierarchical level and by time in the position. (See Exhibit 6.1.) Such a curriculum can be depicted as a training curriculum matrix that depicts all training requirements by department, level, and time in position. For each training requirement, additional issues should be clarified. (See Exhibit 6.2.) Organizations that possess such a training curriculum can plan to meet long-term training needs on a continuing basis.

A *short-term training need* stems from two causes (Rothwell and Sredl, 2000). One cause is organizational change. Whenever the organization changes work methods, equipment, or other processes or equipment with which workers must interact to do their work, then a training need is usually created. Another cause is a shortfall between an individual's abilities and the requirements of a job, which stems from a change in the work methods. For instance, workers who previously used manual processes may find themselves interacting with computers. That creates a training need for computer skills.

It is important to distinguish a *training need* from a *training want*. A *need* is essential to performance. A *want* is something that would be "nice to have"—but is not really essential to performance. Much confusion exists about what to do training on. That confusion often stems from the substitution of a training want for a training need.

A *technical training need* is one form of training need. Recall from Chapter One that technical training was defined as *training intended to help people perform the unique aspects of a special kind of work and apply the special tools,*

EXHIBIT 6.1. TRAINING CURRICULUM MATRIX

Directions: For each job category listed in the left column below, list the *title of a training course* that you feel would be appropriate at each stage of an individual's level of experience in it. "Entry" means "upon entry to the job category and until the end of the first year." "Intermediate" means "from one and up to three years." "Advanced" means "after the individual has been in the job category for three or more years." There are no "right" or "wrong" answers; rather, the aim of the matrix is to begin to organize training requirements. Add paper as needed.

Department Name

Job Category	Entry	Intermediate	Advanced
[List the job categories in the department in the left column below, ranging from the highest level (such as "executive") at the top to the lowest at bottom.]	[List the title of the training course or other training experience from entry-level requirements to continuing requirements in the order in which they should be taken at the level.]		

EXHIBIT 6.2.   COURSE DESCRIPTIONS LINKED TO THE TRAINING CURRICULUM

Directions: Answer the questions appearing below for each course listed on the organization's training curriculum.

1. What is the purpose of the course? State the purpose of the course in one sentence.

2. What should participants in the course know or do upon course completion? (*In other words, what should they know how to do upon course completion that they did not know when the course began?*) List three to five instructional objectives for each course. Use this format for each course:

   Example:

   Given a book describing Deming's philosophy, participants should be able to:

   1. Identify the fourteen points
   2. Describe how the fourteen points apply to Company X's equipment
   3. Describe how the fourteen points apply to their departments/jobs

3. Who are the targeted participants? (*Describe, as specifically as possible, who should take the training and at what point in their period of employment they should take it and why. Specify course prerequisites.*)

4. How should the course be delivered? (*Describe the way the course is presented to participants. Examples of appropriate answers would include "Two-day classroom-based course."*)

5. **(If applicable)** Who should be the instructors, if the course is to be instructor-led? (*Describe, as specifically as possible, the instructors' essential training, education, and/or experience that makes them qualified to teach—and could disqualify those who are not qualified to teach the course.*)

6. What is the course content? (*Provide a topical outline for each course. Use about half a page for each course. Use about half a page for each outline to describe course content. Add paper as necessary.*)

7. How should the course be evaluated? (*Answer these questions: Should participants complete course evaluations? Should participants complete pre-/post-tests to measure their knowledge? Should participants complete six-month post-course evaluations to measure on-the-job learning transfer? Should efforts be made to measure the return on training investments by indicating long-term productivity gains to be realized by the training? Should instructors rate participants, course, and/or other issues?*)

equipment, and processes of that work, usually in one organizational setting. Hence, a technical training need occurs when a difference exists between what individuals know, do, or feel and what they must know, do, or feel to *perform the unique aspects of a special kind of work and apply the special tools, equipment, and processes of that work, usually in one organizational setting.*

Conducting a training needs assessment does not have to be as complicated as rocket science. The real goals are to identify what work results and activities are desired, compare that to what work results people are actually achieving and how they are doing that, and then figure out how to bring the two into alignment. Doing that may be as simple as asking a supervisor what he or she expects, watching a worker perform some activity (such as using a word processing package, carrying out a manufacturing process, using a machine, or attempting to access the company's inventory control system), and then comparing the expressed desires of the supervisor and the actual work behaviors and results of the worker. Of course, conducting a training needs assessment can be as complicated as you want to make it—or as your customers demand it to be confident of the results.

How Are Training Needs Distinguished from Other Needs?

The previous chapter introduced *performance analysis,* a step that usually precedes training needs assessment and is intended to distinguish problems that can be solved by training from problems that must be solved by management action. It is worthwhile to revisit that topic. One reason to do so is that technical trainers are frequently approached by line mangers with training requests. A *training request* is an appeal for a special solution. When a manager says, "My people need training," he or she is requesting a solution. But the problem that prompts that request remains unknown until the technical trainer begins asking questions about it.

Technical trainers simply cannot fill every training request that they receive. If they did, they would probably be functioning as little more than order takers, much like waiters or waitresses in a restaurant who simply write down what meals their customers want and fill any order given to them.

A better approach is to assume the role like a medical doctor who is treating a patient. That requires analytical skill, which is also important to trainees who are subsequently successful in technical careers (Wicklein and Rojewski, 1999). The patient enters the doctor's office with complaints, which are usually considered to be symptoms of problems. But the root causes of the problems are not known, and it is the doctor's job to find out what is the root cause (or causes) of the problem and then prescribe the best therapeutic treatment available to solve a problem.

Incidentally, what doctor would prescribe medicine simply because a patient requested it? Imagine the situation. A patient walks into the doctor's office and asks for chemotherapy! No doctor in his or her right mind would agree, since that would immediately raise the specter of a malpractice suit!

So it is with technical trainers. They cannot simply go along with every request for training from managers. One reason is that the underlying root cause(s) of the performance problem(s) may not be known. Therefore, to apply training as a solution would be potentially unwise, costly, and inefficient. Another reason is that the technical trainer who goes along just to get along may actually be treating a symptom rather than the underlying cause of a problem. That will be a wild goose chase that will ultimately lead to the loss of credibility for the training department, since treating a symptom will not cure the illness.

To apply performance analysis, technical trainers should thus ask many questions about the problem. (Examples of such questions were supplied in Chapter Five.) If the problem is unknown, then they must discover what it is and what causes it. Remember that training will only solve problems resulting from lack of individual knowledge, skill, or attitude. Training will not solve problems that are caused by poorly defined jobs, lack of tools, lack of management planning, lack of rewards or incentives for performance, or other such common root causes. Those problems may only be solved by management action.

Training needs assessment is only conducted when it is clear that a training problem exists. If another problem exists, technical trainers must possess at least sufficient expertise to pinpoint what the causes are and what solution or solutions might be used to address those causes. To continue the analogy with a medical doctor, a doctor must be sufficiently skilled to diagnose the problem. If the doctor does not possess the skills to treat that cause, then he or she will refer the patient to a specialist who does possess those skills. So it is with technical trainers.

What Methods Can Be Used to Assess Technical Training Needs and How Is That Information Used to Build Effective Training?

Conducting a training needs assessment is often a project in its own right. Indeed, many technical trainers find that they must first scope the training that is necessary before they are able to begin designing and developing the training. The challenge is how to do it quickly, since line managers usually want the training immediately (Treichler and Carmichael, 1999).

Methods for Technical Training Needs Assessment

Many methods have been suggested to assess training needs. Generally speaking, training needs assessment can be conducted by any data collection method so long as it:

- Identifies what knowledge, skill, and attitude people are expected to possess to perform their work competently
- Identifies what knowledge, skill, and attitude individuals currently possess
- Pinpoints the *training gap*, which is the difference between what people should know, do, or feel to perform competently and what they currently know, do, or feel

The concept is emphasized by the picture in Exhibit 6.3.

Skill standards are of value in conducting training needs assessment. *Skill standards* express desired skill levels in different industries and occupations and thereby clarify what skills individuals should possess to perform their work competently. More specifically, as noted in *Built to Work*

EXHIBIT 6.3.   UNDERSTANDING A TRAINING NEED

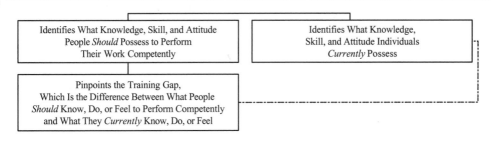

(2000, p. 2): "Skill standards answer two major questions: (1) What does someone need to do on the job to perform competently? and (2) What knowledge and skills will enable them to carry out these responsibilities? What does on-the-job excellence require and what does it take to get there? That's exactly what skill standards will tell us."

Currently, the United States is sponsoring a national initiative to identify skill standards in fifteen industry sectors under the guidance of the National Skills Standards Board (NSSB). The fifteen industries targeted for action are: (1) agriculture, forestry, and fishing; (2) business and administrative services; (3) construction; (4) education and training; (5) finance and insurance; (6) health and human services; (7) manufacturing, installation, and repair; (8) mining; (9) public administration, legal and protective services; (10) restaurants, lodging, hospitality, and tourism, and amusement and recreation; (11) retail trade, wholesale trade, real estate, and personal services; (12) scientific and technical services; (13) telecommunications, computers, arts and entertainment, and information; (14) transportation; and (15) utilities and environmental and waste management. For more information about this initiative and for publications that can be downloaded to describe how skill standards may be used, visit the NSSB website at www.nssb.org. Documents such as *Getting Started* (NSSB, 2001) can help in showing how to use skill standards in establishing benchmarks for work requirements, which can (in turn) be useful in training needs assessment.

Exhibit 6.4 presents a list of possible data-collection methods that can be used in conducting technical training needs assessment. Appendix IV

EXHIBIT 6.4. GENERAL METHODS TO ASSESS TRAINING NEEDS

Method	Advantages	Disadvantages	Comments
Interview	Reveals feelings, causes, and possible solutions as well as facts.	Takes time. For that reason it reaches few people. The results can be difficult to quantify. Participants in interviews may be uncomfortable with the process.	Conduct a pre-test and review interview questions as necessary. Ensure that the interviewer can listen without judging responses.
Questionnaire	May reach many people in a short time. It is relatively inexpensive. It can afford an opportunity for free expression without fear or embarrassment. It generates data easily. If the questionnaire is scaled, data can be easily summarized and reported.	If the questionnaire is scaled, it may afford little opportunity for free expression and unanticipated responses. Questionnaires may be difficult to construct. They may have limited effectiveness in identifying the root causes of problems and the range of possible solutions to them.	Conduct a pre-test. Revise questions and questionnaire format as necessary. Offer and give assurance of anonymity and confidentiality. Use questionnaires only if you are prepared to report unfavorable as well as favorable findings and take action on the findings.
Tests	Tests are useful as a diagnostic tool to identify deficiencies of knowledge or skill. They can help narrow down a group of targeted participants, eliminating those who are already proficient. Test results are usually easily compared and reported.	Valid, work- or culture-specific tests are not available for many occupations. Tests that are valid in specific situations may not be valid in all situations. Test results yield clues, not conclusive results. Tests do not produce the best evidence of work performance.	Those who use tests should know what the tests measure and what they do not measure. They should ensure that test results are worthwhile. They should not use tests to justify difficult or unpopular decisions that should be taken by management.

Group Problem Solving	Group interviews are similar to interviews, described above. They permit a synthesis of views from multiple viewpoints. They promote understanding, agreement, and possible ownership in the results. This approach may be especially effective in organizations functioning with team-based management.	Group problem solving can be time-consuming and expensive. Supervisors, executives, and other key players may feel too busy to participate. (In downsized organizations, even participants may feel that way.)	Do not promise or expect immediate results. Begin with recognized problems, such as group concerns. Identify all meaningful problems for the group. Permit the group to make its own analysis and set its own priorities.
Study of Records and Reports	This approach provides excellent clues to performance problems. It provides more objective evidence of problem consequences than opinions of individuals.	Records and reports rarely reveal the causes of problems or identify possible solutions. They may not provide representative cases. The available information may be outdated or based on special and unusual cases.	Use them to enhance and triangulate other approaches.
Position Analysis and Performance Review	This method can produce specific, precise information about work and performance. It relates problems or needs to real workers.	Conducting analysis in this way can be very time-consuming and expensive. It can be difficult for individuals who are not trained to analyze positions or review performance to use this method. This method may highlight individual but not group needs.	Keep information up-to-date by offering training to those who will analyze positions and review performance. Ensure that analysis focuses on current information and current people.

Source: W. Rothwell and P. Cookson. (1997). *Beyond Instruction: Comprehensive Program Planning for Business and Education.* San Francisco: Jossey-Bass, pp. 136–137. Used by permission of the publisher.

presents a ready-to-go questionnaire that may be used to assess the technical training needs for a manufacturing plant.

How Is the Information from a Technical Training Needs Assessment Used to Build Effective Training?

To reemphasize a point made in Chapter Five, a technical training needs assessment is the starting point for preparing a rigorous, results-oriented technical training program. Recall that training needs are essentially problems. The results of training needs assessment should lead directly into establishing training objectives, which (when met) will satisfy the needs and thereby address performance problems. Objectives are, in turn, the foundation for the testing criteria and methods by which participant mastery of the training can be measured.

What Is the DACUM Method and How Can It Be Used in Training Needs Assessment?

This section provides more detail on the DACUM process and gives examples and exercises that will reinforce your understanding of the approach.

DACUM stands for *Developing A Curriculum*. A particularly promising method for use in conducting technical training needs assessment, DACUM was developed by the Canadian Department of Manpower and Immigration and the General Learning Corporation of New York. The DACUM technique was created to help prepare a curriculum guide that would encourage trainee involvement and goal attainment in training programs. In the early 1970s, both the National Center at Ohio State University and the Center for Vocational, Technical, and Adult Education at the University of Wisconsin-Stout began offering workshops in this technique (Lee, 1990).

The DACUM process, as it is used to analyze jobs or occupations, is based on the following assumptions:

- Expert workers, regardless of their occupation, are better able to identify their job duties and tasks than anyone else
- Any job can be described in terms of duties and tasks that a competent worker performs
- All tasks are directly related to the knowledge, attitude, and performance required of workers to perform the job

In addition, once the DACUM chart is developed it may be used for (Lee, 1990):

- Training needs assessment
- Curriculum development
- Job descriptions
- Employee recruitment

What Is DACUM?

DACUM can be defined as a single-sheet skill profile that serves as both a curriculum plan and an evaluation instrument for occupational training programs. It is graphic in nature, usually presenting definitions of the skills of an entire occupation on one or two sheets of paper. This discourages treatment of any occupational element in isolation. A DACUM chart is subdivided into general areas of competence. Each is then analyzed to identify the skills it contains. The results are independent specifications of each skill or behavior that collectively enable an individual to perform competently in the occupation. These skills are defined quite simply and are structured independently in small blocks on the chart. Each can serve as an independent goal for learning achievement. Performers can then be assessed for their competence in each work activity area.

A DACUM chart contains a rating scale that accommodates evaluation of skills developed for each defined skill or behavior. The chart also serves as a recordkeeping system, as all ratings of skills are reported directly on a copy of the DACUM chart maintained for each employee.

Once an adequate skill profile in the form of ratings has been developed, the DACUM chart becomes a record of individual skill development in an occupation or job. The DACUM chart also has potential application as a guidance tool prior to entry to a training program and a placement tool upon completion (Adams, 1975).

DACUM enables business and industry to (Norton, 1997):

- Design new training programs quickly and cost-effectively
- Assess the relevance of existing training programs
- Reduce the costs and start-up time for designing, developing, and delivering training programs
- Conduct a high-quality occupational analysis in one or two days instead of thirty or more days
- Obtain significant employee involvement and buy-in
- Collect the information needed for development quickly and efficiently
- Design, develop, deliver, and evaluate job- or occupationally relevant training materials
- Identify training program support needs—such as tools, equipment, materials, and supplies—that are directly related to the "condition" spelled out in training objectives
- Develop job descriptions for new or existing jobs
- Provide a legally defensible basis for developing knowledge or performance tests
- Describe job operations and job systems so as to meet ISO 9000 requirements
- Help organizations meet the requirements of the Americans with Disabilities Act

The Role of the DACUM Facilitator

A DACUM facilitator is the person who works with, and provides leadership to, a committee of experienced job incumbents as they participate in the DACUM process. This person should have been trained on the DACUM method and should be able to follow prescribed procedures. The facilitator does not have to be a subject-matter expert but must be able to provide examples of all phases of the DACUM process so committee members can understand the technique.

To be successful, the facilitator must (Adams, 1975, p. 127):

- Possess knowledge and skill in occupation, job, and/or task analysis
- Be able to show sensitivity to both verbal and nonverbal communication
- Demonstrate the ability to motivate and stay focused
- Possess excellent listening skills
- Be able to establish rapport
- Be able to conduct small group process
- Obtain consensus

The DACUM Process

There are seven steps in the DACUM process to produce a chart:

- Define areas or categories
- Identify general areas of competencies
- Identify task statements
- Review general areas of competencies and tasks
- Sequence the general areas of competencies and tasks
- Validate the general area of competencies and tasks

Room Setup

Room setup is important for an effective DACUM process to be carried out. A typical room setup would position the facilitator at the front of the room. Since an important part of the group work is to build a chart on a wall, the room requires a large unbroken wall with chairs facing the wall so that participants can see the chart as it is built. The facilitator—working alone or (more often) with one or more helpers—records the information provided by the subject-matter experts on an index card (if it is a small group) or on $8\frac{1}{2}''$ by $11''$ sheets of paper (if it is a large group) (Nelson, 1988).

Define Area or Occupation

The participants in the DACUM process are selected for their knowledge of the occupation, job, equipment, or process for which the DACUM is being developed. There is no preparation on their part. No reference materials need be used, although it may be helpful to show participants what a finished DACUM chart looks like. When the participants in the DACUM process are brought together, the first step is to explain the process, their role, and the approach to be used. It is usually important to explain also how the results of the DACUM process will be used.

Identify the General Areas of Competency

In this step, the participants in the DACUM process brainstorm the duties and tasks associated with the job. As in classical brainstorming, participants are informed that no idea is too wild—and that they should not criticize remarks made by others. No answer is correct or incorrect. As participants brainstorm, each statement is captured on a piece of paper, placed on a wall, and positioned neatly in a horizontal line. At this time the facilitator does not attempt to order the information. Using large Post-it® Notes will allow the tasks to be moved around later. *Note:* participants should be informed at the outset that all statements should start with an action word (verb). To assist the subject-matter experts, the facilitator may hand out a list of action verbs during the overview session. This step would continue until the facilitator feels the content experts have listed all possible work tasks associated with a job, occupation, work process, or equipment operation. When moving to the next step, experts should be told that if they think of additional tasks at a later time to present them.

See the sample DACUM chart presented in Exhibit 6.5.

Identify the Major Duty Statements

When all the major tasks have been posted on the wall, the facilitator then instructs the subject-matter experts to identify major duties. *Duties* are the main categories into which many of the tasks will fall. On a DACUM chart,

EXHIBIT 6.5. SAMPLE DACUM CHART OF AN ENTRY-LEVEL TRAINER IN CHINA

Duties	Alphabetic Designation	Tasks							
		1	2	3	4	5	6	7	8
Administration	A	Prepare training schedule	Take and confirm course registrations	Deal with vendors	Prepare budget	Manage logistics arrangement	Prepare and distribute training materials	Organize training programs	Develop and distribute training and development reports
		Create and maintain training records	Publish a training and development newsletter	Participate in training-related meetings	Respond to learner or participant requests	Make training and development policy and contracts	Establish and maintain a training library		
Analyze training needs	B	Research company culture and business strategy	Conduct performance analysis	Conduct effective meetings	Become aware of internal/external environment and structure	Identify targeted learners	Analyze performance gaps	Prepare and collect individual training needs surveys	Determine the common aptitude of learners to better serve them
		Classify tasks and develop associated schedules	Work closely with personnel/human resource management function	Assist line managers in developing individual development plans (IDPs) for employees	Assist in developing the training plans and strategies				

(Continued)

EXHIBIT 6.5. SAMPLE DACUM CHART OF AN ENTRY-LEVEL TRAINER IN CHINA (*Continued*)

Duties	Alphabetic Designation	Tasks							
		1	2	3	4	5	6	7	8
Design, develop, source training materials	C	Write instructional objectives	Select training methods (case studies, lecture, activities, information technology)	Establish measurement tools	Develop all training materials (manuals, videos, training aids, participant guides, instructor guides)	Revise training materials and methods based upon evaluation and feedback	Source and develop relationships with instructors, facilitators, content experts, and consultants	Adapt training courses to organizational culture and local context (including translation)	
Market training	D	Gain support for training and development through creating good relationships at all levels	Visit customers at various locations	Discuss training and development/performance issues with line managers	Persuade management to increase investment in training and development	Inform program managers of training and development plan updates and/or changes	Prepare rewards to encourage participants to become involved in training	Influence senior executives to implement training and development reward and recognition systems	Involve top management in instruction and training
		Sell training internally and externally	Coach line management on training and development-related policies and approaches						

E	Deliver and facilitate training	Conduct on-the-job training (OJT)	Analyze participants' profiles	Identify instructional objectives for the course	Facilitate training	Use audiovisual aids and equipment	Administer test items	Monitor participant performance	Facilitate debriefing and course evaluation sessions
F	Evaluate training programs	Prepare evaluation instruments	Assess participants' reaction to course	Determine the transfer of learning	Provide constructive feedback and criticism	Collaborate with other trainers to improve course quality	Collect periodic feedback from business units following training	Perform cost-benefit analysis/ calculate return on investment (ROI) for training	
G	Develop-ing pro-fessionally	Study manage-ment theory (to understand corporate culture and manage-ment style)	Partner with business groups/ functions to gain industry awareness	Exchange experiences with colleagues	Set up and lead a training network	Attend professional development activities	Gain updated training and development trends, new method-ology, etc., through self-learning		

Source: W. Rothwell (1997). *A DACUM Chart of an Entry-Level Trainer in China.* Unpublished research study. State College, PA.

duties always appear in the far left column. They are the categories in which work tasks are placed. For instance, a category may be named "administrative paperwork." A task associated with that would be "prepare employee performance appraisals."

The subject-matter experts identify enough categories in which to organize all the tasks. The subject-matter experts may continue to revise or rethink the major duties as they continue through the process, and that often happens.

Sequence Tasks in Major Duties

In this step the facilitator works with the subject-matter experts to identify what tasks to place opposite the major duties identified previously. (Recall that the wall chart consists of randomly placed tasks.) The subject-matter experts then work through the tasks, placing them into the appropriate duty categories.

This can be a time-consuming activity. After all, some tasks will have been duplicated. As the subject-matter experts work through this step, they may choose to add tasks that were forgotten, combine tasks that are logically related, and subtract redundant tasks (because they were listed more than once on the wall as participants brainstormed). The facilitator often probes task statements during this step to draw out the subject-matter experts to explain tasks that seem to be vague or even cryptic. There is much group discussion during this step, which corresponds to the evaluation stage in classical brainstorming. An important role of the facilitator is to draw out silent group members, since all subject-matter experts should have input during this step.

When this step has been completed, the next step is to sequence the tasks or skills from simple to complex, placing the simplest task from the left and moving to the right. The sequencing could also be arranged according to work flow or job process. For example, it would be necessary to know the machine controls before operating a piece of equipment or process. This would have to be learned first.

A DACUM chart is not, by itself, suitable for conducting a technical training needs assessment. It must be converted into a questionnaire, like the one in Exhibit 6.6., so that individuals may be assessed (or may assess themselves) against any work requirements.

Case Study: Continuation of Case on Technical Training Needs Assessment

This section contains the case study begun at the opening of this chapter, which described how the DACUM method was used to develop job descriptions and identify the skills associated with those descriptions. Recall that a paper format was used to capture the developed information, and it is at this point that the case study continues. A few weeks after completing this task, the technical trainers discussed a systematic approach to training. This topic was the result of the DACUM project in which the technical trainers began to realize that it was possible to complete a project of this size.

For years, the company developed many training programs—some at the corporate level and others at the plant level. Unfortunately, each department used its own format and approach. Some programs were detailed; others were not. The sharing of training across locations was not common, since technical trainers at each location found only their own programs credible. The cost of developing separate training programs also became an issue at this time. During the DACUM project, many levels of the organization were involved—including department managers, plant managers, corporate directors, and the vice president of operations. For many it was the first time they had ever been involved with a training project. Because of this close involvement, managers developed a deeper appreciation of the training process. As might be expected, technical trainers wondered whether collaboration might be useful in other areas as well. They also wondered whether a more standardized approach to the development of training might yield substantial benefits. That set the stage for the technical trainers, both at the corporate headquarters and in the plants, to develop a plan to address standardization of technical training.

Finding the Standard Approach

Seven technical trainers met and brainstormed some key criteria for standardizing training. To them, training standards should:

- Keep the training materials development to a minimum
- Include an approach to training-the-nontrainers (such as supervisors) so that they would understand the approach
- Include some ways to store records electronically
- Include standards for manuals, handouts, lesson plans, hands-on-training operating procedures, and safety procedures

EXHIBIT 6.6. QUESTIONNAIRE TO ASSESS TRAINING NEEDS BASED ON A DACUM CHART

Technical trainers vary in their work duties and in their experience levels. For each work activity listed in the left column below, circle an appropriate response code in the middle column to indicate how important you consider the work activity for success in your work. Use the following scale for the middle column: 1 = **no importance; 2 = some importance; 3 = importance; 4 = much importance; 5 = very great importance.** Then circle an appropriate response code in the right column to indicate how much need for professional development you feel you need in this work activity area. Use the following scale for the right column:
1 = **no need; 2 = some need; 3 = need; 4 = much need; 5 = very great need.**

Activity	How Important?					How Much Need for Professional Development?				
A technical trainer should be able to:	No Importance				Very Great Importance	No Need				Very Great Need
(All items listed below are taken directly from a DACUM chart)	1	2	3	4	5	1	2	3	4	5
1. Prepare training schedule	1	2	3	4	5	1	2	3	4	5
2. Take and confirm course registrations	1	2	3	4	5	1	2	3	4	5
3. Deal with vendors	1	2	3	4	5	1	2	3	4	5
4. Prepare budget for training	1	2	3	4	5	1	2	3	4	5
5. Manage logistical arrangements for training	1	2	3	4	5	1	2	3	4	5
6. Prepare and distribute training materials	1	2	3	4	5	1	2	3	4	5
7. Organize training programs	1	2	3	4	5	1	2	3	4	5
8. Develop and distribute training and development reports	1	2	3	4	5	1	2	3	4	5
9. Create and maintain training records	1	2	3	4	5	1	2	3	4	5
10. Publish a training and development newsletter	1	2	3	4	5	1	2	3	4	5

- Include ways of placing operating procedures online, since the new equipment purchased by the company often included monitors that could be used for troubleshooting any problems with that equipment
- Cover ways of tracking employee training
- Track the skills employees acquired
- Not be costly
- Be easy to use

With these criteria in mind, five technical trainers began benchmarking companies that had systems in place to address these points. The trainers also developed a standard letter that listed the points so that, if a vendor was found that had a system to meet or exceed these points, the vendor could be sent a letter requesting a written proposal. Within several weeks, four companies were selected to present their proposals. To give each vendor the proper time needed for the presentation, interviews were conducted over a two-day period. Each vendor had some way to develop the DACUM charts. But one vendor had a way to develop DACUM charts electronically, and that vendor was selected for this reason.

That concludes the case study.

Type of System

Using an electronic template of the DACUM process, the system supported many other human resources functions. This system enabled technical trainers to develop a computerized technical training management system that

- Contained an inventory of all competencies required to operate a business
- Provided a current training status report for any employee in relation to any competency
- Provided information on job-related training needs by unit, department, group of employees, or position
- Was designed to store and make accessible on-line training materials and key support information for every competency identified within. Example: If the competencies were specific operating procedures or maintenance procedures, the details of the procedures could be accessed directly by any qualified employee using a computer terminal in a control room or maintenance shop. Weekly or more frequent updates of the procedures could be made by authorized personnel.

- Could transfer standard operating procedures or process manuals into accessible and readily updated databases
- Could be used with a pay-for-knowledge system. Employees could view or print out a record of their competencies achieved to date, date of last compensation change, and their current pay rate.

Exhibit 6.7 provides an example of the electronic DACUM template. Note that the chart contains all the duties and tasks associated with a job that is needed to operate equipment or process. The job chart contains three important points of information. The letters CHD located in the lower right hand of each window identifies this. C identifies the classification of the task. The middle letter identifies the training priority, where the letters used are HML. And the performance frequency is identified by the letters DWMP. This information is useful to both the training department and the worker in developing a personal training plan.

Under each task, resource media can be added—the design, quality checks, safety information, operating procedures, lockout procedures, and MSDS information. This information can be presented in the form of electronic file-text, computer-aided design (CAD), computer-based training (CBT), videotape, or audio.

Other Benefits of the Support System

Another benefit of the support system described in the previous section is that it began to create the basis for an electronic performance support system (EPSS). As Gloria Gery (1991, p. 34) wrote, "The goal of an electronic performance system is to provide whatever is necessary to generate performance and learning at the moment of need."

Technical trainers sometimes feel that workers need to have the same training repeated. And they sometimes hear it said that "We keep giving workers the same training, and they still are having trouble doing their jobs correctly." There are many reasons for this problem. One reason is that the training did not transfer from training to work. Another reason is that people may forget what they have been trained to do. A third reason is that the

EXHIBIT 6.7. THE SKILBASE CHART CONCEPT

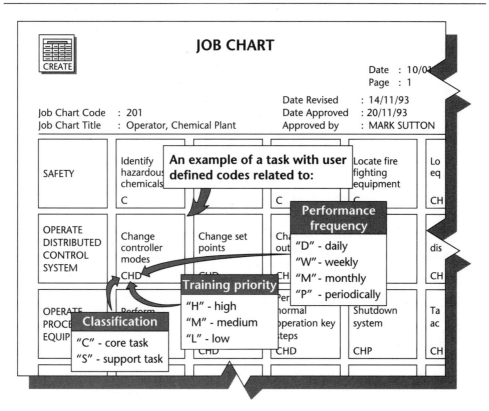

training that was offered was not geared to the needs of the people targeted for it. A fourth reason is that work requirements have changed since the training was designed, developed, and delivered.

It sometimes happens that the people who received training never really needed it to begin with. There is a danger of creating a culture of incompetence in which the organization's leaders begin to take steps to address unproductive behavior and results that fall far short of expectations. The most insidious cost of incompetence is the high overhead associated with supporting those who cannot perform competently. This cost is buried—and it is enormous. And the consumption of resources attendant on paying for work that adds no real value prevents organizational growth and impedes an organization's future survival in a competitive world.

A large national consulting firm recently reported to an insurance company management that, in one strategic business unit (of fifteen) that contributes 65 percent of the company's profits, 60 percent of its employees were involved in work that did not directly add value to the business. More specifically, workers were (Gery, 1991):

- Supervising other people at a 1:5 to 1:7 supervisor-to-employee ratio
- Controlling the work of others
- Reviewing the work of others
- Training others
- Answering questions at help desks or in other expert support functions
- Coaching and correcting others
- Reworking other people's inadequate work
- Compensating for others
- Supporting others by joint work activities when incompetents could not perform independently
- Actually doing the work of others who could perform but chose not to do so
- Conducting damage control activities
- Recruiting, hiring, and orienting new people to replace those who left or were asked to leave because of incompetence

Incompetence is often supported by work environments that make needed information difficult to obtain on a timely, and as-needed, basis. As an earlier chapter pointed out, adults are motivated to learn when they can easily retrieve information that is needed for their work. Having information unavailable when needed is a key reason for repetitious training. All workers do not have the capacity to remember all procedures or steps in a process, especially if they do not perform those steps or procedures frequently.

This kind of support has always required human beings in the past. But now we have the means to model, represent, structure, and implement that support electronically. And it can be made universally and consistently available on demand at any time, in any place, and for any situation, without unnecessary intermediaries involved in the process (Gery, 1991).

The Exemplary Worker

Consider what you would call an exemplary employee. This is the best-in-class worker who learns and remembers whatever information is given to him or her. We are likely to remark about such a person: "If only all the workers were as good as this person, our jobs would be much easier." Because of their ability to retain information, these are the same workers selected time and again to perform those special jobs that management needs to see carried out correctly. They are also selected because of their ability to work with little to no assistance due to their ability to find the necessary information on their own. For the worker who needs more help in finding information, it seems as though we label them as poor workers—or even, in some cases, as untrainable. But if we take a closer look, we sometimes discover that the so-called untrainable worker could be transformed into a valuable one if he or she could find information on demand.

The same general principle holds true for training. Not all workers are gifted with the ability to remember all information. Therefore, when a worker forgets what he or she needs to know to perform, technical trainers are asked to provide refresher training. The first thought that comes to mind when this happens is that the training was not done properly. That is not always true. In some cases, a low-tech method such as a job aid or a procedure manual is all that is needed; in some other cases, a high-tech method such as an electronic performance support system is what is needed.

Types of Information Available Electronically

Electronic performance support systems give workers just-in-time information. In many organizations, equipment and processes are controlled by computers. Electronic performance support systems can be adapted using the same monitors provided by the original equipment manufacturers. These systems have the capability not only to present information in a written text but to show pictures and even videos as well.

Exhibit 6.8 provides an example of how an electronic support system can provide on-demand, real-time access to training and supply performance support information. Workers can retrieve the information quickly,

EXHIBIT 6.8.   HOW A SKILBASE CHART IS USED
FOR EMPLOYEE RECORDKEEPING

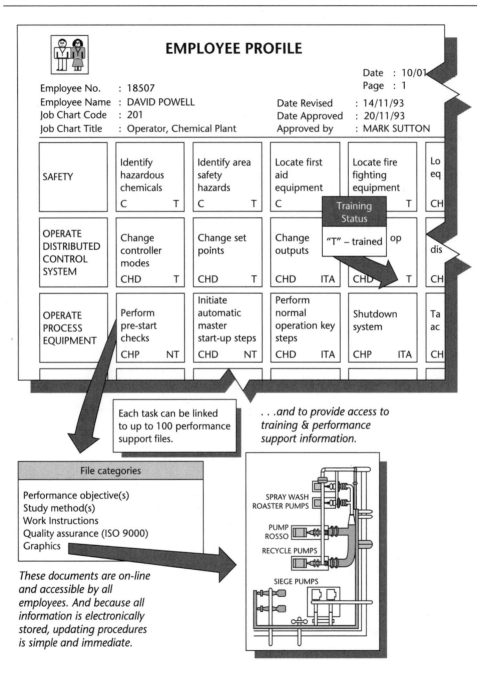

EMPLOYEE PROFILE

Date : 10/01
Page : 1

Employee No.   : 18507
Employee Name : DAVID POWELL
Job Chart Code   : 201
Job Chart Title   : Operator, Chemical Plant

Date Revised   : 14/11/93
Date Approved : 20/11/93
Approved by   : MARK SUTTON

SAFETY	Identify hazardous chemicals C T	Identify area safety hazards C T	Locate first aid equipment C	Locate fire fighting equipment T	Lo eq CH
OPERATE DISTRIBUTED CONTROL SYSTEM	Change controller modes CHD T	Change set points CHD T	Change outputs CHD ITA	op CHD T	CH dis
OPERATE PROCESS EQUIPMENT	Perform pre-start checks CHP NT	Initiate automatic master start-up steps CHD NT	Perform normal operation key steps CHD ITA	Shutdown system CHP ITA	Ta ac CH

Training Status

"T" – trained

Each task can be linked to up to 100 performance support files.

. . .and to provide access to training & performance support information.

File categories
Performance objective(s) Study method(s) Work Instructions Quality assurance (ISO 9000) Graphics

These documents are on-line and accessible by all employees. And because all information is electronically stored, updating procedures is simple and immediate.

SPRAY WASH
ROASTER PUMPS

PUMP
ROSSO

RECYCLE PUMPS

SIEGE PUMPS

especially if computer access is at the workstation or is otherwise close at hand. To retrieve the information, the worker uses a mouse to click on a window. A menu appears that contains all necessary topics related to the task, perhaps organized in a way comparable to a DACUM chart. The information could then be presented in the form of operating/safety procedures, pictures, documents, or video. Having a system that is readily available just in time not only benefits the workers but technical trainers and the organization as well.

Information associated with training no longer has to be delivered in a classroom. Technology has provided technical trainers with tools to manage and support the workers' needs. Electronic performance support systems are successful when they can demonstrably improve worker performance. This is ultimately measured by measurable indicators of quality, productivity, customer satisfaction, and creativity and the cost of the finished product or service.

This means that if performance support is successful, it

- *Should be designed to solve a pressing problem for a work area or an organization.* This means that the system must ease existing pain in an organization or that it must simplify work in a way that is significant to workers.
- *Must make it easier for workers to manage and create problem-solving knowledge more effectively.* This means that the domain must be job- or task-specific.
- *Should be production-centered.* This means that performance support priorities are those likely to have greatest impact on internal or external customer satisfaction. There is not much sense in speeding information access and skill acquisition in an area that does not add value for internal and external customers.
- *Should grow organically, as needs for support grow and change with the business environment.* This means that initial support tools will be narrowly focused on a specific job or department. After proving important to the work of an area, demand for electronic performance support systems will usually grow.
- *Must ultimately cause or contribute to the disintegration of "information islands" on an organizational level.* "Creating, maintaining, and segregating knowledge bases in an organization builds managerial and bureaucratic power, but

it interferes with effective work and fosters inter-work group tension" (Stevens and Stevens, 1995, p. 8).

There are many ways to conceptualize electronic performance support systems. But perhaps the most important to consider is the human interface, meaning how people will use the system. Key issues to consider include the following:

- The ability to analyze human performance needs in the workplace, including job task analysis, discrepancy analysis, and user analysis. This ability is required to answer many crucial questions, among them: What type of support do people need when they are at work? When is reference information the most appropriate support? When do people need performance feedback instead of training? What characteristics must a performance support tool offer to be of greatest value to an audience of users?
- An understanding of the ways in which human beings interact with information and environment at work. This understanding is typified by an understanding of cognitive science. Another type of individual who might bring this asset to an EPSS project is one who is experienced at work process design or process reengineering.
- The ability to understand problems from the perspectives of both the individual worker and the work system, without letting prior paradigms interfere with that understanding. This is to say, whether one has a background in information systems design, instructional systems design, or organization development, EPSS success requires that designers not be so wedded to those conceptual paradigms that they dictate the design of the electronic performance support.
- An understanding of human-computer interface design. If a performance support tool is to be used efficiently, it must function as a natural extension of the worker, rather than be regarded as another tool to be mastered. Performers should not have to "learn" how to use a performance support tool. Interface design is crucial to this effort.
- Finally, but not least in importance, is the ability to design applications for microcomputers in a distributed environment. Most performance

support applications are ultimately delivered on a personal computer of one type or another. The capabilities and limitations of the myriad PC technologies available can dramatically affect the success of an electronic performance support project (Stevens and Stevens, 1995, p. 10).

Summary

This chapter focused on identifying technical training needs, a topic linked in Chapter Five to the analysis step in the ISD model. It is a key topic of importance to technical trainers. The chapter opened with a case study that dramatized the importance of technical training needs assessment and provided an example of the decisions that technical trainers must make as they carry out that assessment.

The chapter addressed several key questions: What are technical training needs? How are training needs distinguished from other needs? What is the DACUM method, and how can it be used as a particularly effective tool in conducting technical training needs assessment? What methods can help assess technical training needs, and how is that information then used to build effective training? The chapter concluded with a continuation of the case study, providing further information about how the case situation involving training needs assessment was managed in a real organization. The next chapter treats the development of technical training programs.

CHAPTER SEVEN

PREPARING TECHNICAL TRAINING PROGRAMS

The results of technical training needs assessment should provide a solid foundation on which to build a training course specification that lists (among other things) the course objectives, targeted participants, and content to be used in the training. It is also essential to prepare evaluative criteria, such as test items, based directly on the information that should be presented to help participants meet the objectives.

Once the course has been planned, technical trainers face an important question, similar to that faced by managers who are making a purchasing decision: *Should the training materials be made, bought, or bought and modified?* To answer that important question, technical trainers must first answer a series of other questions. What is the basis for reaching a make-or-buy decision? And, if the decision is made to prepare (make) the training, how should training materials be prepared? This chapter addresses these questions.

What Is the Basis for Making, Buying, or Buying and Modifying Training Materials?

Reaching a make-or-buy decision is not difficult. Several key questions should be posed.

The first question is this: *Is sufficient time available to prepare training materials?* If, for instance, training must be prepared and delivered to keep a production line on schedule, then timing is of utmost importance. Preparing good training materials takes time. Is there enough time to do it properly? If the answer is "yes," then there may be grounds to design and develop training materials in-house. But if the answer is "no," then technical trainers must explore alternatives that might include purchasing near-fit technical training materials from vendors or other sources or outsourcing, in whole or part, the design and development of training materials to external vendors.

The second question is this: *Do the technical trainers in the organization possess the necessary expertise to prepare the training materials?* Do they know enough about the topic of the training to prepare the materials? While it may be possible for them to acquire the necessary expertise eventually, is it worth the time and expense for them to do so? If the answer is "yes, they possess the necessary expertise," then there may be good reason to design and develop the material in-house. Even subject-matter experts (SMEs) may be used to design training (Mueller, 1997). But if the answer is "no," then they may purchase training materials from outside vendors or else outsource training materials development to vendors.

The third question is this: *Will training materials designed and developed in-house have sufficient credibility with the stakeholders?* That question is not identical to the previous one. There is, after all, a difference between possessing expertise and having credibility. An expert who is not regarded as such will not possess sufficient credibility. Since it is sometimes true that outside vendors are accorded more credibility than their in-house counterparts, the issue of credibility is an important one. If the answer to this question is "yes, in-house trainers possess the credibility," then perhaps they should design and develop the training materials. But if the answer is "no," then the training may have to be purchased externally or else its preparation outsourced.

The fourth question is this: *Will technical trainers be able to prepare the training material in the form in which it is desired?* Various high-tech delivery methods are growing increasingly popular—including web-based instruction. Not all technical trainers can work in all media. Therefore, if the answer is that technical trainers do not possess sufficient knowledge of the media in which the training is to be delivered, then the training material may have to be purchased externally or else the design and development of it must be outsourced.

The fifth question is this: *Can the technical training materials be easily sourced?* Is it obvious that some vendor has best-in-class training materials already available? For instance, if a course on design for manufacturability is being considered for engineers, such a course may already be available from a vendor in a form that could never be duplicated with the same level of quality by in-house technical trainers. If that is true, then the materials should be purchased (or licensed) from an external source, such as a publisher or vendor.

Key issues in reaching a make-or-buy decision for training materials include how much time is available, how much expertise is possessed by in-house technical trainers, how much credibility is possessed by those trainers, how capable the trainers are to work in the desired training format, and how easily the technical training materials are already available. If any of these issues is not favorable, then the training materials will have to be purchased or else their design and development will need to be outsourced. However, if these issues are generally favorable, technical trainers may develop the material. Of course, translation requirements may make some form of outsourcing necessary—even if only for translation from one language to others (Carnevale, 1993).

How Should Training Materials Be Prepared?

To introduce key issues associated with preparing technical training materials, read the case study on the facing page and make notes about what was done in the case to prepare technical training materials.

One trainer, interviewed at length for this book, has seen many training manuals prepared in his twenty years of experience in technical training. The question of what is good and what is not so good depends on who developed the training manual, he asserts. But what about the user? How often does the user have a say in what information should be included in a training manual?

Adult learners have unique characteristics. But which characteristics of special importance to adult learners should be emphasized when developing a training manual? What about the desire to learn? If the information is not user-friendly or easily found, it is fair to say that it is unlikely to be used. What about seeing learning in a meaningful framework? If the information is not presented showing the big picture, again, it might not be used. Finally, what about having the information presented in digestible pieces? If the information is not presented in a logical sequence, it too might not be used. How often are these points considered when developing training manuals? Think about these questions as you read the following case, written from the interview notes of a technical trainer.

Case Study: Developing Technical Training Materials and Manuals

My first experience with training manuals was as a technical trainer in a company that had thirteen plants located throughout the United States. Each plant had a technical trainer responsible for local technical training activities and a corporate technical training department that was responsible for training common to all plants.

The purpose of my first meeting with the technical trainer from the corporate headquarters was to introduce me to the corporate philosophy about technical training and the different methods being used to support the plants' technical training needs. One method was the preparation and distribution of technical training manuals. The technical trainer showed me a shelf filled with manuals covering every imaginable topic, ranging from equipment use, to work processes, to general technical skills. He was very enthusiastic and very proud of the manuals. I was profoundly impressed with the cover layout and the pictures inside the manuals.

In the months following that meeting I found myself looking at training manuals to support the technical training needs of my local plant. Just as the corporate technical trainer showed such pride in the manuals, I came to feel the same way. In developing the manuals, I used subject-matter experts from the plant, and I received positive feedback from the supervisors.

So we continued to develop manuals—but never thought of asking the workers if they were using the manuals or asking what impact, if any, the manuals were having on improving production.

Equipment manufacturers also supplied manuals for most of the machines used in the plant. These manuals also looked great. They further reinforced the value of using manuals for training. All manuals that were developed were given to the supervisors of the departments using the equipment, and it was understood that the manuals would support efforts to meet workers' training needs.

As my job took me more onto the manufacturing floor, I soon discovered that the manuals were not readily available to the workers. Supervisors placed the manuals in their file cabinets or kept them in locked cabinets. In some cases, when training situations arose where the training manuals might have been helpful, the supervisors never thought of using the manuals—or, in some cases, were not even aware that they had the manuals. As I began to ask about this problem, I soon realized that this problem was not uncommon. Many hourly workers were not aware of the manuals, even though those workers were used as content experts for preparing the manuals. As I talked to hourly workers, they told me that the manuals contained too much information to be practical for immediate use and that the information was organized in ways that made it difficult to find needed information on demand. The same problem plagued the manuals prepared by the equipment manufacturers.

Shortly after I became aware of this problem, corporate information systems (IS) developed a manual for a new repair order system. The supervisor whose workers would be using this manual called me to discuss the manual. His concern was that the book was written for IS experts, not for users. It was approximately three hundred pages in length. As I tried to perform an operation described in the manual, I realized that the instructions were difficult to follow. As if to reinforce my conclusion, the supervisor commented, "This manual is too detailed and complex for my people to use." He then asked if I could develop a manual that would be more practical.

As I prepared to revise the manual, I reflected on what I had learned about the manuals I had prepared and what had happened to them. Having learned a hard lesson from that experience, I asked more questions of the supervisor and his workers, using the IS manual as the basis for my questions. That discussion led me to reach the following conclusions about equipment manuals used for training: Only certain sections apply to what is needed to use a machine or perform a work process, and the instructions were written in a form that made it difficult to use them.

Using a flip chart, a worker provided input as to how he would like to see the information presented:

- Use bullet points for each step
- Eliminate unnecessary information
- Use terminology that can be easily understood
- Supply simple troubleshooting procedures

Based on this information, I formed a group of workers to develop a set of procedures as a model. To see whether it would work, a worker who was not involved in the discussion was asked to input the information into a computer. With the exception of one question, she performed the procedure without help. With help from the workers, a new manual was developed that contained only essential information. The completed book was only fifty pages, compared to the original book that was approximately three hundred pages in length.

In reviewing this manual, I noticed that it was developed using principles of adult learning theory. Although the manual was not perfect, it was effective.

Technical Training Strategy: Addressing the Issue of Material Standards

As a result of this experience, I started to look for information on how to design manuals so that they would be readily used by adult learners. I discovered a seminar on "information mapping." I attended the seminar and found answers to many questions I had when developing the IS manual.

As part of a corporate strategy for technical training, technical trainers should develop standards for training materials—including manuals, outlines, leaders' guides, participant guides, and general instructional materials. In my organization, each plant had its own guidelines for developing training materials. Each plant had also experienced problems with users, and technical trainers from many locations had also discovered that materials were not being used as they were supposed to be. Because the strategy planning committee had representatives from a wide range of personnel, their thinking made discussions about materials' standards beneficial. The following points surfaced from their brainstorming:

- Users for whom materials are developed are aware when that material is completed and often never see the materials
- Supervisors do not share the information
- Although the information contained in the technical training manuals is accurate, too much time is required of users to find specific information
- Users have to read too much to find information when they need it
- Material development is an inconsistent process, and information seems to be laid out in a different way every time a new manual is developed
- Instructional materials are rarely available in convenient locations for those intended to use them

After hearing all these points, I realized that these points were exactly the same ones that information mapping was created to address.

Principle 1: Adults Learn in Digestible Pieces

Information should be clustered together in no more than seven facts at a time. That is true because adults tend to be able to remember best about seven facts at once. When developing information maps or mind maps, follow the simple directions described in Exhibit 7.1.

Example: Compare information presented in paragraph format to information presented in visual format. Using the second hand on your watch, keep track of the time it takes to find the cutting speed of cold roll steel in the following paragraph:

EXHIBIT 7.1.   PRINCIPLES OF PROCEDURES MAPPING

Directions: Select a procedure for procedures mapping. Then, use the following symbols:

⌂ **Justification:** Why something is done

□ **Value:** What is gained by doing something

○ **Needs:** Who, what, when, how much

♡ **Action:** How something is to be carried out

Create a description of a procedure using the symbols listed above. Give each team of people assigned to the task a large sheet of flip chart paper. Then ask them to brainstorm a procedure to depict how it is done. Use drawings to represent the procedure.

When using a drill press, remember to use the correct RPMs. If RPMs are too fast, the drill bit will become dull and burn. If it runs too slow, the drill bit could break. To ensure you are using the correct cutting speed, calculate the RPMs. This can be accomplished by using a simple formula. The formula for the cutting speed is CS × 4 over the diameter of the drill bit. CS stands for cutting speed. It can be found in any machinery handbook. For example, drilling a 2-inch hole in a piece of 1-inch flat cold roll steel by looking in the machinery handbook the cutting speed for cold roll steel is 100. Then take that number and multiply it by 4 to give 400. That is then divided by 2 inches, which is the size of the drill bit, so the RPMs would be 200.

Now try a different approach. Again, use the second hand on your watch to find the cutting speed for cold roll steel. Use the information presented in Exhibit 7.2.

As you just experienced, the information was easier to find using the layout techniques in Exhibit 7.2. In reviewing the layout of Exhibit 7.2, there are several main points that are highlighted. First, the title with the specific task is easily identified at the top of the aid. Again clearly identified is the purpose of this instruction—when it should be used and what materials are needed when performing the task. Second, the example shown in Exhibit 7.2 makes it easy to identify what the task is

EXHIBIT 7.2.   LAYOUT OF A JOB CHART

Determine Drill Bit Cutting Speed (RPM)

Purpose: To determine the correct cutting speed for a given material

Step	Action	Example
1. Calculate cutting speed		
2. ***Determine drill bit size**		1/2@, 5/16@, 13/32@, etc.
If material is:	Then cutting speed is:	
Cold Rolled Steel	100	Cold rolled steel = 100
Cast Iron	80	
Tool Steel	70	
Aluminum	120	
		Cutting speed × 4
3. *Use calculator to work through formula		Diameter of drill = RPM
4. Set drill press speed (RPM)		Set at 800 RPM
Result(s):	The result is the correct cutting speed.	

and what action is to be taken. Third, the example provided in Exhibit 7.2 makes it easy to see how to perform the calculation. Fourth, the final results and standards for computing the value are shown in Exhibit 7.2. In addition to the points just covered, the job aid shown in Exhibit 7.2 provided key words located on the left side to help the reader focus on the main points.

If all the information presented in the table were placed in a paragraph format, workers would have to read the information several times to understand it. Finding one item of information would take additional time. But the example shown in Exhibit 7.2 makes the information easily available to users.

To reemphasize some important points, the example appearing in Exhibit 7.2 builds on fundamental principles of adult learning. Adults learn when the information is relevant. The example appearing in Exhibit 7.2 provided only the necessary information needed to perform the task.

Exhibit 7.3 provides another example of how a job aid can be developed when more than one task is required to carry out a procedure. References are provided with the specific page number, which helps to eliminate unnecessary time spent to search for information. If several tasks are included, a cover page can be used as a ready reference to the page with the specific task as shown in Exhibit 7.4.

Principle 2: Adults Learn When the Information Is Consistent

A consistent format should be followed in presenting procedures so that adults do not need to learn a new format before learning a procedure.

Principle 3: Adults Learn Visually

A picture is worth a thousand words. So incorporate visuals into the documentation. If the visual or picture is located on the next page or several pages from the information being discussed and the reader has to page back and forth, not only is this distracting, but there is also a tendency to lose

EXHIBIT 7.3.   CREATING A JOB AID COVER SHEET

Job Aid Cover Sheet

Create a job aid cover sheet if there are several job aids for a task, or if a job aid spans several pages. A cover sheet will allow the worker to reference the material quickly.

Example:

Title the cover sheet with the task name

Note any safety or warning information

If the job aid covers more than one task, write an index.

JOB AID
Adjust Ratchet Alignment

Safety: System must be turned off.
           Safety glasses required.

Job Aid Is: A step-by-step guide for
             ratchet alignment. Use it
             whenever you align ratchets

Ind Task	Page
Preparation	1
Perform	2

HELP: Contact J. Jones at x2222 for help.
NOTE: Certified by J. Jones 1/1/94

Explain the purpose of the job aid and when to use it.

Note who wrote the job aid, where to go for help, and the date the job aid was certified.

EXHIBIT 7.4. SAMPLE COVER PAGE

Warnings

Place a warning before the step it applies to, if performing the step incorrectly could cause injury, or if it is a safety requirement.

Use a warning, caution, or safety message to alert the worker. Put the message in a box to draw attention to it.

Examples:

> WARNING: Turn power off before.

> SAFETY: Earplugs must be worn.

Callouts

Use callouts to highlight important areas in a diagram or picture.

Examples:

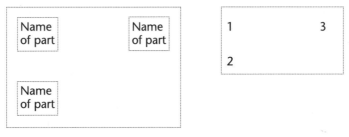

focus. Pictures should be integrated with the text and used to emphasize important information.

Principle 4: Adults Learn When Detailed Information Is Easy to Understand

Use decision tables and other visual representations to make information easier to comprehend. When a complex procedure has to be understood that requires several decision points, use a decision chart or other visual to eliminate confusion. (See Exhibit 7.5.) The same technique can be used when manuals or other training material must be translated into multiple languages (Silverstein, 1997).

EXHIBIT 7.5.   HOW TO WRITE DECISION TABLES

Introduction   As you develop a job aid, you may find a point in a step or action where the worker will need to make a decision. Instead of writing a paragraph to explain the choices or options, you should write a decision table.

People comprehend information much more quickly when it is presented in a visual format. This section will teach you how to write a decision table.

Example   Here is an example of a paragraph describing a decision rewritten as a decision table:

Decide what the employee wants to do. If the employee wants to change life insurance, use form LI-2. If the employee wants to discontinue life insurance, go to step 4 on page 3. If the employee wants to discontinue retirement, use form R-2.

If the employee wants to	Then
change life insurance	use form LI-2
discontinue life insurance	go to step 4 on page 3
discontinue retirement	use form R-2

Let's say the employee wants to discontinue retirement. Which allows you to reach the decision quickest, the paragraph or the decision table?

Components of Decision Tables   A decision table is made up of the following components:

IF (left column) represents conditions or variations in situations that help the worker determine which action to take.

THEN (right or center column) represents actions descriptions of the tasks the worker is directed to perform.

AND (center or right column) represents multiple conditions or actions.

If the AND represents	Then the AND column is
multiple conditions	in the center
multiple actions	on the right

Examples of Headings   Here are some examples of decision table headings:

IF	THEN

	AND	THEN

IF	AND	THEN

EXHIBIT 7.5.   HOW TO WRITE DECISION TABLES (*Continued*)

Guidelines for Writing Decision Tables	Here are some guidelines to follow when writing decision tables:

- Create a separate column for each kind of condition or action.
- Whenever possible, move words repeated for the condition or action into the column header.
- Position the decision table in the step that it applies to.
- Use arrows or dashes to show that a column does not apply for a particular intermediate condition or action.
- An IF should *never* lead directly to two or more THENs, but two or more IFs can lead to a single THEN.

Decision Table Exercises	Decide if each decision table below is acceptable. If a decision table is not acceptable, explain why.

IF	AND	THEN USE
Night Differential		Code 1
Sunday Pay	Overtime	Code 2
Sunday Pay	Regular Rate	Code 3
Sunday Pay	Premium Pay	Code 4

Is this example:

❏ Acceptable

❏ Not acceptable, because _____

THEN	IF
Use form A	Full Time
Use form B	Part Time
Use form C	Special

Is this example:

❏ Acceptable
❏ Not acceptable, because _____

IF	THEN
You have been married less than two years	Sign up for class #1
	Sign up for class #3
You have been employed more than two years	Sign up for advanced training

Is this example:

❏ Acceptable
❏ Not acceptable, because _____

Source: Provided with permission from Claymore Inc. Terry Ogle, President.

Using the Storyboard Format to Develop Technical Training Materials

If technical trainers set out to develop technical training materials without worker involvement or the close guidance of subject-matter experts, the trainers may face problems of acceptance later on. Trainers will have to make sure it undergoes a technical review by those familiar with the details on which workers must be trained. For this reason, it is often wise to find more interactive approaches to developing technical training materials. When such approaches are used, the technical review time is usually dramatically reduced, and the materials enjoy widespread acceptance because those who are targeted to receive training or those with special expertise have been involved in designing and developing the materials.

Definition and Description of a Storyboard. One approach to interactive technical training materials design is the storyboard. A *storyboard* is literally a way to "tell a story." Storyboards have been around a long time, and they have been used in many disciplines. The basic idea is nearly always the same whether a storyboard is prepared by a group working face-to-face or online. A storyboard developed by a group meeting face-to-face is more likely to enjoy immediate support, while a storyboard developed online may require more time for acceptance.

Questions to Be Addressed by a Training Storyboard. Select a series of key questions to be addressed to design the training experience. For instance, consider such issues as these:

- Why should this training be conducted? (What is the business need?)
- What is the problem costing the organization that training is being designed to solve? (How can the cost of the problem be measured or at least estimated?)
- What is the purpose of the training course or experience?
- What are the objectives? (In other words, what should participants in the training know, do, or feel upon completion of the training?)
- How can achievement of the objectives be measured? (How can participants be evaluated?)

- Who are the targeted participants?
- What should participants already know upon beginning the training experience? (In other words, is there prerequisite knowledge, skill, or attitudes that they should possess at the time they begin the training? If so, how can that be assessed so as to screen in only those who possess that knowledge?)
- What subject matter should be covered in the training? What outline of content will help to achieve the instructional objectives?
- How should the training be delivered? Should it be delivered on the job, near the job, or off the job? What pre-work should be given to participants before they begin? What post-work should be given to participants after they finish the training?
- How can the training be followed up to ensure that it was effective and that supervisors hold workers accountable for doing what they have been trained to do?
- How should the training materials be designed and developed to "flesh out" the training outline?
- What is the training budget for the project, and how can it be estimated?
- What will be the gains forecast for conducting the training? (Consider the cost of the problem less the cost of the training = value added or return on investment.)

By answering these questions, subject-matter experts, technical trainers, and managers can begin to clarify exactly what expectations they have for the training. Note that all the journalistic questions—the who? what? when? where? why? how? and how much?—issues are covered by the storyboard format.

Building a Training Storyboard with a Live Group. To build a training storyboard, call together a group of seven to twelve people who share knowledge of an issue to be solved for which training is being designed. Make sure there is a large blank wall in the room and that ample 8½″ by 11″ paper, markers, and masking tape is available. Pose the questions along the top of the blank wall. Then ask the group participants to provide their answers. Ask them to write down what they think, one idea per sheet of paper. Post the paper on the wall underneath the appropriate category.

Continue working until the training course or experience has been designed. Type it up and then later share it for the group for validation.

Once the storyboard is complete, you should have detailed training specifications.

If you wish to continue the project into a second round, reassemble the group. Ask them to focus attention specifically on the course content. Build a detailed course outline, complete with specifications for content to be delivered and activities intended to build participant skill, in the session. Again, have the detailed outline typed up and circulated for validation with group members—and other key stakeholders.

You may also wish to form an *action learning team,* similar to that described by Rothwell (1999), for a project in which trainers, subject-matter experts, and stakeholders work together to design, develop, deliver, and subsequently evaluate the instruction.

Building a Training Storyboard Online. In recent years, much attention has been paid to so-called virtual teams. A *virtual team* is a group of people working together on a project, even though they may never meet face-to-face. Such teams may consist of geographically scattered individuals.

Storyboards can be built online just as they can be built in face-to-face meetings. Either prepare a company website for use by a group or else go online to find a public site that all members of a company group may access. Software such as Groove™ (www.groove.net), which may be downloaded for free, permits groups of people to work together simultaneously on shared tasks in real time. Also available is Ventana for Windows by www.groupsystems.com. Those with a limited budget, and with limited need for privacy, may find it good enough simply to set up a free club at http://clubs.lycos.com/live/Directory/ClubsHome.asp?Area=2.

An advantage of some online message boards is that they are asynchronous, meaning that virtual users can log on and make their comments when they have free time. That is especially advantageous for virtual teams that function internationally due to time zone differences.

The results of either storyboard are the same. They permit groups to work together, and thereby build involvement in the content and delivery methods to be used in technical training.

Summary

This chapter focused on addressing the question: *Should training materials be made, bought, or bought and modified?* To answer that important question, technical trainers must first answer a series of other questions. What is the basis for reaching a make-or-buy decision? And if the decision is made to prepare (make) the training, how should training materials be prepared?

Generally speaking, five key questions should be considered to decide whether to make or buy training materials: (1) Is sufficient time available to prepare training materials? (2) Do the technical trainers in the organization possess the necessary expertise to prepare the training materials? (3) Will training materials designed and developed in-house have sufficient credibility with the stakeholders? (4) Will technical trainers be able to prepare the training material in the form in which it is desired? and (5) Can the technical training materials be easily sourced? If the answer to any of these questions is "no," then it will most likely be necessary to purchase the materials from outside. Otherwise, technical trainers may be able to prepare the training materials.

This chapter also provided information about preparing technical training materials. Of particular note was a case study, written by one of the book's authors, about his experience with preparing usable technical training materials. The chapter closed with a description of how storyboards may be developed with groups, either in live or online settings, to prepare training specifications and even to begin preparing tailor-made content.

CHAPTER EIGHT

DETERMINING AND USING DELIVERY METHODS

Technical trainers today often face the challenge of dealing with line managers who are increasingly aware of technological options by which to deliver training yet are unaware of what costs, time frames, and other tradeoffs are involved to apply that technology. Likewise, many technical trainers who are promoted from within may not know what time will be required to prepare training for online delivery, compared to preparing training for classroom delivery. For instance, it may require between 80 and 350 hours to design just one hour of good, interactive, web-based instruction (Eline, 1998c), a fact unknown to many novice trainers. (Of course, bad training can be designed much faster!)

This chapter turns to the topic of choosing and using delivery methods. That is an important task, since many technical trainers start on the plant floor, helping new hires become productive. They enter the training field with their primary emphasis on delivery, rather than on analysis, design, development, or evaluation.

What issues should be considered in determining what training delivery method(s) should be used? How can training be delivered effectively in classroom settings, and how do technical trainers differ when they play the role of instructor or group facilitator? How can training be delivered effectively near the job? How can training be delivered on the job? And how can training be delivered effectively online or through alternative delivery methods? This chapter addresses these questions.

What Should Be Considered in Determining the Training Delivery Method(s) to Use?

Increasing amounts of training are going online. The evidence of that is quite clear. At the end of 1998, an estimated 147,800,000 people were Internet users worldwide, and 52 percent were living in the United States (Treese, 1999). The WorldWideWeb has been gaining momentum as a delivery vehicle for teachers and trainers, although the use ranges from the low-level (such as placing course syllabi online) to sophisticated uses such as courses offered entirely online. In 1997, about 80 percent of 150 Fortune 1000 companies responding to a survey indicated that they were using some form of multimedia courseware (Barron, 1997). McMurrer, Van Buren, and Woodwell (2000) estimate that 55 percent of all training will be offered through technology-based methods by 2002. The WorldWideWeb will thus be more often used as a platform or vehicle for training.

However, great care should be taken in selecting the appropriate training delivery method. Often the choice is not *what one method* should be used. Instead, it may be more appropriate to think of *what combination of methods* may be most cost- and time-effective and also is most likely to encourage learning and application (see Marx, 1999). Trainers in the authors' small-scale survey indicated that much technical training in their organizations is still delivered in the classroom, a fact borne out by the results of an earlier survey of IT training (Information Technology Training, 1998). From the authors' survey, popular approaches for delivering training included the classroom, videotapes, manuals, and in-house experts offering planned or unplanned on-the-job training. (See Exhibit 8.1.)

EXHIBIT 8.1. DELIVERY METHODS USED IN TECHNICAL TRAINING

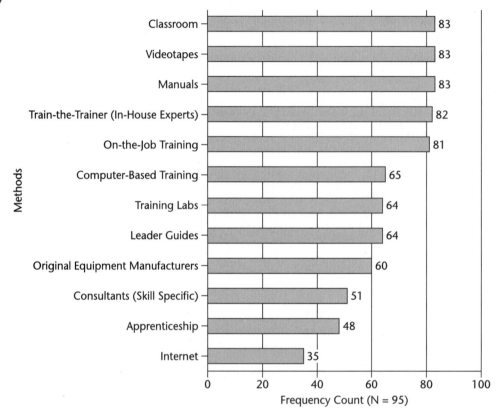

Source: J. Benkowski and W. Rothwell. (2001). *Successful Technical Training Practices.* Unpublished survey results. Stout, WI: The University of Wisconsin.

While various tools (both automated and print-based) are available to help trainers decide what delivery method(s) would be most appropriate (see Mallory and Steele, 1995), it is often an artistic decision. No research conclusively demonstrates that any one delivery method is better than others. However, trainers may discover from experience that some methods are better than others in their unique corporate cultures to encourage learning and application.

Basically, issues that are similar to those that should be considered when reaching a make-or-buy decision for training materials should also be considered when determining what training delivery methods should be used. Consider:

- How much time, money, and staff are available to prepare and deliver training in the media desired?
- What expertise in various delivery methods do technical trainers in the organization possess?
- What range of delivery methods are possible? How much should they be used in isolation or in combination?

Use the worksheet in Exhibit 8.2 to brainstorm on the range of training delivery methods that are available and select one or more that may be appropriate for an instructional experience. As an alternative, use a training course outline and, for each course section, describe how (that is, what delivery methods) each might be most appropriate. Then consider how training delivery methods may be used in isolation or in combination.

How Can Training Be Delivered Effectively in Classroom Settings?

When most workers think of training, they often think of classroom settings first. It is a legacy from their formal education in which they recall—perhaps with painful memories—what it was like for them to be students in elementary or secondary school or in college. Despite the growing use of online instruction, it is doubtful that classroom instruction will ever fade from the scene entirely (Ruyle, 1995). One reason is that many people are social learners who require a social support network—meaning other people—before they can engage in a learning experience. They are ill-equipped, by inclination, to sit alone in front of a computer and access online instruction. They just will not do it.

Technical trainers may play two roles in group-based (classroom) instruction. One role is that of instructor. Another role, increasingly important in today's workplaces, is that of facilitator.

EXHIBIT 8.2.   WORKSHEET TO STRUCTURE YOUR THINKING
ON DELIVERY METHODS

Directions: Use this worksheet to structure your thinking on how many ways you could use to deliver instruction. Of course, obvious examples might include off-the-job, classroom-based training, on-the-job, one-on-one training, or self-study. But how many other ways can you think of? Use this worksheet to brainstorm a list of delivery methods.

Write your list here:

The Technical Trainer as Instructor

The instructor role is most familiar to most technical trainers, whether they are carrying out training on technical topics (such as equipment repair) or technical applications (such as use of a spreadsheet program on a personal computer).

What Is an Instructor? Like teachers, instructors are usually subject-matter experts (SMEs). They "tell" people what they should learn. They are perhaps best-known for lecturing. "Instruction," write Rothwell and Sredl (2000, II, p. 166), "is the process of transmitting information, conveying knowledge, and building skills so that individuals learn and can later apply what they have learned to improve their performance."

The problem is that adult learners are generally not willing to be passive participants in their own learning. They do not like to sit and listen to someone talk. They grow restless, bored—or even fall asleep!—if they are subjected to lecture for long periods of time.

What Should Instructors Do? Effective instructors are competent in a specialized range of competencies that are comparable to those of the public speaker (King, King, and Rothwell, 2000), and these competencies have become the foundation for the Certified Technical Trainer (CTT+), a certification focused on technical training in information technology (see www.comptia.org/certification/cttplus). They will, for instance (Rothwell and Sredl, 2000):

1. Identify key ideas.
2. Develop them through details.
3. Create a logical overall structure based on the central ideas and on audience analysis.
4. Prepare notes and other instructional aids, such as visuals and exercises.
5. Rehearse delivery.
6. Modify delivery if necessary.
7. Plan for giving participants reinforcement and feedback.

Technical trainers who find themselves cast in the instructor's role will carry out these steps. They will also use a range of strategies that are associated with effective public speaking. They may also use various "active training techniques" to ensure that their presentations are more active than passive (Dowling, 1996; Schaaf, 1999), and they may appeal to emotional intelligence as well (Laabs, 1999). They should also have some familiarity of how to arrange a learning facility in ways conducive to the learning process (West, 1995).

A Key Point About the Instructor's Role. It is important to understand that, for the most part, instructors are transferring knowledge and information. They are spokespersons for their organization, and that means they have ethical obligations to speak what management expects them to speak. What is more, they are usually in the business of conveying information that is the fruit of organizational experience. They transfer what is known to those who do not know it.

The Technical Trainer as Group Facilitator

The group facilitator role is less familiar to most people. Think of a technical trainer working with a process improvement team and you can begin to get a sense of what a facilitator does—and how that differs from the traditional instructor role.

What Is a Group Facilitator? Group facilitators do not play the same role that a traditional teacher plays. They do not need to be subject-matter experts to be effective. They "ask" people what is important. They are perhaps best-known for asking questions and unleashing group involvement and the creativity of group thought. "*Facilitation,*" write Rothwell and Sredl (2000, II, p. 198), is a process in which trainers "help group members to: (1) establish a purpose and desired outcomes of a group experience; (2) provide a structure for group problem solving; (3) create a climate conducive to group activity; and (4) test or help group members test results produced by group activity."

What Should Group Facilitators Do? Effective group facilitators apply special skills. They help group members to (Rothwell and Sredl, 2000):

- Establish a purpose and desired results from a group experience
- Meet the responsibilities typically expected of facilitators

- Work together for problem discovery and problem solving
- Provide a structure for group activities
- Create a climate that is conducive to group problem solving

In this process, their greatest responsibility may perhaps be summarized in one key sentence: "A good facilitator asks group members questions to help them think, help them discover, and help them identify and solve problems." Good facilitators do not necessarily provide "right answers," as instructors do. Instead, they focus on helping group members develop their own problem-finding and problem-solving skills.

A Key Point About the Group Facilitator's Role. When technical trainers help team members work together more cohesively, lead process improvement efforts, or clarify how a new machine might be used, they are functioning as group facilitators and not as instructors. It is important to understand that, for the most part, group facilitators are engaged in creating new knowledge. They are spokespersons for their groups and are usually in the business of helping group members work together more effectively. They help group members discover new knowledge and new work processes, sometimes through experiential learning methods (Phoon, 1996).

How Can Training Be Delivered Effectively Near the Job?

Near-the-job training (NJT) is not as well-known as either off-the-job or on-the-job training.

What NJT Is

Sometimes called *vestibule training,* NJT literally occurs near—but not on—the job. If you think of a machine used during downtime to train workers, or else a second machine directly next to one used in production that is used for training, you begin to understand the notion of NJT. Any time you set up training in a location close to where people work, you are using it.

When NJT Should Be Used and When NJT Should Not Be Used

NJT is especially appropriate for giving workers a taste for what it is like to work under real conditions—but without the pressures of meeting production standards. You might think of it as "practice near the work setting."

NJT should be used when supervisory support and reinforcement is critical to ensure that training transfers from the instructional to the work setting. When training is given near the work site, workers are usually under the supervisor's watchful eye and receive direct feedback from their supervisors about what they are doing well and not so well. That is rarely true when training is delivered off the job.

NJT is also appropriate when working conditions are difficult to simulate in classroom environments, and workers need to experience what the actual working conditions are like if they are to master the work. Often, expensive machinery is only available on the work site. The company may be unwilling to purchase additional, and expensive, machines for use in training. Consequently, training may have to be given near the job or during downtime.

NJT is not appropriate, however, when the clumsy performance of novice workers can pose a health or safety hazard to others. Under those conditions, the work may have to be simulated or else workers have to be given extensive safety training before they are turned loose for practice. Often, trainers must be with them during their initial work efforts to ensure that they do not hurt themselves or others as they learn.

How Effective NJT Is Designed, Developed, and Delivered

Effective NJT will often be designed and developed in ways comparable to on-the-job training. That means an approach such as the DACUM method, described in Chapter Six, can be most useful to structure a learning plan for workers who participate in NJT. Often, the learning plan will be formatted in a checksheet that tracks the sequence of tasks or activities in which individuals must be trained. The advantage of that approach is that it gives workers a clear sense of exactly what they must learn and in what order.

When a checksheet is used to guide the training, it can encourage consistency to ensure that all people who receive training are given exposure to the same basic skills, concepts, and ideas. Nothing is forgotten or left out due to the spur-of-the-moment problems that trainers may face as they train workers while also trying to meet their own production requirements.

It is also important during NJT to plan for supervisory involvement. The trainee's immediate supervisor should be involved in periodic updates about what workers have learned, how well they are performing, and what encouragement they may need.

How Effective NJT Is Evaluated

Like OJT, NJT is very much applied to the workplace. That means that trainees' progress can be evaluated against actual work expectations and tasks. Indeed, some organizations establish measurable training standards which are rationally related to work production standards. These organizations may also train and certify those who conduct OJT (Walter, 1998). These organizations may also evaluate workers regularly against actual work standards.

How Can Training Be Delivered On the Job?

On-the-job training (OJT) is well-known. However, there are two basic kinds. *Structured OJT* is planned around what people must learn to become productive in their jobs. *Unstructured OJT* is not planned around the needs of the learner and usually involves "following Joe around the plant" or "sitting by Nellie." The latter type of OJT is notoriously ineffective, though still widely used (Rothwell and Kazanas, 1994).

What OJT Is

OJT literally occurs on the job—that is, in the place where the worker is stationed. Think of a worker being trained right on the assembly line or at his or her workstation in an office. That is what OJT is. Often such training is conducted one-on-one, and sometimes the term *one-on-one training* is used synonymously with OJT. The learner is trained in real time (Marsh, 1996).

When OJT Should Be Used and When OJT Should Not Be Used

OJT is even more appropriate than NJT to give workers a sense of what it is like to perform under actual working conditions. Workers are expected to learn while doing—and do while learning. OJT can contribute to the realization of the learning organization (Hamilton and Hamilton, 1997).

OJT should be used when supervisory support and reinforcement are critical. Unlike off-the-job or near-the-job training, OJT is usually carried out directly under the watchful eye of the worker's supervisor. Suppose, for instance, that you wanted to train a worker to use a difficult software application. If you did that, and you did it by sitting with the worker to show him or her what to do and how to do it, you would be using OJT.

OJT, like NJT, is also appropriate when working conditions are difficult to simulate in classroom environments and when workers need to experience what the actual working conditions are like if they are to master the work. But OJT is not appropriate when learners may pose a health or safety hazard as they learn or when OJT will significantly affect customers' perceptions of the organization's performance.

How Effective OJT Is Designed, Developed, and Delivered

OJT, even more than NJT, lends itself particularly well to checksheet-based instruction in which the on-the-job trainer is given a checksheet that is intended to guide the training process. When that is done, OJT is said to be *structured*. The DACUM process, as described in Chapter Six, can yield a *training protocol* by which individuals are systematically instructed on what to do, how to do it, when to do it, and why it is worth doing. The training protocol can be organized on a checksheet that requires trainers to follow a systematic process of instruction. As learners are trained, both trainee and trainer initial the checksheet to show that the trainee has received instruction. Exhibit 8.3 presents an example of the format of such a checksheet.

EXHIBIT 8.3. SAMPLE CHECKSHEET FORMAT TO GUIDE ON-THE-JOB TRAINING

Name of Mentor	**Name of Mentee**	**Period Covering Mo/Yr to Mo/Yr**

Directions: Use this checksheet to plan for mentoring and coaching new workers or those who are being trained on the job. For each activity listed in column 1 below, indicate in column 2 whether you (as mentor) have coached the mentee on how to conduct the activity. (Be sure to explain what to do, why it is worth doing, and how it is done.) Then, both you as mentor and the mentee should initial column 2 below. Mentors and mentees should use column 3 to make any comments about the quality of the mentoring given or received.

Column 1	***Column 2***					***Column 3***
Have you, the mentor, coached the mentee on:	**Yes** ☒	**No** ☒	**N/A** ☒	**Mentor's Initial**	**Mentee's Initial**	**Comments**
1. *Begin each action with a verb and take each action directly from a DACUM chart*	☐	☐	☐			
2.	☐	☐	☐			
3.	☐	☐	☐			
4.	☐	☐	☐			
5.	☐	☐	☐			
6.	☐	☐	☐			
7.	☐	☐	☐			

As in NJT, supervisory involvement is of key importance in OJT. The trainee's immediate supervisor should be involved in periodic updates about what workers have learned, how well they are performing, and what encouragement they may need.

How Effective OJT Is Evaluated

Like NJT, OJT is very much hands-on training. Trainee progress can be evaluated against actual work expectations, activities, and desired results.

One trainer, interviewed for this book, once faced the challenge of improving OJT in a production facility. Read over the case study that follows. As you do so, make notes on key points in the case that dramatize the importance of OJT and approaches that are especially useful.

Case Study: The Power of Effective OJT

The Case Situation

One of my first assignments as a technical trainer was to develop a training program for a specific piece of equipment. I can still picture talking to the plant manager who gave me that assignment. He started as an hourly worker and, over the years, worked his way up to plant manager. He had held jobs as varied as supervisor, superintendent, packaging manager, maintenance manager, production manager, and, finally, plant manager. Most of his career was spent at this plant, although he spent several years as a plant manager at a different plant before returning. By spending almost twenty years at the same plant, he developed a good relationship with all levels in the plant. If the production department had problems or if supervisors had problems with individual workers or the union, he always seemed to hear about those problems. To him, nothing was a secret.

I was the first technical trainer in this plant. I owed my job to a mandate, issued from corporate headquarters, that all plants would have a technical trainer. A new training manager was also assigned to this plant from the corporate offices. The last training manager had been let go. I remember the plant manager telling me that the last training manager had little direct contact with hourly and supervisory personnel.

When I was told to develop a training program, I asked the plant manager if I could work with a supervisor in that area. He agreed but assigned me not to a supervisor from that department but to a manager who was responsible for the plant's manpower. I soon found out that the manager with whom I was working was a close acquaintance of the plant manager and a key person on the staff. Over the next week we met for an hour or so a day to familiarize me with the plant environment. I asked many questions.

I soon learned that a clear training need existed for one machine in the plant. It was a complex machine, it was used on three shifts, and the number of people who could operate it was limited. That created a problem when workers went on vacation or called in sick. No standard operating procedures existed for using that machine. In the past, the plant manager had tried an unstructured OJT approach to train workers on that machine. The unstructured approach turned out to be a dismal failure.

I reviewed my assessment and asked the following:

- Could I spend several days with a knowledgeable operator who also might be willing to be a trainer?
- Could I work with the skilled operators on the other shifts who were content experts and could be utilized as trainers?
- Could I ask to have machine operators brought to first shift for one week to help me develop a structured training program on the machine, and could I give them a brief train-the-trainer course?

I made these requests in a meeting with the plant manager. Although he agreed to the plan, I had the most difficulty explaining why I needed all three machine operators transferred to the first shift. He felt that my work could be accomplished by meeting with each subject-matter expert on his or her shift. But the manager with whom I had been working was finally able to convince the plant manager to permit these transfers so as to develop standard operating procedures for the equipment.

That manager pointed out what many technical trainers learn the hard way: Training is useless if no standard operating procedures exist. The manager had a chart showing the production time lost due to operator error from incorrect settings. That problem alone, which stemmed not from a training need but from a management need to clarify work expectations and requirements, finally convinced the plant manager to transfer the second-shift and third-shift machine operators to the first shift.

The manager I was working with informed the supervisors on all three shifts about the process we planned to use. We prepared a written plan to guide the training process. I also met with each subject-matter expert to answer any questions they might have and build rapport with them.

We planned a week-long schedule. It included a process for developing training on the machine and a train-the-trainer program. I spent time with the second-shift operator to familiarize myself with how the equipment operated and to build a relationship with that operator. I devoted three eight-hour days with the operator. I used what I learned to develop a working outline for the training.

During the training session of one week's duration that followed, I spent three days working with the group to develop the training program. The group consisted of the three subject-matter experts (machine operators), the manager assigned to the project, and myself. My greatest challenge was keeping everyone focused. The working outline provided some guidance in this process. The chief problem was reaching consensus on the standard operating procedure. After working on this equipment for several years, each operator had developed his or her own way of doing things. If a procedure had no effect on the operation, we agreed to let each operator train a new operator according to his or her own way of performing. But in procedures that affected the manufacturing operation or the quality of the product, the discussion became heated.

It helped me to have the manager present in these meetings. He was able to supply examples when the lack of agreed-on procedure caused production problems. He also referred to the corporate quality assurance standard when procedural issues related to machine operation affected quality. We used flip charts to keep track of the discussions and the program development process. That proved to be useful as a means of summarizing what agreements had been reached when the training program was finalized.

The training we developed outlined such key topics as the procedures for start-up, running, shut down, basic troubleshooting, and cleanup. A detailed outline, including course materials, was developed for each step. Since the outline and materials were processed after each day's meeting, the final training program was ready for review on the last day. At that point, only minor changes were needed.

On the fourth and fifth days, I gave the subject-matter experts a train-the-trainer session. I covered such topics as how to work with peers, how adults learn, how to conduct on-the-job training, how to use the course outline, how to reinforce learning, how to answer questions clearly, and how to use questioning techniques. The training session included hands-on exercises on each topic that I covered.

At the end of the training session, we devoted about three hours to planning how the training would be delivered on the job. We focused attention on each major procedure on which workers would be trained when they learned about the machine. The subject-matter experts were asked to estimate how much time should be spent on training workers for each major procedure, both in the classroom and on the job. We captured on a flip chart how much time the machine operators estimated the training should take. The estimated time was thirty-two hours—with the content experts setting the training at five days, including breaks and lunches.

A typical training day was designed to start with two hours in the classroom covering the theoretical aspects of machine operation. That was to be followed by hands-on practice and experience. To do a thorough job of training, we decided to train only two workers at a time. This would afford the trainer the opportunity to permit one person to operate the equipment while showing and explaining the operating procedures to the other person before his or her hands-on experience. By limiting the trainee group to two people at a time, we ensured that the trainer would have control over both the equipment and the trainees. The technical trainer would be present throughout the week of training to observe and coach each machine-operator-turned-trainer.

The machine operator was also made responsible to ensure that all procedures would be covered during the training—including procedures that were not normally part of daily routine.

The first training session took place on the first shift, followed by the second, and then third shift. The technical trainer was present on all shifts. Each trainee would also be required to operate the equipment at least one day a week for four weeks after the initial training session. This approach proved to be very successful. As a result, additional training programs were developed for other equipment, and they made use of the same training methodology. The company eventually expanded this approach to training to include employees in other parts of the plant.

Lessons Learned from the Case

Here is a summary of the key lessons that you should learn from this case. The training was successful because:

- Key stakeholders—plant manager, manager, supervisors, and hourly trainers/ subject-matter experts—were involved in designing, developing, delivering, and even evaluating the training.
- The training was planned and did not proceed on a catch-as-catch-can basis.
- The technical trainer was involved in the training throughout the process.
- The training plan included both classroom training and hands-on on-the-job training.
- The training was not handled as a one-shot process; rather, workers were required to be involved in follow-up hands-on experiences to keep their training fresh in their minds.
- The subject-matter experts were given training on the training process.
- The plant manager supported the training plan by backing it up with resources and not just by paying lip service to it.

How Can Training Be Delivered Effectively Online or Through Alternative Delivery Methods?

Technical trainers find themselves increasingly tasked to deliver instruction through alternatives to traditional off-the-job, near-the-job, or on-the-job methods. There are four basic categories of alternative delivery methods. One is called *group-based technology methods*. A second is called *individualized technology-based methods*. A third is called *self-directed learning*. And a fourth and final type is called *generally structured experiences*. But what are these methods, and how might they be effectively used?

Group-Based Technology Methods

Personal computers have become essential to the daily work of many people. When training is offered in a group setting—often in a room crowded with computers so that learners may be given hands-on experience with the software—we call it group-based technology.

Many features of this kind of training resemble traditional classroom-based instruction. But there are some key differences. First, if this training is to be effective, the learners must face the trainer. Equipment should be arranged so that the trainer's computer screen is projected at the front of the room, learners face that, and learners can see exactly what the trainer does to use the software. Trainees should be given step-by-step guidance on how to use the software, usually backed up with easy-to-read handouts that walk the learner step-by-step through what to do and with visual aids of the computer screen to represent what should happen as the learner proceeds through using the software.

There are several common problems likely to occur in this kind of training that will render it less than fully successful. If trainees cannot see what the trainer does, or if their equipment or software does not match up exactly to what the trainer is using, problems can surface. If trainees are crowded into the room, two at a terminal, then the hands-on value of such training is diminished. Finally, trainers who move with lightning speed through screens, failing to walk around the room to see how learners are faring, will also find that their training is not effective.

Individualized Technology-Based Methods

Many organizations have invested in *learning centers*, defined as rooms loaded with computers and staffed by full-time trainers. They can be temporary as well as fixed (Piskurich, 1999). Workers can wander in as they have downtime and learn on their own. It is an approach that is often used for learners who have individualized needs that are not shared by a group (Reynolds, 1995).

The writers of this book have yet to see a fully successful learning center. Many sit empty, with the trainer having nothing to do. Why? One reason is that learning centers are sometimes positioned too far away from work sites, making it less than convenient for workers to use them. Another reason is that, in downsized or lean-staffed organizations, workers have no downtime—or have so little of it that they are discouraged by supervisors or co-workers from leaving their work areas. The result: Many learning centers are not as effective as they could be.

A key to overcoming this problem is to make the use of a learner center convenient. Find ways to attract learners to it. Alternatively, find ways to take the learning center to those who need it.

Self-Directed Learning

Self-directed learning includes a broad range of methods (Rothwell and Sensenig, 1999). Workers can be encouraged to participate in off-the-job educational experiences, conferences, trade shows, professional or industry association work, and much more. They may also borrow educational resources, such as books, videotapes, technical manuals, periodicals, or other information and read them and study them on their own.

Self-directed learning is likely to be more important to the work of technical trainers in the future as organizations scramble to remain competitive, look for an edge everywhere they can find it, and pressure workers to assume more responsibility for taking charge of their own careers and their own development.

Generally Structured Experiences

Like self-directed learning, generally structured experiences include a broad range of methods. They exclude planned off-the-job, near-the-job, or on-the-job training. However, they may include just about anything else. A *structured experience* is any planned learning event. It may occur anywhere. But usually it does not include the interaction of a trainer and trainee, as off-the-job, near-the-job, and on-the-job training do.

Much online instruction could be classified as a generally structured experience. It is possible that the instruction is delivered through a range of methods. Such instruction can be prepared by an organization or can be purchased from others. Finding online training has never been easier. A case in point: "Log onto the SkillsPoint.com website, use the reseller's search engine to seek out desired classes, and pay online. Or, buyers have the option to integrate SkillsPoint's service with their corporate Intranets, allowing all the electronic purchases to be tied in with the buyer company's accounting and approval systems" (Brunelli, 2000, p. 97). Many vendors now offer online instruction, on many topics, that can be easily accessed from the desktop.

Use the worksheet in Exhibit 8.4 to structure your thinking on the various self-directed experiences that may be used effectively in technical training to substitute for, or complement, technical training efforts.

The struggle to meet the technical training needs of employees is a key challenge facing technical trainers. Over the years, theories on successful adult learning have focused on providing information that trainees need when they need it. Yet, despite all the information that has been provided on this subject, many technical trainers still must shorten the length of the learning cycle. The main reason is that, as society is transitioning from manual and highly functional craft-based skills to the information processing and analysis skills of a new information age, the workplace is also in transition. Knowledge workers are becoming the dominant workers, and the industrial workforce will become a minority in the industrialized nations of the West. The effective employment of knowledge workers will become the critical success factor for increasing productivity in the knowledge-driven organization. As Naisbitt (in Watson, 1994, p. 129) predicted: "In an information society, human resources are any organization's competitive edge." Despite these changes, it is important to remember that, while technology will always be changing and has become a driving force in business today, the way adults learn will probably not change all that much.

Nor, in all likelihood, will the instructional design process change all that much, as it is based on proven ways of helping adults learn (see www.learningcircuits.org/feb2000/feb2000_webrules.html). In the early days of computer-based training (CBT), there was an initial rush to pour content into electronic tutorials. A few innovative instructional designers made the most of the limited engaging simulations, quizzes, and even games. They tried to preserve the experiential nature of adult learning, proven effective in

EXHIBIT 8.4. WORKSHEET TO STRUCTURE YOUR THINKING ON SELF-DIRECTED LEARNING ACTIVITIES

Directions: Use this worksheet to structure your thinking on alternatives to planned off-the-job or on-the-job training. In the space below, brainstorm a list of as many ways as you can think of that an individual could develop himself or herself through methods other than training. There are no "right" or "wrong" answers. Examples of such approaches might include job rotations, short-term task force assignments, and reading.

Write your list here:

classroom instruction over the years, in the new world of so-called e-learning. But their efforts were often the exception to the rule of exalting content and information over the learning process, and most learners were forced to read the text on the screen. Programs of this type came to be known, rather derivisely, as "page turners." Page turners tainted the early days of e-learning, and they often affect it even to this day. With the advent of interactive videodiscs and multimedia CD-ROMs, instructional designers were equipped with the means to add graphics, animation, audio, and video to e-learning. But such tools are not effective if they are not used to increase learner interaction. Technical trainers who evaluate e-learning should know that learner interactivity—that is, the process of involving the learner in the learning process—remains the key to effective instruction in any medium. Therefore, when technical trainers examine e-learning, they should pose such questions as these (www.learningcircuits.org/feb2000/feb2000_webrules.html):

- Does the program immediately capture a learner's attention?
- Does the program explain its own relevance? Does it answer the learner's question: "What's in it for me?"
- Are the learning objectives presented? Are they specific and measurable?
- Is the presentation of content engaging through both design and media?
- Does the learner have an opportunity for practice and recall (beyond stale multiple-choice questions)?
- Does the program include a final post-test or other device to indicate mastery?

Laying the Foundation for Successful Partnerships Between the Training and Information Technology Departments

Until recently, the training and development function has enjoyed a high degree of control in developing and implementing training solutions. Today, as technology is leveraged for training delivery, the training department must work with IT professionals to implement training solutions. Partnering between IT and training is critical to the success of technology-related solutions.

However, the training department and the IT department differ in culture, political environment, and past history of collaboration. According to Mayberry (see www.learningcircuits.org/jan2000/mayberry.html), it is important to create mutual understanding, whatever the current relationship may be. Mayberry compares the difference between the traditional approach to training solutions and that of an IT request for training. It is in the implementation phase in which leveraging technology comes into play. If training and training content are to be delivered through the company's information system, technical trainers must rely on the expertise and assistance of the IT department. If this stage of development requires solutions to such technical problems as server space, software installation, customization, application, maintenance, and ongoing support, and if those are beyond the trainer's expertise, that is where the assistance of the IT department becomes critical.

In developing an IT request for training, the following four phases should be considered: proposal, development, implementation, and updates and maintenance. The *proposal phase* involves the request for a solution to resolve a performance gap or problem. It includes negotiation regarding the deliverable between the IT department and the training department. The *development phase* involves the creation of solutions and materials, and technical trainers should oversee this phase and negotiate the solutions, functions, and features. The IT department should agree to software installation, customization, and application development. The *implementation phase* involves bringing the product to the client, including beta testing and debugging tasks. And the fourth and *final phase, updates and maintenance,* includes the tedious and labor-intensive portion of technology-related solutions, maintenance, and ongoing support.

Building a successful partnership is often a necessity for technical trainers if they wish to move into the age of e-learning. That is especially true in situations when the training function must reach a diverse and highly distributed global workforce. Building a partnership may take time, and in some cases it can be immensely frustrating. In many cases the training department and the IT department have not had the opportunity to work together on a project. And the stakes are high, since an unsuccessful partnership may sour relations for years to come.

Mayberry gives good advice to trainers faced with working with the IT department (see www.learningcircuits.org/jan2000/mayberry.html):

- Meet with the IT developer face-to-face to discuss the problem or solution before submitting a request for new or unique applications of technology
- Clarify what the IT developer knows and can do relative to the proposed solution
- Present the IT developer with a visualization of the outcomes through a prototype or storyboards of the application
- Form an idea of the IT department's current obligations regarding other requests, projects, or priorities
- For large requests, again top management commitment in the form of funds and personal support before beginning a dialogue with the IT department

The new technology available to technical trainers is powerful. But the key to using it is careful planning and buy-in from the organization.

System Development: A Key Learning Is Used

The process of developing an information system is the same whether it is for technical training, manufacturing, human resources, or some other activity. Understanding the process is important to all professionals who rely on information technology, not just those working in the IT field. In today's businesses, managers and employees in all functions work together and use business information systems. As a result, users of all types are helping with development processes. Effective systems development requires a team effort. The team usually consists of stakeholders, users, managers, systems development specialists, and support personnel. The development team is responsible for determining the objectives of the training system and for delivering a system to meet the needs of the organization.

Key issues to consider in the selection of the media or medium for technical training include all of the following (Stair and Reynolds, 2001):

- *Quality or usefulness of the system.* Can the training system present the information close to, or better than, a live trainer, or can it simulate the same effects if the system is meant to simulate a training exercise?
- *Quality or usefulness of the format of the output.* Is the output generated in a form that is useable and easy to understand? Will the user have difficulty learning how to use the system?
- *Speed at which the output is generated.* If the systems are to be used with a server, how many stations can be connected and in use before the response rate is slowed down? Trainees may lose interest if the response rate is too slow.
- *Compatibility with a system already used by the organization.* If the organization has an information system, can a training system be retrofitted to work in or with the legacy system?

These are just a few examples of what to consider when selecting the media or medium.

The strategic goals of the organization should also be considered. Management buy-in is critical for several reasons. The cost associated with developing e-learning systems can be high, so it is important to have a sound rationale. Some associated developmental costs a technical trainer should consider when thinking about using e-learning include all of the following (Stair and Reynolds, 2001):

- *Costs related to the uniqueness of the system application.* If the versatility of the system is important, trying to save money with a less expensive system can decrease the flexibility and could end up costing much more in the future to add needed features.
- *Fixed investment in hardware and related equipment.* Consider costs associated with such items as computers, network-related equipment, and environmentally controlled data centers in which to operate the equipment.
- *Ongoing operating costs of the system.* Operating costs include costs for personnel, software, supplies, and such resources as the electricity required to run the system.

High technology in the form of computers, telecommunications networks, and databanks, as well as imaging and automatic diagnostic systems, multimedia applications, expert systems, artificial intelligence, and CD-ROMs, are all important aspects of many modern education and training systems. Each form has it pros and cons. In the selection of any of these technologies, technical trainers have to keep in mind some basic questions:

- *What is the cost?* What is the cost of this technology, and can it be justified in its application? The cost goes beyond the development of the training, as one must consider the equipment to support the technology.
- *Who is the intended audience?* Will the workers be able to use this technology? Do they have the computer skills to use the equipment? Do they have computers?
- *How will it be used?* Will the technology be used as a part of training, or will it be the total training? What impact will it have on the learning process?
- *Will it be used?* Are the workers willing to use new technology?
- *Does management support this technology?* If so, is it part of the company's strategic plan, and does it fit into the overall information system?
- *What impact will it have?* Will this technology have the impact expected?

These questions should be answered before making a decision to use e-learning, or any other medium for that matter, in delivering instruction.

A task force can be formed to help in the decision making. When selecting the task force members, technical trainers should consider the following:

- Who will be using the training?
- What department(s) will have access to the training?
- Who are the managers of the departments?
- What senior manager(s) support this media?

By using a task force, technical trainers are building support for the decision within the rest of the organization.

Summary

This chapter focused on determining which delivery methods should be used in technical training. It also examined how several such methods—off-the-job training, near-the-job training, on-the-job training, and training delivered online or through alternative delivery methods—could be effectively used. Many technical trainers spend all or most of their time in delivery, and this chapter thus served as a brief introduction to key topics associated with effective training delivery.

The next chapter examines evaluation, a topic of perennial interest to trainers because line managers and other stakeholders of training often want to know what impact training had on learners, work groups, and organizations.

CHAPTER NINE

EVALUATING TECHNICAL TRAINING

Ask any technical trainer to list the most pressing issues in training today, and you are sure to hear evaluation on the list. Why is that? One reason is that trainers are asked to justify their existence as never before. Another reason is that line managers and other stakeholders have learned, often through bitter experience, that training is no panacea. Therefore, evaluation is—and is likely to remain—a pressing issue for some time to come. And there are already excellent tools for use in evaluating technical training, if only trainers would use them (Brinkerhoff, 1995; Marrelli, 1993).

But what is evaluation, and what is unique about the evaluation of technical training? Why is evaluation important? How much effort is devoted to training evaluation? How is it carried out in technical training? This chapter addresses these key questions.

What Is Evaluation, and What Is Unique About the Evaluation of Technical Training?

What is evaluation? What should be evaluated? This section answers these questions.

Definition of Evaluation and Training Evaluation

Evaluation simply means "the process of placing or estimating the value." *Training evaluation* is thus the process of placing or estimating the value of training. Training evaluation hearkens back to the training needs assessment process, since estimating value is linked to the worth of the needs that were met—or were at least attempted to be met.

Unique Aspects of Technical Training Evaluation

Technical training usually focuses on developing *hard skills,* which can be seen and observed in workplace settings. For that reason, evaluating technical training is somewhat easier than evaluating less tangible soft skills training, such as interpersonally oriented training or supervisory, management, or executive training. Technical training lends itself to many evaluation approaches (Falletta and Combs, 1997).

Technical trainers probably favor performance tests more than most other forms of evaluation. In a performance test, individuals must demonstrate that they can do what they have been trained to do. A performance test is usually based on a checksheet, like that described for OJT in Chapter Eight. Basically, the skills, work procedures, or equipment use is listed out on a checksheet. The trainee is asked to demonstrate the skill, procedure, or equipment use in compliance with what he or she has been trained to do. As the trainee proceeds through the demonstration, a trainer observes and checks off what he or she did.

Performance tests may take other forms. If an individual is trained to troubleshoot equipment, for instance, then he or she may be asked to troubleshoot an actual piece of equipment that has broken down. Success on the test is equated to success in actual application.

Why Is Evaluation Important?

Training and development programs are pervasive. One study revealed that about fifteen million U.S. workers participate in 17.6 million courses each year (Chakiris and Rolander, 1986). One of eight workers attends a formal training course each year. More than a decade after this study, investments in HRD have grown dramatically as intellectual capital becomes an increasingly proven source of competitive advantage (Bassi and Van Buren, 1998). At present, the American Society for Training and Development (2000) estimates that the corporate and government training market totaled more than $98 billion in 1998 (ASTD, 2000). It should therefore not be too surprising that investments of this magnitude should command attention—and demand accountability for results.

Stakeholders in training want to know if they got their money's worth. As Delisle (2001) pointed out, training evaluation is important for many reasons:

- Since no more than 20 percent of training investment actually results in transfer to the job, decision makers want to know what they got for their money
- There is a lack of alignment of many training programs with the strategic direction of the company, and evaluation may help keep training on target
- There is a neglect of action in the pre-training and post-training phase
- There is a lack of training support systems to manage the transfer process
- Training evaluation will ensure the training programs meet the predetermined performance goals; link up learner achievement to organizational strategic plans; and help the training departments demonstrate their values in the organizations

How Much Effort Is Devoted to Training Evaluation?

Evaluation remains a vexing problem for trainers. A 1968 study of 110 companies, conducted by Catanello and Kirkpatrick and cited in Burgoyne and Cooper (1975), revealed that few companies evaluate more than how much trainees liked the training. The results of one survey, cited by Galagan (1983) and Del Gaizo (1984), indicated that 30 percent of the respondents pointed to training evaluation as the most difficult part of their job.

How Is Evaluation Carried Out in Technical Training?

Evaluation for technical training resembles, in most respects, evaluation for any kind of training. The difficulty is often in isolating how training contributed to improvements in performance and keeping those contributions separate from other kinds of changes that could affect individual productivity (Thompson, 2001).

Several models should be described in any discussion of training evaluation, since they can help trainers conceptualize key issues.

Donald Kirkpatrick's Hierarchy of Training Evaluation

The most famous model used to describe training evaluation was first developed by Donald Kirkpatrick. For Kirkpatrick (1994), there are four levels of training evaluation.

The first level is *reaction*. How much did trainees like the training in which they participated? That is the focus of this form of evaluation. It is usually measured by end-of-course evaluations, which are sometimes called smile sheets because they rely on "smiley faces."

The second level is *learning*. How much did trainees learn from the training in which they participated? This level may be assessed through pretests, post-tests, and midpoint tests. Tests may focus on knowledge, and these tests are called paper-and-pencil tests. Tests may also focus on skill, and these tests are usually called performance tests and require individuals to demonstrate that they can do what they have been trained to do.

The third level of Kirkpatrick's hierarchy of evaluation is *behavior change*. Evaluation at this level focuses on how much trainees change their on-the-job behavior as a direct result of the training they received. Change of this kind can be measured through written questionnaires administered to individuals to assess their own perceived behavior change or to other people, such as subordinates or co-workers, who are positioned to assess how much an individual has changed his or her behavior on the job.

The fourth and final level of Kirkpatrick's hierarchy of evaluation is *organizational impact*. How much did an individual change, and what impact did that have on the organization's productivity, profitability, error ratios, or other bottom-line measures of performance? This level is usually associated with return on investment (ROI), in which the cost of the training is added up, subtracted from real or perceived improvements in organizational productivity, and the net results are the return on investment.

According to Brown (1998), 94 percent of training courses in business are evaluated at Level I, 34 percent at Level II, 13 percent at Level III, and only 3 percent at Level IV. The popularity of rating participant reactions (Level I) is evident in several online services for evaluation of training such as ACT: Training Evaluation Services at www.act.org., Enquire Within at www.enquirewithin.co.nz, PERMISS at www.cpol.army.mil, or NPS at www.nps.navy.mil. At least one case study has been published to describe how decentralized training was evaluated across nations for its cost-effectiveness (Johnson, 1993).

Evaluation Based on Time

Nickols (2001) points out that training may be evaluated before training, during training, after training but before an individual's return to the workplace, after training and after an individual's return to the workplace, and upon leaving the workplace. For Nickols, a key issue is the stakeholder of evaluation, and a bottom-line issue is "Who wants to know the results of training?" and "What do they want to know?" These questions can be posed at different points in time and addressed from the standpoint of different stakeholders.

Evaluation Based on the Process

How will training evaluation be carried out? That question has preoccupied many people as they have pondered the issue.

Most often, training evaluation is approached much like a research problem. Trainers clarify what they want to know, establish a methodology by which to carry out the process, and then report results. Stated another way, as Sieloff (2001) describes it, trainers (1) plan and design the evaluation type, approach, and protocol; (2) collect data; (3) organize the data; (4) examine the reliability and validity of the evaluation design; and (5) report the results and plan future improvements based on them.

A particularly interesting, and recent, approach to training evaluation has been suggested by Lee (1996). Called "pay forward," it describes benefits from training investments that may perhaps not be best expressed in financial terms. The notion is that training may actually yield benefits other than those expressed financially—such as improvements in culture, long-term customer service, and others. To use this method, trainers must collect information by interviews and opinion surveys.

Issues Influencing Training Evaluation

How training evaluation is carried out is influenced by many organizational issues. As Sieloff (2001) points out, those include: (1) the goal of the client or sponsor; (2) interpersonal relationships among evaluators, participants, and decision makers; (3) ethical considerations of the evaluation (such as confidentiality and anonymity); (4) the organization's political environment; and (5) the decision made or actions to be taken by the training stakeholders based on the evaluation results. Successful training evaluation therefore addresses each issue appropriately, as exemplified by a case written up about the Prudential Insurance Company (Hardinger, 2001).

A study by Warr, Allan, and Birdi (1999) revealed that several individual characteristics greatly influence training outcomes. One was the trainee's learning motivation. A second was the trainee's confidence about his or her ability to cope with the learning task. The most significant organizational characteristic that predicts the training outcomes is the *transfer climate*, the perception that the training can be applied in an organization. The transfer climate is associated with how much supervisors and co-workers encourage and reward the application of training. A training course was studied on twenty-three occasions over a seven-month period, and the study participants included technicians employed by a motor-vehicle dealership. The manufacturers supplying vehicles to the dealers offered the training course. The training course involved lectures and practical demonstrations about the operation of, and interpretation of output from, an electronic tool. The piece of equipment permitted diagnostic checks on engine performance and could present detailed information about particular models. Trainees were asked to complete a knowledge test and questionnaires on arrival at the training course (T1) and at the end of the training course (T2). The study revealed that three levels of training evaluation, measures of trainees' reactions, were associated with learning outcomes. But the reactions were generally unrelated to subsequent job behavior. In addition, both immediate and delayed learning strategies were predicted by trainees' motivation, confidence, and use of certain learning strategies, and changes in job behavior were independently predicted by transfer climate and learning confidence.

Problems That Plague Training Evaluation

Clark (1995) identified five reasons that training evaluations are sometimes less effective or useful than they could be.

The first reason is that those who conduct the evaluation do not comprehend the full scope and complexity of the training evaluation process. The second reason is that evaluators are not savvy about the nature and type of organization in which they are carrying out the evaluation. Third, the perspectives of evaluators may vary, depending on whether they work inside or outside the organization. Fourth, evaluators have not been properly trained on approaches to conducting training evaluation. Fifth and finally, evaluators do not have sufficient resources, such as time, money, and staff, to conduct rigorous evaluation.

Summary

This chapter addressed four key questions. First, what is evaluation, and what is unique about the evaluation of technical training? As the chapter pointed out, evaluation means assessing value. It is closely linked to needs assessment, since a training experience should be deemed successful if a training need is met. Second, why is evaluation important? Evaluation is important because it proves that the organization received benefits from the funds invested in training. Evaluation is likely to remain a front-burner topic for some time to come. Third, how much effort is devoted to training evaluation? Although trainers are often asked about the impact of training, the reality is that decision makers often reward training activity more than they do evaluation studies. Trainers are pressured to do training, not spend time on evaluating training. Striking a balance is a challenge for technical trainers today. Fourth and finally, how is it carried out in technical training?

The chapters in the next part of this book focus on special issues in technical training. The next chapter examines the important role that is—and can be—played by vendors and original equipment manufacturers (OEMs).

PART IV

SPECIAL ISSUES IN TECHNICAL TRAINING

The chapters in this section focus attention on issues of special interest to technical trainers. It

- Describes how to manage and work with original equipment manufacturers (OEMs)
- Describes how to work with hands-on equipment manufacturers
- Describes how to use training suppliers to develop instructional materials
- Examines requirements for effective apprenticeship programs and safety training programs
- Explains how to work with unions to offer technical training
- Discusses useful alternatives to technical training that may be used to enhance performance

Exhibit 5 is the blueprint for Part IV within a schematic diagram representing the book.

EXHIBIT 5. PART IV WITHIN THE SCHEME OF THE BOOK

Chapter 1: **What Is Technical Training?**	**Part I:** **Foundations of** **Effective** **Technical** **Training**
Chapter 2: **What Are the Characteristics of Effective Technical Training?**	
Chapter 3: **Establishing an Organizational Plan for Technical Training**	**Part II:** **Planning and** **Managing the** **Technical** **Training** **Function**
Chapter 4: **Leading and Managing the Technical Training Department**	
Chapter 5: **Basic Principles of Instructional Systems Design**	**Part III:** **Key Issues** **in** **Training** **Course** **Design**
Chapter 6: **Identifying Technical Training Needs**	
Chapter 7: **Preparing Technical Training Programs**	
Chapter 8: **Determining and Using Delivery Methods**	
Chapter 9: **Evaluating Technical Training**	
Chapter 10: **Using Vendors and Managing Original** **Equipment Manufacturers**	**Part IV:** **Special Issues** **in Technical** **Training**
Chapter 11: **Operating Apprenticeship and Safety** **Training Programs and Working with Unions**	
Chapter 12: **Achieving Results with Alternatives to Technical Training**	
Afterword	**Part V:** **Concluding** **Thoughts**

CHAPTER TEN

USING VENDORS AND MANAGING ORIGINAL EQUIPMENT MANUFACTURERS

This chapter examines how to use vendors and how to manage original equipment manufacturers (OEMs). The word *vendor* has several meanings when applied to technical training (Doyle and Van Tiem, 1995). It can refer to the company from which equipment is purchased, and in this sense *vendor* means the same as OEM. In a company that purchases simulators to teach systems for electrical, mechanical, and computer skill building, vendors can also mean *training simulators* or *hands-on equipment manufacturers*. Vendors can also mean organizations that develop such training materials as videos, and these are also known as *suppliers*.

This chapter is organized in three parts. The first part describes how to manage and work with OEMs and devise a certification program for them. In the second part, we describe how to work with hands-on equipment manufacturers. In the third part, we describe how to use training suppliers to develop instructional materials.

Managing and Working with OEMs

In today's business environment, companies rely on others for services or products as part of their operations, and that trend toward partnering is likely to continue in the future (Barron, 1999). Take one case in point. Henry Ford's River Rouge Plant was a self-manufacturing facility. All materials used to manufacture cars were produced at that plant—including paint, steel, glass, and some automotive equipment. Eventually it became economically unprofitable to produce the materials at that plant due to the exorbitant costs associated with the research and manufacturing processes to support this operation. With the divesting of these processes from the plant, many specialized companies were founded to produce equipment to support large manufacturing companies. These companies are referred to as *original equipment manufacturers* (OEMs).

In most situations OEMs design and build equipment and carry out work processes for diverse operations. Example: Packaging is a key issue for many companies. Many companies require packaging to send out their products. OEMs build specialized packaging equipment designed for different (and unique) products, and almost all companies manufacturing consumer products require special packaging equipment. OEMs manufacture most equipment used by the beverage industry, for instance, and this equipment can also be found in every phase of the work process.

The Technical Trainer's Role with OEMs

Although the engineering department usually makes the purchasing decision for OEM equipment, technical trainers play a key role. Training people how to use the equipment has always been an issue for OEMs, but it has become more important as OEMs increasingly build machines that require computers to operate and maintain equipment. OEMs usually provide some training to companies purchasing their equipment. The training ranges from planned to unplanned. The quality of training depends on the size of the OEM's operation. Large, well-known OEM companies such as HandK, Douglas, Krones, and R.A. Jones operate sophisticated, well-established training programs for their clients. Because these companies supply equipment to many businesses, they enjoy sufficient economies of scale to warrant investments in first-rate training materials and programs. Normally, each company has full-time, professionally prepared technical trainers to support their efforts. On the other hand, smaller OEM companies simply do not have the budget to support quality training programs because they lack the economies of scale to make them feasible.

Whether the OEM is large or small, the technical trainer of the client company has an important role to play in making sure that workers know how to use equipment purchased for their use during the work process.

Training and Large OEMs

Even when technical trainers are dealing with large OEMs that have sophisticated training programs, trainers should be involved in designing, developing, delivering, and evaluating the technical training to workers in their organizations. The department purchasing the equipment is the main point of contact for OEMs, and so technical trainers may need to be involved with such varied groups as engineering, management information systems, production, or other groups. No matter who purchases the equipment, trainers should be involved soon after a purchasing decision is contemplated.

Technical trainers will usually find that those who make purchasing decisions on equipment will focus their attention on how the equipment will help them perform their work. They will seldom pay much attention to the training requirements for the workers who will ultimately have to use the equipment. Nor will they usually scrutinize how the OEM will organize or deliver the training. Indeed, many times training will not surface as an issue until the equipment is already on-site and being used and workers are struggling to figure out how to operate the equipment. If that happens, the training usually ends up planned on an as-needed basis to meet immediate problems with worker performance. The result is that the value of the equipment is lost due to downtime and employee error.

There is even a term for this problem. It is called the *productivity paradox*. It is the belief that technology or equipment will end up yielding higher production when, in fact, it does not because the human side of the enterprise was forgotten during implementation. The inability of workers to use (or repair) equipment becomes the weak link that saps full realization of the productivity improvement that should have been yielded from the equipment. *The paradox is that technology that should have yielded higher production may actually end up resulting in lower production.*

But the productivity paradox can be avoided if training is planned at the same time that an equipment selection decision is made. That is a proactive approach. If technical trainers are involved in the selection decision, they should pose the following questions before the equipment arrives and take active steps to get answers:

- What training does the OEM have available?
- What training materials have been prepared by the OEM?
- What is the content of the training?
- How does the training content match up to the work expectations of the organization?
- What training is offered to those interacting with the equipment in different ways? (In other words, has training been prepared for operators? For maintenance crews? For other groups as needed?)
- What assumptions have been made by OEMs in their training about the skills possessed by workers? (In other words, do OEMs assume specialized skills? If so, do workers in the organization possess that prerequisite knowledge and skill?)
- How will training be scheduled and carried out by the OEM? Will the OEM deliver the training at the employer's location, at their location, or in some other way (such as by videotape or by web-based instruction)?
- How easily can the OEM's training be modified so that it is tailored to any unique customer/user requirements?

Training and Small OEMs

Technical trainers should be more actively involved in planning and installing equipment with small OEMs than with their larger counterparts. While the same problems exist with the installation of equipment, small

OEMs are less able to supply quality training. As a consequence, it is important to involve technical trainers from the outset of the decision-making process so that they can clarify what training will be needed. After all, the purchaser may have to develop training from scratch. Budgets might need to be adjusted to plan for the necessary training funds, since they are usually part of the project's capital budget. An example of one company's process for new equipment start-up can be found in Exhibit 10.1.

OEM Training Certification Program

Companies that are heavily dependent on OEMs for their manufacturing capabilities are more likely to demand greater input in OEM-prepared technical training materials and methods. For this reason, many companies develop an OEM training certification program to help OEMs comply with company-mandated training requirements. Even when OEMs have state-of-the-art, professionally prepared training programs, client companies still want greater input in the development of training materials. One reason is that companies have found that, by having training standards, employees can be better trained because of consistency in the way training is conducted. That practice is also consistent with a key adult learning principle, which is to *keep the learning environment consistent.* When adults become familiar with an approach to training and that approach is used consistently, the learning curve is reduced. But if new methods are used, adults require time to adjust to them, and that can make the learning process more time-consuming. In addition, once a training standard has been developed, the training process becomes easier to evaluate and improvement processes becomes more effective.

Deciding when an OEM Training Certification Process Is Warranted.

A training certification process is warranted when three conditions are met. First, the organization is a big purchaser of OEM equipment. That provides leverage in the way training is developed and delivered. Second, the organization needs to find ways to help OEMs comply with its certification process. If no direction is provided or reason is given for this request, it will be difficult for OEMs to justify.

EXHIBIT 10.1.   PROCEDURES FOR PLANNING TRAINING
FOR EQUIPMENT INSTALLATION

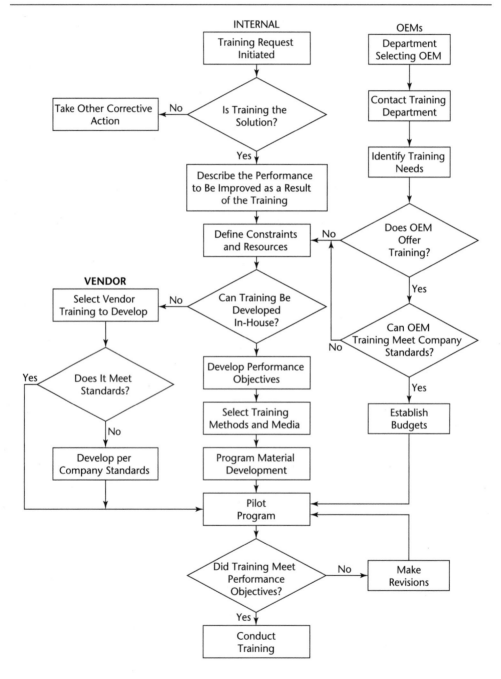

Third and finally, the organization should establish a trainer certification process and build support for it across departments. If any one of these three conditions is not met, it will be difficult to establish and implement an effective, consistent, OEM training certification process.

Justifying the OEM Training Certification Process. A certification process will not just happen on its own. The need must exist—and be felt as a need. An OEM training certification process can help correct widespread problems identified in training course evaluations, employee discussions, supervisory feedback, and technical trainers' opinions. Discussing an OEM training certification process with key stakeholders is a useful starting point to help technical trainers judge whether such a process is worth the time and expense required. If a consensus exists to establish an OEM training certification, technical trainers should depict the process steps through a flow chart. A flow chart depicts in a simple way how the process works.

Reviewing Training Materials and Methods. Depending on what standards are established for technical training, technical trainers will need to establish guidelines for training material, training objectives, lesson plans, course outlines, training aids, activities, and other components of training.

Approving Training Materials and Methods. Technical trainers should notify the department that is heading up the project when an OEM's training materials are approved and should then notify the OEM that approval has been granted.

Rejecting Training Materials and Methods. Technical trainers should notify the department that is heading up the project when an OEM's training materials are rejected. Corrective action should be provided in a timely fashion and with specific corrective action required.

Implementing the OEM Training Certification Process. As part of implementing the OEM training certification process, technical trainers should develop standards for technical training. To help OEMs meet the standards, technical trainers can develop a manual that provides examples of the requirements. Technical trainers may also develop and deliver training for OEMs on the meaning and application of the standards. A list of all OEMs meeting the certification requirement should be kept for future reference.

Certifying Instructors. Instructor certification should usually be part of an OEM training certification process. Technical trainers should evaluate the instructors' presentation skills. Not all OEMs employ full-time professional trainers, and some use sales or service representatives to do the training. In some cases, training is an afterthought. A key responsibility of the service representative is to install the equipment and/or process and, if time permits, provide training. Under these circumstances, the service representative may not possess good presentation skills. As part of the OEM training certification process, technical trainers can provide train-the-trainer instructions or a manual for service representatives as necessary. That must be done before the training is delivered.

Because an OEM training certification process takes time if done correctly, technical trainers should give the matter careful consideration before implementing a process. However, a key advantage of an OEM training certification process is that it ensures some quality in the training subsequently given. That is more likely to mean that the company derives maximum benefit from OEM training—and from the expensive machinery the company has purchased.

Working with Hands-On Equipment Manufacturers

In one sense, technical training means the process of upgrading the technical skills needed by virtually everyone in an organization—including managerial and professional employees—and is usually associated with hands-on training. The association of technical training with hands-on training comes primarily from its relationship with the training of maintenance workers and those who operate equipment or work processes. The required personnel who work with the maintenance or operation of equipment must possess a sound foundation in the systems making up the equipment. These systems include electrical, mechanical, and pro-grammable logic components. Today's technology is so sophisticated that operators and technicians must know how these systems function. To build the necessary skills, technical training must go beyond the machine and address the systems making up machine operations.

Using equipment specifically for training can be costly. It is often impractical to tie up equipment that could otherwise be used in production. For that reason, several companies have developed *universal training simulators* as a foundation for training on high-technology equipment. These simu-lators allow training to be conducted without requiring use of the actual equipment. One such company, Amatrol, has developed many simulators to enhance the skills needed to troubleshoot and repair systems. Some com-panies even help establish technology laboratories for use by organizations or colleges (Agrawal, 1995).

When selecting such hands-on equipment, technical trainers should take precautions to ensure that the simulators will yield good training experiences. In many respects, the issues that technical trainers face when evaluating hands-on equipment resemble those faced when assessing the quality of OEM training. For instance:

1. What training is provided with the simulator? Example: Is a train-the-trainer provided?
2. What instructional materials come with the simulator? Example: Is a leader's guide provided?
3. Have the instructional materials been developed in ways consistent with the ADDIE model?
4. Will the simulator support the hands-on training needed for the inten-ded equipment? Example: Exercises that represent the systems?
5. If exercises are not available, is the staff capable of developing exercises to support use of the equipment?
6. Does the company have personnel who are professionals in the systems field?
7. Will the manufacturer of the equipment review the intended instruc-tional applications of the equipment?

Working with companies that can enhance the learning of high-technology systems by providing simulators can be an effective way to train personnel in the necessary skills in today's competitive market. Downtime is, after all, very costly. Reducing how long it takes for operators and technicians to troubleshoot problems can yield a significant competitive advantage to organizations.

Using Training Suppliers to Develop Instructional Materials

Technical trainers may have occasion to use outside experts for many activities. *Outsourcing*—which generally means "sending the work out" or "bringing in someone other than full-time employees to do the work"—is increasingly common. While training suppliers may be used in many ways, perhaps the most common use in technical training is for instructional materials development. Instructional materials can be quite time-consuming and expensive to develop, and they include participant manuals, videotapes, audiotapes, leaders' guides, web-based instruction, and multimedia courses. Whatever the need, technical trainers should take care in selecting suppliers (Simpson, 1996). Even organizations possessing a large staff of professionally prepared trainers frequently turn to outside training suppliers for design and development expertise, especially if the material to be prepared requires specialized skills in multimedia design. If a company plans to use outside suppliers as part of its long-term plan, then establishing a strategic alliance with a small number of such external suppliers may be cost-effective. Since partnering exists beyond the completion of one project, the supplier develops a strong commitment to help the client successfully implement many programs. Partnering can be advantageous to both client and supplier.

Before selecting suppliers for partnership, however, a formal selection process is worthwhile. Interview several suppliers. The interview process should involve key personnel from outside the client organization's training department—such as managers and supervisors from departments that will rely on the training. By gathering input from others on the choice of a supplier, technical trainers will find that the relationship will ultimately be more productive. Depending on how many projects are to be scheduled over one or more years, technical trainers may consider allowing several suppliers to bid on the projects and give several of them the opportunity to do a project. Although interviewing can give a good indication of what the supplier can deliver, it does not necessarily reveal how well the supplier and client will interact during a project. By using several suppliers for different projects, technical trainers can assess the compatibility of the technical trainers, supplier, and organizational customers. After a project, suppliers may be more accurately evaluated. Although this approach takes more time, it can lead to more effective long-term relationships.

Another issue to consider is the supplier's location. Generally, it is better to select a supplier that is geographically close to the business. Although much can be handled by phone or by computer, travel is usually involved in any project, and a face-to-face relationship is important to maintain. Travel can be expensive.

Technical trainers will find that working with a small number of suppliers for the development of training materials will yield at least the following benefits:

1. Reduced bidding and management costs
2. Increased consistency and effectiveness of the training curriculum resulting from improved coordination and communications
3. Better service, as the client represents a significant share of the supplier's current and potential business
4. Reduced learning curve costs

The supplier will realize these benefits:

1. Increased efficiency as a result of having a predictable, long-term flow of work
2. More cost-effective operation due to increasing familiarity with the industry conditions and practices
3. Project management and designers' dedication to a single client on a long-term basis

Careful selection of suppliers is critical to the success of any training department and the organization it represents. Having the right supplier can be a tremendous benefit to any organization. When dealing with a supplier for a one-time project, the same selection procedures should be taken as when looking for a long-term partnership.

Summary

This chapter examined how to use vendors and how to manage original equipment manufacturers (OEMs). As the chapter pointed out, *vendor* has several meanings. First, the word can refer to the company from which equipment is purchased. Second, the word can refer to *training simulators*. Third and finally, the word can mean organizations that develop training materials.

Each category vendor requires special management. Technical trainers cannot just trust any vendor to perform without any guidance. The chapter provided recommendations for managing relationships with each vendor category.

The next chapter examines two special topics of growing importance to technical training. The first is apprenticeship programs. The second is safety training.

CHAPTER ELEVEN

OPERATING APPRENTICESHIP AND SAFETY TRAINING PROGRAMS AND WORKING WITH UNIONS

This chapter focuses on three issues of importance to technical trainers. The first issue is setting up and operating apprenticeship programs. The second issue is safety training. The third issue is working with unions to conduct technical training.

An Introduction to Apprenticeships

The word *apprenticeship* and the phrase *technical training* have much in common, and some people regard them as going hand-in-hand. The principles used to train apprentices are identical to those on which technical training is based. Many such technical training principles have been described in this book already.

Since apprenticeships are closely related to technical training, the first part of this chapter will discuss in detail how apprenticeship programs work. To appreciate the rich heritage that apprenticeships have enjoyed in the development of skilled workers, you must understand the history. How far back does apprenticeship go? People have been transferring skills from one generation to another in some form of apprenticeship since before the beginning of recorded history. Four thousand years ago, the Babylonian Code of Hammurabi provided that artisans teach their crafts to youth. The records of Egypt, Greece, and Rome from early times reveal that skills were being passed on in this fashion. When an apprentice achieved the status of a craft worker, he was regarded as an important member of society. (We say "he" because apprentices were almost always men until recent times. [See Berik and Bilginsoy, 2000])

The system of apprenticeship established in Babylon was carried over to European countries. In Europe, many crafts had well-established guilds, which are predecessors of modern craft unions, and such crafts as shoe-making, carpentry, stonemasonry, and silversmithing were among the most common indentured skills. The apprenticeship tradition continued when America was settled, and craft workers traveled to the New World from England, Germany, and other European countries. The word *indentured* derived its name from the English practice of tearing indentions or notches in duplicate copies of the apprenticeship agreement (contract) (U.S. Department of Labor, 1991). The master would keep a copy, and the apprentice would keep a copy. Upon completion of the apprentice-ship, the apprentice would receive the master's copy. Having both copies with the same indenture marks was an apprentice's way of showing that he was a journeyman. Only when he could purchase the tools of his trade did he become a master.

Crafts in Family Tradition

The apprenticeship tradition in America was also a part of a family busi-ness in which fathers passed down their crafts to their sons from one gen-eration to the next. Some of America's most famous early families apprenticed their children in the family business (U.S. Department of Labor, 1991). Paul Revere and his brother learned the craft of silver-smithing from their father. Benjamin Franklin was indentured in 1718 at the age of twelve to his elder brother James to learn the printing trade. Daniel S. Glackens learned the printing trade from his father. Glackens published the newspaper, *The Lafayette,* in the 1820s in Pottstown, PA.

One of his sons, Henry O., became a craft worker in the shops of the Pennsylvania Railroad after serving an apprenticeship, and he later became a manufacturer and business executive. Another son, William J., was engaged in the art of plastering and worked on the capitol building in Washington, DC.

Many other industrial and governmental leaders began their working careers as apprentices. Charles E. Sorensen was a skilled pattern maker, and he became a production genius who worked for Henry Ford and was often considered his right-hand man. Sorensen formulated the concept of the moving assembly line. He was credited for laying out the economics of the $5 day, built Ford's River Rouge Plant, and built Ford's mile-long Willow Run bomber plant that became famous in World War II for turning out a B-24 every hour. Ralph E. Flanders of Vermont, who served an apprenticeship as a machinist in 1897, later became a distinguished U.S. senator. Patrick V. McNamara of Michigan served an apprenticeship in plumbing before becoming a U.S. senator. Apprenticeship, in many cases, was the stepping stone from poverty to prominence for many of America's earliest leaders (U.S. Department of Labor, 1991).

But, although there are many success stories, early apprenticeship training also had its dark side. Poor children were indentured as apprentices and exploited as cheap labor, working many hours each day for as long as twelve years to learn a trade. In colonial New England, many youngsters under ten years old whose parents could not support them were indentured to masters who agreed to teach them a trade.

Legislation Governing Apprenticeships

Although apprenticeships were well-established in the United States at the turn of the 20th Century, the terms and conditions were established by the company hiring the apprentice. It was not until 1911 that Wisconsin enacted legislation to promote an organized system to monitor apprenticeships (U.S. Department of Labor, 1991). The law placed apprenticeship programs under the jurisdiction of an industrial commission, and the purpose of that commission was to ensure that the terms of the apprenticeship agreement would be upheld by both company and apprentice. The law also contained a clause that required apprentices to attend five hours of classroom instruction each week. That was done in conjunction with local vocational schools.

In the 1920s, the federal government—along with national employers, labor organizations, and educators—began a concerted effort to establish uniform national apprenticeship systems to meet the needs of a growing economy. This prompted the federal government in 1934 to promote apprenticeships on a national level. The Federal Committee on Apprenticeships—composed of representatives of government agencies—was appointed by the Secretary of Labor to serve as the national policy-recommending body on apprenticeships in the United States. It was authorized to assume responsibility for apprentices and their training under industrial codes formulated by the National Recovery Administration. This act, known as the National Apprenticeship Law or as the Fitzgerald Act, helped establish a system of labor standards, policies, and procedures governing the registration, cancellation, and de-registration of apprenticeship programs. Under the National Apprenticeship Act, unions and employers can determine their own apprenticeship programs within a framework of standards laid down by state apprenticeship councils (SACs) or the Bureau of Employment and Training, U.S. Department of Labor. If an apprentice program meets these standards, it is registered and persons who successfully complete the training receive certificates of completion that entitle them to be called certified journeymen in that trade (U.S. Department of Labor, 1991).

Apprenticeships Today

The range of apprenticeship programs available today spans more industries and occupations than was true in the earliest days. Early apprentice programs focused on the needs of an agricultural economy that encouraged the production of household goods such as furniture, clothing, and shoes. Today, apprenticeship programs can be found in manufacturing, transportation, communications, wholesale and retail, printing and publishing, finance, insurance, real estate, and services. Even childcare workers and optical dispensors have apprenticeship programs. The United Brotherhood of Carpenters (UBC) has the most apprentices in the United States, numbering some 52,000 at this writing, and invests more than $100 million per year in apprenticeship programs. The U.S. military has the second largest group of apprentices, and the United Brotherhood of Electricians is the third largest employer of apprentices.

But, more often than not, apprenticeship programs are associated with organizations needing highly skilled workers. With the ever-changing need for skilled workers, the U.S. Department of Labor in its publication *Apprenticeship—Past and Present* (1991) cited a new apprenticeship that was created to train orthotic and prosthetic technicians. As the need for skilled workers increases, the number and types of apprenticeships will also increase. More attention continues to focus around apprenticeship programs (Cantor, 1997; Dolainski, 1997; Evanciew and Rojewski, 1999; Hong Vo, 1996; Kazis, 1995; Kelly, 1995; Paquin, 1995; Reid, 1993; Rowley, Crist, and Presley, 1995; Verespej, 1996). There is particular interest in best-practice examples of apprenticeship programs (Blume, 1991; Cheney and Jarrett, 1997; Lucadamo and Cheney, 1997; Sooy, 1993).

Why Apprenticeship?

As U.S. companies compete in a fiercely competitive global economy, many are introducing new technologies that require more educated and trained workers. In the present economy, employers are searching for, and often having a most difficult time finding, qualified workers possessing the skills they need. This problem has been exacerbated by a U.S. unemployment rate that has been at its lowest point in thirty years. The demand for skilled workers is rising even as there is an increase in technical graduates from technical and community colleges (Cantor, 1994). Organizations are using apprenticeship programs to develop the skilled workforce they need to stay competitive. Sometimes organizations are also looking internationally for lessons learned from effective apprenticeship programs abroad (Frantz, 1994; Gitter, 1994; McCain, 1994).

There are key advantages to using apprenticeship programs as a way to build a pool of qualified applicants for entry-level jobs in the crafts:

- Apprentices can be selected from individuals in the organization's present workforce.
- There is a six-month trial to see if an apprentice wants to learn the trade.
- The starting pay is approximately 60 percent of a journeyperson, with increases based on the total numbers of years of the apprenticeship program.
- Training is primarily on-the-job and can be tailored to meet the unique needs of a specific organization.
- Apprentices may receive related instruction at a technical college to support on-the-job learning.
- Apprentices are motivated in learning skills and are recognized for their achievement when the apprenticeship is completed because they receive a Certificate of Completion of Apprenticeship.
- The certificate of completion is valuable, since it can help an apprentice find a new job with a new organization in the event that he or she is laid off from an employer. It thus provides portability of skills for workers at a time of increasing uncertainty about the duration of employer-employee relationships.

How to Start an Apprenticeship Program

The size of the organization need not matter when starting an apprenticeship program. A small company can do it as well as a large company. The process is the same. If a skill shortage is of concern to an organization (see Huey and McCallar, 2000), technical trainers can play an important role by looking at the feasibility of establishing a formal apprenticeship program.

Before any outside contacts are made, technical trainers should first discuss with management that they would like to investigate the requirements for establishing an apprenticeship program. Key to the research is to focus on critical skill and talent shortages, both present and future, to meet business needs. Provide company managers with an overview of how the research will be conducted (U.S. Department of Labor, 1989):

- *Contact other companies that have an apprentice program.* If the technical trainer is not familiar with any companies that have such programs, then the next step would be to contact the U.S. Department of Labor, Bureau of Employment and Training regional office. Each state has an office located in their largest city. If this cannot be found, the location of the regional office can be obtained by contacting the U.S. Department of Labor, Secretary of Employment of Apprenticeships and Training in Washington, DC, or by surfing the web.

- *Once the regional office has been located, set up a meeting to discuss the steps in establishing a program.* Let the person know this is just an information meeting. (Note: Take care how this is handled. The authors have seen situations in which a contact was made just for the information and before long the word is out that the company is establishing an apprenticeship program. The program is killed before it gets started.) If the technical trainer is planning an apprentice program in a unionized organization, the union should be notified of the research, since a program of this nature will have implications for any existing or pending collective bargaining agreement. If that is the case, it should be one point brought up during collective bargaining negotiations that management wants to research the possibilities of an apprenticeship program. The union can ask to be included in the research process, and some highly successful programs are jointly sponsored by management and labor organizations.

- *Clarify the questions to ask the regional officer of the Labor Department.* Prior to meeting put together a list of potential occupations that are being considered for apprenticeships, since the length of the required training and schooling varies for each trade.

- *Establish an apprenticeship committee.* Form a committee and clarify the responsibilities of the sponsor.

- *Establish apprentice qualifications.* These will depend on the physical, mental, or health requirements of the occupation. Included in the qualifications is the level of education in a certain subject. A tool-and-die maker may require a certain level in mathematics, while a steamfitter may require a certain level in mathematics and science. The U.S. Department of Labor regional office personnel can help in establishing this requirement. In any case, such educational requirements must be clear and objective to be in compliance with equal opportunity laws.

- *Specify the number of apprentices that can be trained at one time.* A key principle of apprenticeship training is to have the apprentice work alongside a journeyperson. The advantage of having several journeypersons is that apprentices can learn from people with different experiences. Depending on the size of the company and the specific trade, apprenticeships may be possible with only one journeyperson.

- *Set apprentice wages.* Apprentice wages are based on the prevailing rate of journeypersons, which usually starts at 50 percent to 60 percent of that wage (unless that is lower than the minimum wage, in which case the prevailing rate will be the minimum wage). The wages are progressively increased every six months throughout the apprenticeship with the final pay period amounting to 85 to 95 percent of the journeyperson rate.

- *Ensure appropriate supervision of apprentices.* One person must be responsible for the apprentice to ensure that the agreement in the contract is adhered to. Usually the person in charge of the department where the apprentice is assigned bears this responsibility. This responsibility governs apprentice job assignments, tracking the hours worked to develop specific skills, receiving proper classroom training, and overseeing the apprentice's progress. If the company has a technical trainer, it is important that apprentice, supervisor, and trainer work closely during the apprenticeship effort.

- *Establish and manage the time for classroom instruction.* The time assigned to classroom instruction will depend on the type of apprenticeship, the company, and the Bureau of Apprenticeship regional office. The minimum number of hours is 144 as mandated by the Secretary of Labor. The purpose of classroom instruction is to complement hands-on (on-the-job) training. Courses taken at a local technical college (or other sources of classroom training) should address the theory to support the hands-on training. Classroom training can also include hands-on instruction at the school. Although regional apprenticeship offices and the schools sometimes predetermine the classes, the company can require courses meeting unique organizational needs.

- *Establish and manage a consistent method by which to grant credit for previous experience.* If the apprentice has earned related credit through attending technical college or through gaining military experience or prior work experience, the apprentice may be given credit toward the apprenticeship time. Credit should not be based on time, but should be based on the skills that the individual acquired as those skills relate to the apprenticeship. (Note: Developing a chart, such as a DACUM chart, can be most helpful in determining the relevant skills and providing a basis for assigning credit for them.)

- *Remain sensitive to equal opportunity.* All apprenticeships, in conjunction with the state apprenticeship office, must comply with both the federal and state equal opportunity laws—and that includes testing and selection procedures as well as the training designed and delivered. Individuals should be eligible for apprenticeships regardless of race, color, creed, sex, or national origin.

Apprenticeship Committee

Depending on the size of a company, an apprenticeship advisory committee can benefit both the apprentice and the organization. This committee consists of individuals representing both management and employees. They may include production supervisors, personnel staff, craft supervisors, and skilled workers. Its primary functions include setting standards for training, establishing selection procedures for apprentices, determining the number of apprentices to be trained, ensuring that apprentices are receiving the proper training, reviewing the apprentices' progress, and acting as a liaison when problems occur between apprentice and supervisor. The number of committee members is usually left to the organization but should include an equal representation from both sides. Member selection should also be based on those who want to serve. If selection is not done voluntarily, then the value of the committee to serving the best interest of the apprenticeship program is questionable.

The Technical Trainer's Role in Apprenticeships

Most apprenticeship requirements make good sense. They are consistent with key principles required for any effective technical training. To be most useful, apprenticeship programs require organizations to develop a list of tasks associated with classroom and on-the-job training, provide train-the-trainer experiences, and build apprentice competence.

Technical trainers can provide essential input to ensure the successful design, development, and delivery of an apprenticeship program. Whether the apprentice program is just starting or has been in existence for many years, technical trainers can provide valuable insight. The better an apprenticeship program is organized, the greater will be the benefits it brings to the company and to apprentices enrolled in it.

Developing a List of Competencies and Tasks

The length of an apprenticeship is based on the number of hours worked. This length of time includes both on-the-job and off-the-job training. Since the Bureau of Apprenticeships already determines the time required for most apprenticeships, a common problem is that many companies overlook the hour requirements. In addition to total hours worked, the Bureau of Apprenticeships also provides a recommended list of time that should be given to building major competencies. For instance, a tool and die maker apprentice may be required to operate several precision pieces of equipment. Each piece of equipment may be linked to a competency or competencies that have specific hours attached. Under each competency is a list of tasks that breaks down all the work processes into smaller parts. For example: Under a competency labeled "Die Repair" would be a suggested list of hours (1,000 hours). Under this would be a list of tasks required to demonstrate that competency as well as specific information with which the apprentice must be familiar—such as sharpening the die, replacing broken parts, and checking for proper clearances. Each competency could have as many as fifteen to twenty tasks linked to it.

The DACUM method, discussed in an earlier chapter, could be used to develop the trade competencies and tasks. By developing a DACUM chart, companies can more accurately determine the competency, task, and time for their apprenticeships and have greater ownership in the training. The DACUM chart can be used as a guide to track the progress of the apprentice; and the company—to ensure that an apprentice is consistently trained on all skills—can also use it. With the chart completed, one additional step can be taken to get a more specific time that should be devoted to each task. Since some tasks are easier to learn than others, the time spent learning the skills will vary. Developing approximate times for mastery of each competency and task will also provide guidance to the supervisor in charge of the apprentice. Times for each task can be estimated simply by assessing how difficult each task is and how often it is performed. If the difficulty is great, it might take a longer time to learn and more time should be devoted to this task. If it is done frequently and is repetitious, less time might be needed.

Developing a Train-the-Trainer Program

Since apprentices receive their training from journeypersons, journeypersons should possess a basic understanding of how to conduct training. Often, people are selected as trainers because of their expertise. Although the person assigned to do the training should have the skills to do the work, he or she should also want to function as a trainer, command skills in communicating, and possess a good attitude. Even when a trainer is selected who possesses these skills, additional training may be required. Consideration should be given to offering a basic train-the-trainer course. In fact, a train-the-trainer program can itself follow the apprenticeship model.

If the company has a training department, it should be involved in providing this service. If not, various schools and organizations can offer this training. Having a qualified trainer will give structure to the hands-on training and should improve the quality of that training. The training does not have to be detailed, but it should at least cover such topics as how adults learn, the four-step method of instruction, coaching procedures, and techniques for planning and delivering on-the-job training. The trainer should be provided with all the necessary information to be an effective trainer, and company managers should be sensitized to the opportunity costs (lost production time) that will be necessary to provide the training. A case study of an exemplary train-the-trainer program for apprenticeship, sponsored by the International Association of Bridge, Structural, and Ornamental Ironworkers, has been published and can prove instructive for organizations that contemplate establishing an apprenticeship program (Wircenski, Robertson, and Sullivan, 1993).

Classroom Instruction

Classroom instruction is another important aspect of an apprenticeship program. Apprentices will usually be required to attend a technical college (or other source of training) for this instruction. One might think that, since the training is being offered by a school, the company needs to have little to no involvement with it. But that is far from being true. Since the classroom training is a key element of the apprentice program, companies should take note of what instruction is given and how the apprentice is performing in class. The school predetermines many classes that an apprentice will take. These classes should be reviewed prior to the apprentice's first class. The class list should be reviewed along with the DACUM chart. If a class is not pertinent to the apprenticeship, the company should see whether the school offers another course more appropriate to the needs of the apprentice.

Apprenticeship programs are just one way companies are meeting the needs of their skilled workforce. But, like any training, how effective they are depends on how well they are organized and managed. Technical trainers can play important roles in apprenticeship programs by helping to develop the tools to make them successful.

Safety Training

Technical training and safety training are often linked, for any time training is being conducted for equipment and/or processes, safety is a key element and needs to be given top priority. Since 1970, when the Occupational Safety and Health Administration (OSHA) was founded, the mission of the agency has been *"to assure so far as possible every working man and woman in the nation safe and healthful working conditions."*

Since 1970, the overall workplace death rate has been cut in half. But despite the efforts of OSHA, every year over six thousand Americans die from workplace injuries, and six million people suffer non-fatal workplace injuries. Safety problems are a major cause of death in the workplace (Leigh, 1995). Injuries alone cost the U.S. economy more than $110 billion a year. In addition to these costs, OSHA also fines companies for failure to comply with standards. Therefore, safety training cannot be taken lightly and is essential to ensure safe workplaces.

Developing a Safety Strategy

In a previous chapter, we emphasized the importance of developing a technical training strategy. Safety training should be considered in that strategy. The nature of the safety strategy depends on the size of the organization and the OSHA regulations that apply to it. In some companies only a few regulations apply, and developing a safety strategy would not be necessary. In other organizations, where OSHA regulations figure prominently in daily operations, a safety strategy may be worth the investment. With training requirements coming from all parts of an organization, it is easy to lose sight of how much time is spent on meeting OSHA-required and company-required safety training.

Selecting a Task Force

Since many departments and personnel are involved in safety, consideration should be given to using a task force when developing a safety strategy. Trying to develop a plan without the input of workers could result in a waste. Support is the key to any successful plan and knowing the customers' concerns as well as safety needs can result in an effective strategy. When you select task force members, focus on departments requiring safety training. Such departments should be represented on the team. Be sure to include workers representing all levels—hourly, middle management, and senior management—since safety affects everyone. Diversity in the task force members will also bring a better understanding of safety throughout the organization. Once members are selected, an initial meeting should be held to provide the task force members with the purpose of this committee and their expected role in it. Once the discussion is completed on the purpose, the task force members can work together to develop a list of objectives as one way of involving them in the processes. What follows is an example of how the objectives may be written:

- Evaluate existing safety training requirements and develop recommendations to make training more efficient, effective, and less costly while meeting all business and legal requirements.
- Evaluate how safety-training programs are presently being developed and recommend a more efficient method of developing them.
- Evaluate how safety training is presently being facilitated and recommend alternate methods of instruction while meeting all legal requirements.

Safety Training Requirements

An early step in developing a safety training strategy is to make a list of all the training currently being conducted by the organization as part of meeting OSHA, local plant, and corporate requirements to determine what is necessary. What follows is an example of what that may look like:

Currently there are forty-two safety-training subjects identified as necessary for compliance with OSHA regulations, OSHA directives, the OSHA standard digest, and the Corporate Safety and Health Policy manual. Five required training programs are presently delivered on safety-related subjects. These are monthly employee safety talks, periodic HR/safety personnel development training, and new employee safety and health training.

Thirty-eight of the identified training subjects are required by OSHA regulations or are essential elements of OSHA compliance. The other regulations are considered essential to a specific compliance such as accident prevention or to develop knowledge of OSHA requirements. One example would be National Electric Code requirements.

Once all the safety training is identified, it should then be classified into two categories: (1) new employee training or (2) periodic retraining requirements.

There are two categories of new employee training. One category applies to all new employees. A second category applies to special training required by an employee's assigned department to meet specific requirements. In addition, department requirements may vary according to job classification. An example is that an operator may require two hours of training, while a maintenance employee may require seven hours of training because their work differs. Other considerations are specialized training, such as respiratory protection and confined space entry, which might add additional hours of training. The point worthy of emphasis is that training requirements depend on the industry.

The best approach is to begin by listing all the training and the hours required. What follows is an example of what that might look like:

- Fire Extinguisher Training—15 minutes annually
- Emergency/Hazmat plans—15 minutes annually
- Hearing Conservation—15 minutes annually
- Lockout/Tagout—15 minutes annually
- Ergonomics—15 minutes annually
- Machine Guarding—15 minutes annually
- Personal Protective Equipment Requirements—15 minutes every two years.
- Hazard Communications—60 minutes every two years.

All eight of the subjects are necessary for the organization to be in compliance with OSHA requirements. Three of the eight have a specific annual OSHA requirement. Five address performance-related OSHA requirements. Hazard communication is an example of a standard for which OSHA does not specify a training frequency but does require employees to be kept updated on their understanding of the hazards to which they may be exposed.

Other training to consider is the specialized training requirements applying to specific job duties. Consider this example:

- Forklift Safety—15 minutes annually, and 1 hour every three years
- Powered Hand Truck—15 minutes annually
- Respiratory Protection—30 minutes annually

Once all training is identified, a matrix can be developed to spell out all safety training. The matrix should summarize all the safety training requirements for the organization. That helps managers and workers alike see all requirements at a glance. The matrix should include all safety courses and should clarify who should receive that training, how often they should receive that training, how long the training lasts, what OSHA or other requirements the training satisfies, and other information of value.

Developing a Safety Training Plan

Developing a matrix puts all the necessary safety information in a concise picture for all task force members to see. It also serves as a working document to determine whether training is being duplicated. This is important if employees switch from one department to another, and the same safety training is required. Instead of giving a transferred employee the same training, a refresher course might be all that is needed. That reduces the amount of training required. The matrix can also be useful in tracking employee safety training. Remember that the purpose of developing a safety strategy is not to eliminate safety training but to eliminate unnecessary duplication and focus attention on the key issues surrounding safety. Exhibit 11.1 provides an example of what a safety matrix might look like.

This is just one format that can be used for a safety matrix. A task force may come up with another format that is better suited to meeting an organization's safety needs. Having a matrix provides a clearer picture about how many hours a plant or corporation is devoting to safety training, how much it is costing in employee salaries and instructor costs, and what delivery methods are most appropriate for meeting specific safety-training requirements. Because of the laws surrounding OSHA requirements and the

EXHIBIT 11.1.   SAMPLE SAFETY MATRIX

Name of Course	OSHA Required	Corporate Required	Plant Required	Department Required	Type of Job	Hours Required	Frequency of Training	Number of People Needing Training
Fire Extinguisher	x		x	x		15 min	yearly	300
Emergency/ Hazmat Plans	x	x	x	x		15 min	yearly	300
Hearing Conservation	x	x	x	x	all employees	15 min	yearly	300
Lockout/Tagout	x	x	x		operators, machinists, and electricians	15 min	yearly	50
Ergonomics	x	x	x	x		15 min	yearly	100
Machine Guarding	x	x	x			15 min	yearly	100
Personal Protective Equipment Hazard	x	x	x	x	all employees	15 min	once every 2 years	300
Communications	x	x	x	x		60 min	every 2 years	300
Forklift Safety	x			x	employees working in warehouse	15 min to 60 min	yearly every 3 years	50
Powered Hand Truck	x			x		15 min	yearly	50
Respiratory Protection	x			x		30 min	yearly	35

consequences of lawsuits facing companies for not meeting the requirements, training is sometimes given just for the sake of training. But a matrix can help to answer many questions concerning safety training and OSHA requirements.

Making Recommendations

Once the matrix has been evaluated, recommendations should be developed that will spell out the task force findings. This may include a variety of actions necessary to improve the way safety training is addressed. What follows are some typical examples of how recommendations could be stated:

- Safety training must continue to be targeted at OSHA compliance, accident prevention, or other business requirements such as control of Workers' Compensation costs.
- A corporate-wide standardized format for the preparation of safety training should be developed and utilized. A lead facility concept to develop training courses should be used to control costs, quality, and standardization of courses.
- Facilities must develop in-depth annual safety training plans for each department. Additionally, monthly safety talk programs should be used to complete most employee safety training requirements.

A Model to Guide Safety Training

OSHA has developed guidelines to help employers design, conduct, evaluate, and revise safety training programs:

- Determine whether safety training is needed
- Identify safety training needs
- Identify goals and objectives
- Develop learning activities
- Conduct the safety training
- Evaluate safety training program effectiveness
- Improve the safety training program

Do these steps sound familiar? They should, since they are related to the ADDIE model described in Chapter Five of this book.

An excellent way to reinforce the safety message to employees is to have them involved in each step of the safety training model. As with any training, employee support is critical. Employee input, suggestions, and even co-teaching in the delivery of the safety training will increase the motivation needed for the training to be successful, and the training—as well as other performance improvement interventions designed to enhance safety (Lermack, 1999; Pollock, 2000)—will also benefit from the expertise of incumbent workers. The delivery of safety training, far from an exciting topic, need not be boring (Boyd, 1999). Some organizations take safety matters so seriously that they even provide incentives for suggestions to improve it (Allen, 1997; Laabs, 1997) and take special care to translate safety training material so that safety can be managed consistently across company global locations (Tompkins, 1996).

Boyd (1998) identified seven key requirements for effective safety training. It should: (1) be based on applicable training requirements established for the organization's industry by OSHA; (2) pinpoint hazards in the organization's workplace and create a hazard and abatement program; (3) be based on an appropriate analysis of training needs and the establishment of a training plan; (4) be carried out on a timely basis; (5) provide for an audit of programs and a means by which to examine learner performance in line with application of the training; (6) provide for the documentation of employee safety training; and (7) be cooperative during OSHA inspections and investigations (see Eyres, 1998).

Of course, organizations are seeking to avoid the pain caused by workplace accidents. They are also seeking to avoid the litigation that goes with them (Koury, 1996; Sample, 1993; Sample, 1995; Sample, 1996).

Determining Whether Safety Training Is Needed

There are three common occasions when technical trainers may need to consider developing safety training. The first is the installation of new equipment or the implementation of a new work process. The second occurs when the organization experiences an increase in accidents or when mounting evidence exists that employees are not following proper, and safe, work procedures. The third occurs when employees have not been previously trained on safe work procedures, as in the case of new hires, transfers, or workers who are making other job changes. In short, when the work changes or when the people change, safety training may be necessary.

For safety training associated with new equipment, the original equipment manufacturer (OEM) is the first source from which to gather safety information. Such information can often be found in the training or operation manuals provided at the time of equipment purchase. If a manual is not available, the OEM should be required to supply that information before a contract is signed to purchase the equipment. After all, if employees are injured on the equipment, the company and the OEM are usually held liable. When OEMs conduct training on their equipment, the training outline should be checked to ensure that safety training is covered in accordance with OSHA regulations.

If a supervisor or employee notices that someone is not following the correct safety procedures, the individual operating the equipment should be given immediate, corrective feedback. At that point the supervisor or company safety officials should investigate why proper safety procedures were not followed. Appropriate corrective action should then be taken to avoid a recurrence. If the problem can be solved by training in whole or in part, then the next step is to determine *what* training is needed.

Safety training should also be provided to contingent workers as well as to full-time employees (Rousseau and Libuser, 1997). Managing contingent workers, who may not be as familiar with equipment or work methods as full-time workers, is important.

Identifying Safety Training Needs

Identifying safety training needs requires a thorough investigation of what employees are expected to do and how they do it. That can be accomplished in several ways. One way is to conduct a "Job Hazard Analysis." This procedure requires an intensive examination of each job step. The purpose of the procedure is to identify existing or potential job hazards and determine the best way to perform the job to reduce or eliminate safety risks. The information obtained from a job hazard analysis can then be used as the basis for training. Information on how to conduct a job hazard analysis can be obtained from the OSHA Office of Training and Education. A second way is to interview employees, review safety training outlines to see what is already covered in the training, and determine whether employees are being trained properly. A third way is to check company accident records to isolate trends and their possible causes and then review standard operating procedures. That information can, in turn, be used to pinpoint safety training needs.

Once safety training needs have been identified, it is equally important to determine what training is *not* needed. Employees should be aware of all steps involved in a task or procedure, but training should focus only on those steps on which improvements are needed. Training for the sake of training will demotivate workers and result in diminished credibility for the training effort.

Identifying Goals and Objectives

Objectives are an important part of the safety training process and should be written to address specific training needs. Writing an objective that merely requires an employee to be "aware of" a machine hazard or "understand" the lockout/tagout procedures is not good because it's not specific. Each expected outcome should be written as a measurable objective.

For machine hazards, for instance, a well-written objective would take this general form: "The machine operator will identify by pointing out the nine-pinch point on machine xx." A second example: "The machine operator will demonstrate the proper method to lockout/tagout machine xx using his/her lock."

Whether safety is part of an overall training program on machine operation and maintenance or is specifically tailored to safety issues alone, objectives should be written for each key learning activity.

Developing Learning Activities

Once the objectives are written, then learning activities can be identified and described. Learning activities enable employees to demonstrate they have acquired necessary skills and knowledge. To ensure that the employees transfer the skills or knowledge from the instructional site to the work site, the learning situation should simulate actual working conditions as closely as possible. Arrange objectives in the specific order in which the task or safety procedures are to be performed. For instance: (1) shut down the machine and clear out the product; (2) turn off the master switch; and (3) lockout/tagout machine. When developing learning materials, remember that they should reinforce learning and not serve as filler for content, an afterthought, or entertainment.

Videotapes are used frequently for safety training. When using videotapes, keep several key points in mind. Before showing the video, explain its purpose and emphasize key points in the tape. After the videotape is shown, guide the learners to discuss the key points of the video and how those points relate to their work. When purchasing a videotape, always review it first to see if the information is pertinent to the organization's working conditions. If it is not, then the videotape will not be useful for training.

Conducting Safety Training

The key to conducting safety training is to be prepared. Even when all the parts needed to conduct the training are in order—such as materials, training aids, and room conditions—the training will not be successful if the trainer is not prepared. Employees can tell within a few minutes whether or not the trainer is capable of delivering the information. If the trainer is not prepared, employees will sense that the information is not important and will promptly lose interest. On the other hand, if the trainer is prepared, employees will sense that the information is important and will usually pay attention to it.

Evaluating Program Effectiveness

The most common way to evaluate a course is to gather employee feedback through a prepared written evaluation sheet, called by such varied names as a *participant evaluation,* a *reaction sheet,* or a *smile sheet.* This evaluation form can be helpful in determining employee interest in the training. What it does not tell the trainer is whether the participants learned anything.

To measure learning, trainers must prepare and administer tests or watch hands-on activities given to participants. Another method is to ask participants' supervisors to observe the behavior of their employees on the job. That is usually a good indicator whether learning took place and the safety training was effective. Safety training results are usually measured by the reduction in company accidents.

OSHA research has linked a disproportionate share of injuries and illnesses at the workplace on the part of employees to the following issues (see www.osha.gov/oshinfo/priorities/overview.html):

1. The age of the employee (younger employees have higher incidence rates).
2. The length of time on the job (new employees have higher incidence rates).
3. The size of the firm (in general terms, medium-sized firms have higher incidence rates than smaller or larger firms).
4. The type of work performed (incidence and severity rates vary significantly by SIC code).
5. The use of hazardous substances (by SIC code).

If technical trainers remain sensitive to conditions prevailing in their organizations, they can be more effective in identifying issues most requiring safety training.

Prior to the Occupational Safety and Health Act of 1970, safety was an issue for all companies—but, admittedly, some companies were more concerned than others. The awareness of how important safety training has dramatically increased since the 1970s. There are still ample opportunities to reduce the number and severity of accidents in many companies. Safety training can make a difference in reducing accidents. The key is to establish and maintain ownership, since employees who are involved in safety training will make it more useful and more grounded in the reality of the workplace.

Working with Unions

There have been many articles and books written on unions, and some cover the training of union members. Unions are one of the strongest supporters of training, recognizing that training is one way to give their members a competitive advantage in the labor market. Many union contracts include language about training, including how many hours of training employees should receive per year or the percentage of wages that should be invested into a training fund. Some unions even have their own training facilities and vigorously support apprenticeship programs. All in all, unions have led the way in many companies to ensure that workers are properly trained. Using a variety of data, most studies on training economics focus on the relationship of training to wages and other employee demographic variables, as well as descriptions of training practices within firms. Mincer (1983, 1988), Brown (1983, 1988), and Lillard and Tan (1986) used data on training obtained from surveys of individual workers in the United States. Their findings, summarized by Lynch (1990), indicate that working in a union significantly raises the probability that an individual will receive on-the-job training or will participate in an apprenticeship program.

In another study, the Human Resources Development Institute designed and implemented five demonstration projects that developed jointly administered skill training in aerospace, industrial manufacturing, and health care industries. All projects involved unionized workplaces. Three lessons were learned from this experience:

- *Lesson 1*: Training programs will function more smoothly, and are more likely to be successful, if structured in a manner that complements the official union structure.
- *Lesson 2*: Workers are keenly interested in career advancement and highly committed to work-related training, especially if developed jointly by management and labor.
- *Lesson 3*: Interdependence occurs between work reorganization and continuous skill training. The implementation of a high performance

workplace organization, with its emphasis on broader job categories and acute concern for quality, creates anxiety among workers accustomed to more authoritarian approaches. Continuous skill training programs create a supportive atmosphere where workers have access to the resources needed to maintain their employment security (Cooke, 1990).

In a three-year study conducted by Rosow and Zager (1988), they addressed five aspects of training for new technology. Their second report, *Toward Continuous Learning Outlines,* found several characteristics when unions are involved in the continuous learning process. First, management policy actively invites and supports an important partnership role for the union. Second, the collective bargaining agreement between management and labor defines their respective roles and establishes the lasting basis for cooperation. Third, the parties act jointly in program control, planning, design, and direction of learning programs at national, regional, and plant levels. Fourth, unions and workers participate fully in needs analysis and course content decisions, and they share the responsibility for successful results. Fifth, instructors are selected from the regular workforce; they are assigned equal status and full-time duties to develop content, deliver courses, and evaluate results. Sixth and finally, a jointly administered fund provides for the financing of training programs and assures a long-term commitment to goals and objectives.

Each study has shown that unions are strong supporters of training. Not only are they interested in training but they are actively involved in the training process.

Joint Training Committee

A joint training committee is one way of involving a union in the training process. The primary function of such a committee is to ensure that employees are receiving the correct training and that the training meets company needs. A training committee is a joint venture between management and labor, with both parties playing an active role in the decision-making process.

There are several advantages that such a committee can bring to the organization. First, since training is a non-threatening activity, management and labor can have an open dialogue on training issues. That increases the chance that the organization will supply the proper training.

Second, training is beneficial to both parties. Working together should have a positive impact on how training is received by employees and management. Third, communications between both parties are increased, training problems are more accurately addressed, and each side has a better understanding of the other's needs. Fourth, opportunities for addressing and correcting performance improvement problems are increased. Fifth and finally, evaluation of training is not always successful because there is a disconnect as to what happens when the employees return to their work. Feedback is more likely to occur with a training committee.

Having a joint training committee can help avert many problems that can be created when only a few people are involved in the training process.

Technical Trainers Working in a Union Environment

One key point for a technical trainer to remember when working in a union environment is to *understand the contract*. Knowing the language not only as it relates to training but also to other aspects of the contract can be a benefit to ensure training meets the needs of both parties. Although training language is included in labor contracts and may include such points as the number of hours each employee receives training, who does the training, and whether training is done during work or outside of work, it may not consider the problems that can occur under different situations. Since technical trainers are involved on a day-to-day basis with training, they are better positioned than others to determine what implication certain language can have on the training process if they know the agreement. In addition to understanding the labor contract, technical trainers in many situations are placed in the middle between management and labor when it comes to training. Handling the conflict that can result is no easy task. To be effective, technical trainers must ensure that training meets the needs of both management and labor and must preserve good working relations with both groups.

Summary

This chapter focused on operating apprenticeship programs and safety training programs and working with unions. These are important issues for many technical trainers.

The next chapter, the final one in the book, examines alternatives to technical training that may be used to improve employee performance.

CHAPTER TWELVE

ACHIEVING RESULTS WITH ALTERNATIVES TO TECHNICAL TRAINING

Recall from the discussion in Chapter Five that not all performance problems lend themselves to training solutions. However, some technical trainers—and, admittedly, some line managers—see training as a solution to every problem. But training is really a short-term change strategy intended to equip individuals with the knowledge, skill, and attitude they need to do their work effectively. Training will not prove effective to solve problems rooted in issues that are beyond the ability of individuals to change or that reside in the work environment. These issues can only be solved by management action. The trend in the training and development field has for some time been focused on doing more than just training people. Instead, trainers should be focused on improving workplace performance (an outcome), and not just offering training (an activity) (Fertal, 1996). Generally speaking, the trends point toward technical trainers becoming *performance consultants,* sometimes called *human performance improvement specialists* (Hallberg and DeFiore, 1997), whose job it is to isolate the root causes of human performance problems and then match one or more appropriate solutions to address underlying causes.

The challenge, however, is that human performance problems can stem from many possible causes. It has been estimated that only 10 percent of all human performance problems stem from deficiencies in individual knowledge, skill, or attitude (Rothwell, 2000b; Rothwell, Hohne, and King, 2000). The remaining 90 percent of all human problems stem from causes linked to working conditions or the work environment, and these can only be solved by management action. Human problems that can be solved only by management action include any of the following:

- *Selection.* Does the person responsible for doing possess the ability to do it?
- *Incentives and rewards.* Are people rewarded for doing what they are supposed to do?
- *Goals and objectives.* Are people clear what results they are expected to achieve?
- *Responsibilities.* Are people clear on what they are supposed to do, and do their opinions match up to what their supervisors expect them to do?
- *Feedback.* Are people given clear, timely, and specific feedback when their performance does not match expectations?
- *Discipline.* Are individuals counseled when they deliberately refuse to perform or deliberately fail to follow orders?
- *Information.* Are people given the critical information they need to perform on a timely, specific basis?
- *Tools and equipment.* Are people given the tools and equipment they need to do their work?
- *Consequences.* Does something happen when people fail to perform?
- *Resources.* Do people possess adequate time, money, and staff to achieve desired results?
- *Practice.* Are people given real-time guidance to help them perform when the work or task is done so infrequently that they forget how to do it?
- *Expertise.* Can experience with solving problems—such as troubleshooting machine problems—be captured and organized electronically through so-called expert systems or through more elaborate electronic performance support systems?

See Exhibit 12.1 for a visual depiction of these ideas, and see Exhibit 12.2 for a worksheet to help you organize your thinking on how problems caused by each issue might be solved.

Many organizations have recently been attempting to improve their performance management systems. A *performance management system* has two possible meanings. On the one hand, it can mean the same as traditional employee performance appraisal. On the other hand, performance management can be equated with pursuit of a *high performance workplace* (HPW). Much research has been done around the characteristics of the HPW. The idea is to establish a workplace that encourages people to perform to their peak ability. That means that people have the knowledge, skills, and attitudes to do the work and a work environment that completely supports their efforts to meet or exceed customer expectations.

This chapter examines possible alternatives to technical training as a means of improving human performance and of establishing, and maintaining, a performance management system. In other words, it examines other ways—apart from training—that may help people perform. Perhaps the most important of these alternatives include job aids, feedback systems, recognition and reward programs, and work redesign

EXHIBIT 12.1.   THINKING ABOUT THE ROOT CAUSE(S) OF HUMAN PERFORMANCE PROBLEMS

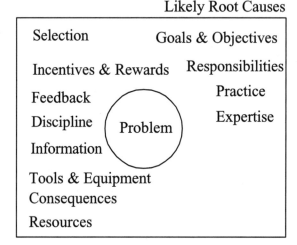

EXHIBIT 12.2. WORKSHEET FOR CONSIDERING INTERVENTIONS

Directions: Whenever you encounter a problem with human performance, consider which one (or how many) of the following root causes may be the reason for the problem. Then, in the right column below, brainstorm how many different ways that root cause may be addressed. There are no "right" or "wrong" answers to this worksheet in any absolute sense, but some answers may be better than others.

Root Cause(s)	Solution/Intervention?
1. **Selection** (Does the person or the people responsible for doing the work possess the ability to do it?)	
2. **Incentives and rewards** (Are people rewarded for doing what they are supposed to do?)	
3. **Goals and objectives** (Are people clear what results they are expected to achieve?)	
4. **Responsibilities** (Are people clear on what they are supposed to do, and do their opinions match up to what their supervisors expect them to do?)	
5. **Feedback** (Are people given clear, timely, and specific feedback when their performance does not match expectations?)	
6. **Discipline** (Are individuals counseled when they deliberately refuse to perform or deliberately fail to follow orders?)	
7. **Information** (Are people given the critical information they need to perform on a timely, specific basis?)	
8. **Tools and equipment** (Are people given the tools and equipment they need to do their work?)	
9. **Consequences** (Does something happen when people fail to perform?)	
10. **Resources** (Do people possess adequate time, money, and staff to achieve desired results?)	
11. **Practice** (Are people given real-time guidance to help them perform when the work or task is done so infrequently that they forget how to do it?)	
12. **Expertise** (Can experience with solving problems—such as troubleshooting machine problems—be captured and organized electronically through so-called expert systems or through more elaborate electronic performance support systems?)	

efforts. But what do these terms mean? How can each be used as an alternative to training? When should they be used, and when should they not be used?

Job Aids

A *job aid* is anything that can help people perform in real time (Reynolds, 1998). We are literally surrounded by job aids. Signs are job aids that tell people what to do—or what not to do. Procedure manuals, in print or online, are job aids. Checksheets are job aids. Warning lights and machine dials are job aids.

How Job Aids Can Be Used as Alternatives to Training

Prepare a job aid by examining how the work is performed. Then list out the steps in a procedure or task in step-by-step fashion. It is often helpful to come up with ways to help people remember what to do by giving them a simple acronym to remember.

When to Use Job Aids and When Not to Use Them

If people need to know what to do in real time, then a job aid may be warranted. Generally, job aids are most appropriate when they can be kept simple. An ideal is a job aid that contains one page—or less—of instructions and that can be used the moment a performer must carry out a task or work activity. Job aids are most effective in helping people remember what they learned to do in training.

Job aids are usually not appropriate if the work task is very complicated or if the use of a job aid would hinder the credibility of a performer to do his or her work. (That is why we don't see brain surgeons referring to them as they operate.) Nor are job aids effective if the task is so simple that almost anyone could do it.

Feedback Systems

Workers often get feedback on what they do. Feedback occurs when a worker is told about his performance by a customer, co-worker, supervisor, or other person. For instance, if a customer says "That's not what I want," the performer has received feedback.

Feedback may come from people or from machines. If a worker performs, someone may comment on the performance. Alternatively, if a worker adjusts the flow of water into a machine, a dial may provide that worker with feedback on what he or she did.

If you poll supervisors and managers about how much and how often they give feedback to their workers, they will probably tell you that they do so regularly. However, many workers feel that they only receive feedback when they do something wrong. If their perception is true, then feedback should be the focus of attention in an organization. It may be necessary, for instance, for the organization to establish a plan to gather feedback from customers and give it to the performers.

How a Feedback System Can Be Used as an Alternative to Training

Feedback can be used as an alternative to training if workers know what they are supposed to do, know how they are to do it, and can assess the quality of the information they receive from others about what they did. One way to examine it is to ask workers:

- What kind of feedback do you receive?
- How often do you receive that feedback?
- How could the quality of feedback you receive from your customers be improved?

The answers to these questions may provide a starting point to think about ways to encourage workers to find and use feedback more effectively.

When Feedback Systems Should Be Used and When They Should Not Be

Feedback is a powerful intervention. It empowers workers by giving them the information they need to adjust their own behavior. Feedback is only useful, however, if it is timely, specific, and concrete. To be timely, it must be given to a performer soon after the action is taken. To be specific, it must lay out exactly what the performer did right or did wrong. And it must be concrete in that it must be provided in language that is clear to the person receiving the feedback.

Feedback is not useful when the worker is not authorized to change what he or she does. In other words, feedback will only impact performance if the worker has some discretion in what he or she does and how he or she does it.

Recognition and Reward Programs

A *reward* is something given after performance to reinforce behavior and results. Rewards may be either financial or nonfinancial. *Recognition* means paying attention to people, usually for performance that exceeds expectations. A *recognition and reward program* is a systematic effort to give people reinforcement and attention for performing as desired.

How Recognition and Reward Programs Can Be Used as Alternatives to Training

There is an old saying that "you get more of what you reward." People will tend to do that which they are rewarded for doing. They will also tend to avoid, or do less of, that which they are punished for doing.

A key to developing effective recognition and reward systems is to examine what people are really rewarded for. One way to do that is to ask people. Another way is to watch how rewards and recognition are given out—and for what.

Recognition and reward systems may be a substitute for training in those cases in which motivation is a cause of performance problems. If people are rewarded and recognized for achieving results, then they will do more of that. But if they are rewarded and recognized for other things—such as seniority or effort—then there may be a mismatch between what is rewarded and what is actually desired.

When Recognition and Reward Programs Should Be Used and When They Should Not

Many organizations could realize substantial improvements in performance if they would only clarify and communicate what results they desire and then provide rewards for those who achieve performance targets. The problem is that many times performance goals are unclear or are so complicated that performers cannot figure out what they are really expected to do. In these situations, making improvements in recognition and reward programs could lead to quantum leaps in productivity improvement.

However, recognition and reward programs will not work effectively if promised reinforcement and attention is not forthcoming when performers do, in fact, achieve desired results.

Work Redesign Efforts

Work redesign simply means restructuring the work that people do. A simple way to think of it is to revise job descriptions so that work responsibilities are reassigned or are reorganized.

How Work Redesign Efforts Can Be Used as Alternatives to Training

To use work redesign, identify clearly what the workers actually do. Then ask who can do what best. Using the results of that analysis, pinpoint activities to be performed by individuals. That can simplify or even eliminate training requirements for those who do not have to perform a specific work activity or task.

When Work Redesign Efforts Should Be Used
and When They Should Not

Work redesign is an appropriate strategy to improve performance when the work is so complicated that nobody could learn it or perform it effectively. It is also effective when an individual, otherwise disabled, is unable to perform job duties and the organization is willing to make reasonable accommodations under the Americans with Disabilities Act.

Work redesign is not, however, appropriate when all workers must perform a work activity or task due to the way the work is structured. If each worker has a specific role to play, then it may not be possible to reassign the work. In those cases, work redesign will not be effective in improving human performance.

Summary

As this chapter has emphasized, training will not prove effective to solve problems rooted in issues that are beyond the ability of individuals to impact or that reside in the work environment. In those situations, alternatives to training must be used. The chapter examined several key questions that can be posed to examine performance problems. Among them: (1) Does the person responsible for doing possess the ability to do it? (2) Are people rewarded for doing what they are supposed to do? (3) Are people clear what results they are expected to achieve? (4) Are people clear on what they are supposed to do, and do their opinions match up to what their supervisors expect them to do? (5) Are people given clear, timely, and specific feedback when their performance does not match expectations? (6) Are individuals counseled when they deliberately refuse to perform or deliberately fail to follow orders? (7) Are people given the critical information they need to perform on a timely, specific basis? (8) Are people given the tools and equipment they need to do their work? (9) Does something happen when people fail to perform? (10) Do people possess adequate time, money, and staff to achieve desired results? (11) Are people given real-time guidance to help them perform when the work or task is done so infrequently that they forget how to do it? and (12) Can experience with solving problems—such as troubleshooting machine problems—be captured and organized electronically through so-called expert systems or through more elaborate electronic performance support systems?

This books ends with an Afterword, which shares the authors' insights about their experience with technical training. Following the Afterword, you will find a series of Appendices that provide additional, and helpful, tools for you as you work as a technical trainer.

PART V

CONCLUDING THOUGHTS

The last part of the book offers the lessons of our experience as authors. We leave you with seven lessons we have learned from experience. Exhibit 6 is the blueprint for Part V within a schematic diagram representing the book's total scheme.

EXHIBIT 6. PART V WITHIN THE SCHEME OF THE BOOK

Chapter 1: **What Is Technical Training?**	**Part I:** **Foundations of Effective Technical Training**
Chapter 2: **What Are the Characteristics of Effective Technical Training?**	
Chapter 3: **Establishing an Organizational Plan for Technical Training**	**Part II:** **Planning and Managing the Technical Training Function**
Chapter 4: **Leading and Managing the Technical Training Department**	
Chapter 5: **Basic Principles of Instructional Systems Design**	**Part III:** **Key Issues in Training Course Design**
Chapter 6: **Identifying Technical Training Needs**	
Chapter 7: **Preparing Technical Training Programs**	
Chapter 8: **Determining and Using Delivery Methods**	
Chapter 9: **Evaluating Technical Training**	
Chapter 10: **Using Vendors and Managing Original Equipment Manufacturers**	**Part IV:** **Special Issues in Technical Training**
Chapter 11: **Operating Apprenticeship and Safety Training Programs and Working with Unions**	
Chapter 12: **Achieving Results with Alternatives to Technical Training**	
Afterword	**Part V:** **Concluding Thoughts**

AFTERWORD

Lessons Learned from Experience in Technical Training

This book is an introduction to technical training. It is not intended to answer every question or solve every problem you may have under this topic. Our goal as authors has been to supply you with a practical, how-to-do-it guide, based on research and best practice, to provide an orientation manual for you, especially if you are a new technical trainer. Allow us to share our insights and the following lessons that we have learned from experience in technical training:

Lesson 1: Make the focus results, not activities

Lesson 2: Align technical training with business goals and needs

Lesson 3: Work to become part of the strategic planning process

Lesson 4: Build partnerships and involve others

Lesson 5: Demonstrate a sense of urgency

Lesson 6: Become a means for continuous improvement

Lesson 7: Strike a balance among speed, cost, and learning effectiveness

Lesson 1: Make the Focus Results, Not Activities

Working as a technical trainer is not easy. To be successful, you must be a special type of person. You should possesses a well-rounded knowledge of training, an appreciation for adult learners, an understanding of business, and exceptional interpersonal skills. But, unfortunately, not all technical trainers think or act—or are rewarded by their organizations—for results.

Technical training is not about "offering courses" or "getting people to attend courses." Instead, it is about "getting results." Results equate to knowledgeable, skilled workers who possess appropriate attitudes for the work they do.

The goal of technical trainers should not be to measure "number of classes offered," "dollars spent," "participant ratings," or even "butts in seats." A better way to think about it is to put oneself in the position of a senior manager, think about all the money spent on training, and ask this question: *Is technical training in this organization worth the investment, and is it making a difference?* If you must honestly answer *yes,* make note of *how* and *why* training makes a difference. But if you answer *no,* then ask this: *What must be done for technical training to add value to the organization?* If you do not know how to answer that question, then ask this: *What gets in the way of achieving results?*

Lesson 2: Align Technical Training with Business Goals and Needs

Chapter Three discussed the importance of aligning technical training with the organization's goals and business needs. That should be the acid test for any project: *Does it meet business needs?* Aligning training with meeting business needs will move training from being superfluous to being a critically important effort. Technical training has tremendous potential to achieve quantum leaps in productivity improvement. However, that potential is not realized in many organizations.

Lesson 3: Work to Become Part of the Strategic Planning Process

If technical trainers are successful in aligning what they do with what the business needs, they should be able to become part of the strategic planning process. But that will not happen on its own. Technical trainers must be proactive to earn a seat at the table of the strategic planning process. They must understand the business from the most detailed (microscopic) to the most global (macroscopic) levels.

Lesson 4: Build Partnerships and Involve Others

Building partnerships with supervisors and managers will show them that technical trainers are interested in understanding their problems and their issues. Partnerships lead to trust, which leads to more open communication and greater insight into the root causes of performance problems facing the organization. When this happens, technical trainers will find that it is easier for them to get to the heart of problems. Once the technical trainer is recognized as a partner, artificial boundaries between the training department and the production (or operations) department will disappear.

Building partnerships serves another purpose. Along with trust comes the technical trainer's ability to communicate his or her role as a trainer in the business. Managers and hourly personnel are more likely to listen to the trainer's opinion and find ways to remove barriers that may exist for training. Having a good partnership will keep the technical trainer updated on strategic and operational changes that will enhance the trainer's ability to be proactive, to make surgical strikes at production hot spots and bottlenecks, while giving trainers a global view of where those surgical strikes will have greatest impact.

Additionally, avoid attempting to do all the training. That only invites problems. Training will never be successful if technical trainers believe they must do everything. Training has greatest impact when others are involved in the process. Unless others are involved with training, they will never know the roles they are playing—and should be playing—in it. Training can be explained many times to managers, but they will miss the point if they are not involved. The more others are involved, the greater the chance training can leverage its impact by gaining support.

Incidentally, partnering does not mean "working with one person or a few people." It means working with all key divisions in an organization—such as engineering, industrial engineering, management informational systems, human resources, quality, maintenance, production, and others. In any business environment it is a common occurrence that several divisions work together on a business project. Because many projects require the expertise of multiple people or groups, technical trainers must find ways to assemble and effectively work with project teams. That can only be accomplished by spending time where the work is being done— and avoiding the charge that training is "thought up in an ivory tower" or "in a vacuum."

Lesson 5: Demonstrate a Sense of Urgency

Time has become a strategic resource. Effective technical trainers understand that, and they demonstrate a sense of urgency that leads to just-in-time training. Business decisions are being made faster than ever, with a goal in mind of slashing cycle time and beating competitors to the punch.

Time has also become critical for training. It would be nice to have the time to follow each step in the instructional systems design process. Unfortunately, that is not always possible. Effective technical trainers are creative in their applications, looking for ways to shortcut steps while still obtaining good results. While training should never be designed in a haphazard way, it should also strike a balance between efficiency and effectiveness. This requires technical trainers to be creative and flexible.

If technical training is to be truly effective, the trainers must partner with managers from the outset of changes in production or operations. If technical trainers are not called in until after the decisions are made, then they cannot be as effective as they would be if called in during the decision-making process. To that end, technical trainers must demonstrate to others that they are willing to work *hard* and *fast*.

Lesson 6: Become a Means for Continuous Improvement

Make technical training a means to the end of continuous improvement. Do that to build additional credibility with management. Think of training as a process improvement technique—which it is. But if technical trainers can combine knowledge of process improvement techniques with knowledge of the business and training, they can become invaluable.

Lesson 7: Strike a Balance Among Speed, Cost, and Learning Effectiveness in Training Materials

Managers and workers alike have become more sophisticated in their requests for training. Today it may even be more likely to hear someone say "put that on the Web" as it is to hear them request a classroom course. The trouble is that not all delivery methods can be rolled out on the same timeline. Nor do delivery methods cost the same or are equally effective in helping people learn.

With all the availability of sophisticated, computerized delivery methods, technical trainers can become overwhelmed with technology. Before making commitments about how training will be delivered, consider the following:

- Is the training really needed, or would it just be nice to have?
- Will the training really help the organization achieve its strategic objectives and business needs?
- How will the training be used?
- Who was involved in selecting delivery methods, and what did they consider when making their decisions?

Use the same methods for involving others as you would expect to see if others were asking for your help. Consider the costs and usage before committing. Remember: Sometimes the best training materials are the simplest and least costly.

Final Remarks

That concludes the book. But before you close it, turn to the Appendices and glance through some material that you may find most useful as you work as a technical trainer.

APPENDICES

APPENDIX I

Assessing and Building Competence as a Technical Trainer

This form is designed to help you assess your level of competence and identify professional development needs related to technical training. You can use the results of this assessment to develop your own plan for developing yourself.

For each competency linked to the work of the technical trainer listed in the following questionnaire, check the box in the right column indicating the most relevant self-rating. An explanation of the scale follows.

DK   You don't know the relationship between the issue and your current level of competence

LO   Your current competence related to the listed area is especially low but could be raised

MD   You believe past experiences have provided part of the desired competence and some learning experiences would develop the remainder

HI   You believe you have substantially established competence in the
     listed area

After you complete the self-assessment, discuss it with others—such as
your immediate organizational superior, stakeholders who depend on you
in your organization, and technical trainers in your organization or in other
organizations. To develop yourself, you may need to prepare a learning
plan that describes when and how you could build competence in areas
that are rated below HI.

Self-Rate Your Competency	DK	LO	MD	HI
1. Awareness of what technical training is and why it is important	☐	☐	☐	☐
2. A grasp of the characteristics that lead to effective technical training in organizational settings	☐	☐	☐	☐
3. Ability to establish an organizational plan for technical training	☐	☐	☐	☐
4. Ability to lead and manage the technical training department	☐	☐	☐	☐
5. Familiarity with the basic principles of instructional systems design	☐	☐	☐	☐
6. Ability to identify technical training needs	☐	☐	☐	☐
7. Ability to prepare technical training programs	☐	☐	☐	☐
8. Ability to determine or select appropriate technical training delivery methods	☐	☐	☐	☐
9. Ability to evaluate technical training	☐	☐	☐	☐
10. Knowledge of how to use vendors and original equipment manufacturers (OEMs) to meet an organization's technical training needs	☐	☐	☐	☐
11. Ability to establish and operate apprenticeship programs	☐	☐	☐	☐
12. Ability to establish and deliver safety training programs	☐	☐	☐	☐

Self-Rate Your Competency	DK	LO	MD	HI

13. Knowledge of how to select and use alternatives ☐ ☐ ☐ ☐
    to technical training, either in isolation or in
    combination with technical training

If you have additional needs, please describe them in the following rows and estimate your level of competence on each.

	DK	LO	MD	HI
14.	☐	☐	☐	☐
15.	☐	☐	☐	☐
16.	☐	☐	☐	☐

APPENDIX II

Guidelines for Technical Training Development and Delivery*

This appendix contains the following material:

Training Development and Delivery Overview

Development Process

Delivery Process

Reinforcement Process

Summary

Sample Forms

    Title Page Form

    Phase 1: Overview

    Phase 2: Learning Objectives

    Phase 3: Reinforcement

*Miller Brewing Company, Milwaukee, WI.

Blank Forms

Title Page Form

Phase 1: Overview

Phase 2: Learning Objectives

Phase 3: Reinforcement

Training Development and Delivery Overview

Introduction

Learning how to do something while on the job is a great way to learn important job skills. Learning by doing helps most people remember how to do their jobs because they see the link between what they need to learn and why they need to learn it.

Not all training is successful. It can fail if you leave out important information or if the training lacks structure.

Purpose

The purpose of these guidelines is to help you develop and present structured, on-the-job training in your plant. The guidelines will help you set standards of quality and effectiveness while ensuring usefulness of the training.

Objectives

The objectives of the guidelines are:

- To provide the manufacturing process with the ability to document, transfer, and perpetuate the knowledge and skills necessary to perform key tasks within job functions.

- To provide the manufacturing process with the ability to reinforce the knowledge and skills that were transferred.

- To utilize a process across the organization that is consistent enough to allow maximum effective use of people in the development, implementation, and reinforcement of training.

Process Flow

A standard process flow is used in the transfer of knowledge and skill from those who develop and deliver the training to those who need to learn or operate the equipment or process.

Process Flow Diagram

The following is the process flow diagram for developing, delivering, and reinforcing training. Each area will be described in more detail as you go through these guidelines.

NOTE: Sample and blank forms for all three areas are provided for you to use as you go through the process, or you can create your own to fit your needs.

In This Document

This document covers the following topics:

Topic	See Page
Development Process	296
Delivery Process	300
Reinforcement Process	302
Summary	303
Sample Forms	304
Blank Forms	305

Development Process

Introduction

A defined process for development is used to maintain consistency. In this process the need for the training is stated, the specific audience is determined, an overall training objective is written, and the specific physical tasks, called "Learning Objectives," are defined.

In reverse order, the "Specific Learning Objectives" are the physical action a student must perform which will accomplish the "Overall Objective" for the specific "Audience," thus fulfilling the "Training Need."

This helps the developer and requester to reach agreement before organizing the job duty content material.

Development Process Flow Diagram

The process flow diagram below shows the stages for the development process.

Identify Training Needs

This stage simply states the need for training.

Example: Develop training for the operation of the packer.

Determine Audience

This stage identifies who will receive the training. It determines a frame of reference from which the development and delivery of training is specific for the intended audience.

Example: The audience is the packer operator.

NOTE: This training, for example, would contain only the skills and knowledge for the operator and not the mechanic or electrician.

Write the Overall Job Duty Objective

This stage identifies the overall objective for the training.

Example: The training should teach the operator how to start, stop, and maintain the packer as well as how to respond to various problems that occur during production and make minor machine adjustments for continuous operation.

This training must provide a means for reinforcing the skills and knowledge that were transferred to the student.

List Specific Learning Objectives

This stage lists the specific knowledge or skill the student must learn and demonstrate to successfully complete the training.

Example: Listed below are some typical examples.

NOTE: Make statements active by beginning with action verbs such as start, repair, clear, isolate, adjust, and so forth.

- Identify packer components by proper name.
- Perform before start-up procedure.
- Start up packer.
- Shut down packer.
- Perform required safety procedures.
- Clear jam at infeed.
- Clean machine components.

Write and Organize Content Material

This stage details the specific learning objectives in terms of listing references, providing definition, creating an exercise, and making suggestions as to how the training should be reinforced on the job.

Create the Training Document

Now that we have identified the need, the audience, the overall objective, the specific learning objectives, and written and/or organized the content, a training document should be created.

This document will help to ensure standardization, consistency, and structure to the training. The document should include the following:

NOTE: Blank forms are provided on pages 305–309 for your use or you may create your own.

Section	*Description*
Title Page	Lists the name of the training.
Table of Contents	Lists the contents (optional).
Overview/ Introduction	An overview or introduction to the training may be given, but should list the training need, audience, and overall training objectives, as well as the specific learning objectives.

Section	*Description*
Learning Objective Detail	For each specific learning objective: • List the specific learning objective. • List approximate training time. • List supporting reference material for instruction. • List tools required to perform the objective. • Provide the training resource for the learning objective. This may be provided in the document or refer to other documentation such as equipment manual pages, check sheets, job aid, etc. • List an exercise that demonstrates the learning objective.
Reinforcement	A checklist to ensure that the objectives learned are transferred to the job. NOTE: Once created, use the document to perform the delivery and reinforcement process.

Delivery Process

Introduction

A defined process for instruction has been developed to aid in the transfer of knowledge and skill. This process contains five stages.

Instruction Process Flow Diagram

The instruction process flow diagram looks like this:

Number	Stage	Description
1	Restate the Learning Objectives	A learning objective is a physical action to be learned by the student. Restating the objective focuses the thoughts of the student on a single objective.
2	Provide Definition (Training Resource)	The instructor provides the student with a definition of the objective. This may be provided by reading or reviewing an operator manual, training manual, equipment manual, spec sheet, job aid, or checklist or by a subject-matter expert, trainer, or instructor. This stage provides *who, what, why, where,* and *how* as it pertains to the learning objective.
3	Address Safety Concerns	Before any physical action can begin, the instructor must point out any safety concern, that is, pinch points, lockout/tagout, slip hazards, and so forth.

Number	**Stage**	**Description**
4	Instructor Demonstration	Adults learn by doing; therefore instruction should include a physical action to aid in learning.
		At this point, the instructor performs an exercise to demonstrate to the student how to use the knowledge and skill. At times you may have to be creative and cause jams, flip switches, or turn knobs to devise an effective exercise.
		NOTE: Be careful to create an effective exercise, not a trick.
5	Student Demonstration	Once the student understands the learning objective, have him or her *approve it* by performing the exercise before moving on to the next learning objective. Allow the students to perform the exercise without any verbal or physical help. Let them try again until they have mastered the exercise. (Of course, keep their safety and the safety of the equipment in mind.) This provides positive feedback to the students that they are learning. When the students have performed the exercise successfully, you may move on to the next objective.

Reinforcement Process

Introduction   A reinforcement process is a three-stage process that flows like this:

Number	Stage	Description
1	Reinforcement on the Job	Schedule the student to perform the duty that was taught on the job. After two to four weeks, evaluate the student's long-term memory by having him/her perform the exercises without help. Students may, of course, use available resources. Use a checklist to verify completion.
2	Recognition	Give positive reinforcement and recognize accomplishments to emphasize importance.
3	Documentation	Document completion and skill mastery for department or plant record keeping.

Summary

Description

Follow the leader training is the primary method used to transfer knowledge and skill. We need something better.

Formal training is a shock to our culture. We have used follow the leader training for so long that we are shocked to find that more structure is necessary.

Benefits

By providing structure and standardization to the development and delivery process while maintaining flexibility in the resources and method used to organize the content, several benefits can be realized.

- Identification of standardized skills and knowledge needed to perform successfully.

- Improvement in yields, defects, overfills, and labor costs can be achieved.

- Easier method for documentation and tracking.

- Communication of job expectations are more clearly defined.

Sample Forms

Description

The following sample forms have been filled in with examples of the type of information needed to make them effective.

Forms

The following sample forms are included:

Title	*See Page*
Title Page	305
Phase 1 B Overview	306
Phase 2 B Learning Objectives	307
Phase 3 B Reinforcement	308

Title Page Form

(Company Name)

(Company Logo)

Plant:

Department:

Training Course:

_____

_____

_____

Date:

Phase 1 B Overview

Job Title:

Training Need: _____

Audience: _____

Overall Objective: _____

Specific   1. _____
Learning
Objectives   2. _____

               3. _____

               4. _____

               5. _____

               6. _____

               7. _____

               8. _____

               9. _____

              10. _____

              11. _____

              12. _____

              13. _____

              14. _____

              15. _____

              16. _____

              17. _____

              18. _____

              19. _____

              20. _____

Phase 2 B Learning Objectives

Job Title:

Learning Objective Number:

Approximate Training Time:

Reference:

Tools:

Definition (Training Resource):

Exercise:

Phase 3 B Reinforcement

Learning Objective Complete:

Job Title: _____

_____

Student: _____

Instructor: _____

Date Started: _____

Phase	**Description**	**Date Completed**
Phase 1	Overview	_____
Phase 2	Learning Objectives	_____
Phase 3	Reinforcement	_____

*Scheduled on Job (2 to 4 Weeks)   Dates: _____

Reinforcement Checklist

Exercise	#1	_____
Exercise	#2	_____
Exercise	#3	_____
Exercise	#4	_____
Exercise	#5	_____
Exercise	#6	_____
Exercise	#7	_____
Exercise	#8	_____

Exercise   #9 _____

Exercise   #10 _____

Exercise   #11 _____

Exercise   #12 _____

Exercise   #13 _____

Exercise   #14 _____

Exercise   #15 _____

Exercise   #16 _____

Exercise   #17 _____

Exercise   #18 _____

Exercise   #19 _____

Exercise   #20 _____

APPENDIX III

Examples Representing the Work of an Organization's Strategic Planning for Technical Training Committee*

---

*Miller Brewing Company, Milwaukee, WI.

VISION FOR TECHNICAL TRAINING

Management Commitment of Resources to Learning That Drives Business Results	Culture Is One of Learning Organization	A Standardized Approach to Technical Training Used Throughout the Company	Job Descriptions That Identify Required Skills
Management believing and providing resources to increase learning as a driver for business success	Learning organization: philosophy has: • Built trust • Increased morale • Increased productivity • Increased safety awareness	A standardized approach to technical training will be embraced and used throughout the corporation	People using job descriptions to identify training needs and knowing that they will be certified for that job
Champion for technical training within corporate organization B direct tie-in to CEO	Learning is viewed as a continuous process and rewarded	Vendors/OEMs as partners using our standard format for design, development, delivery of training	All jobs have skills identified for them that include core skills and all support skills needed
Adequate resources will be provided and seen as an investment in future of our company	Training will be a core value	Standardized training approach	Skills requirements change as roles change
Importance of technical training will be recognized at all levels in the organization	Company is recognized as a leader in continuous learning	A consistent training process for all plants that utilizes the same format/structure/process	Skills inventory for each work station supported by training
Adequate resources—dollars, time (develop, deliver, attend) budgeted	Top management talk highly of technical training	All company operations follow a standard approach to training	Qualification standards supported by technical training
Adequate resources committed	A training council at each facility that tracks and ensures that training occurs, is resourced, and is useful	People being trained on the job following a structured, competency-based approach	Basic skills needs are met
		Competency-based training will exist and be accepted by unions	Employees understand business goals and how we will get there
		Documented process for technical learning exists	
		Continuous improvement of the training process	

OUR VISION FOR TECHNICAL TRAINING

The Ability to Tie Technical Training Delivered with Performance Impact	Effective Use of Technology in Delivery of Training	Individuals Have Responsibility and Control Over Their Skill Development Needs	Involvement and Ownership Across All Levels in Design, Development, Delivery of Training
• Process in place for measurement of ROI/success of learning	• High-tech delivery systems for training	• Performance review/IDP for all employees to identify opportunities for training	• Ownership by Operations for technical training down to operators
• Technical training will lead to improvements in all areas of operation	• Standard computer methods for training and other information on each line	• A university type setting where individuals identify their own schedule of training for the year	• Employees assessing training needs, developing training, evaluating training
• Suppliers providing competency-based training guarantees with the products they sell	• Interplant satellite downlink to support training needs	• Training is self-driven by employees	• People learning skills and knowledge from peers, through computer-based training, multimedia, etc.
	• Accessible information	• Development plans exist	• Apprenticeships
	I/S system that supports tracking of all training requirements	• People assessing their skills and forming their own development plan	• Employees designing, developing, delivering training using standard process and tools provided by the organization
	• People utilizing I/S systems to track, identify, and evaluate training	• Peer evaluation/assessment	• Documented procedures/processes for Operations
	• A computerized tracking system will exist	• Training that is self-identified and can be accomplished within the employees' power	
	• A tracking system in place that tracks a person's training, job training, updates, and signals retraining	• Bargaining units multi-skilled with rewards, pay for skill supported by technical training	

TECHNICAL TRAINING: GOALS AND STRATEGIES

Management Commitment of Resources to Learning That Drives Business Results

❖ GOAL: By [insert date] [insert %] of employees' time to be spent developing needed skills

Strategies—Technical and soft skills plus business knowledge

❖ GOAL: By [insert date] the performance review of everyone with direct reports includes people development

Company's Culture Is One of Learning Organization

❖ GOAL: By [insert date] we need to develop strategies that will motivate people to acquire the job skills they need

Strategies

- Tuition reimbursement for hourly and salaried
- Obtain job-related skills outside (tech schools)
- Incentives to local tech college to develop classes

❖ GOAL: By [insert date] training is an integral part of company's strategic planning

Strategies—Establish a corporate training council

- Have in place a process for prioritizing the training need
- Training not an afterthought, but an integral part of our planning
- Integrated process where the planning, delivery, and support of training exists
- Technical training staff together with Operations, Engineering, etc., at decision points

A Standardized Approach to Technical Training Used Throughout the Company

❖ GOAL: By [insert date] have selected and adopted a standard approach to technical training

Strategies

- Standardized approach that includes:
  - Type of design
  - Type of delivery
  - Type of evaluation
  - Type of documentation
  - Needs assessment
  - Who will develop
  - Guidelines for vendors/OEMs
- Define what else this process includes
- Obtain buy-in for new process throughout company
- Choose one of existing approaches
- Define method for process review
- Establish method for identifying and categorizing job competencies flexible for each plant's requirements

(Continued)

TECHNICAL TRAINING: GOALS AND STRATEGIES (*Continued*)

❖ GOAL: By [insert date] people from all affected departments within the company are oriented in this process
(standard approach)

❖ GOAL: By [insert date] vendor/OEMs as partners using company standard process for development and delivery of training

Strategies

- Purchasing requirement to this as contract provision
- Engineering to include in specs
- Engineering to include in start-up process

❖ GOAL: By [insert date] have in place a process for individual plants to assess and prioritize their training needs

Job Descriptions That Identify Required Skills

❖ GOAL: By [insert date] have in place a complete list of job skills needed to operate and maintain all equipment in our plants

Strategies

- Build a standard for defining job competencies
- Can't make job descriptions constraining
- Start with several core processes/positions
- Divide up task among all plants

❖ GOAL: By [insert date] have complete inventory of all the skills and proficiencies within a plant

Strategies

- Who has the skills?
- Levels of proficiency
- Basic skills

Effective Use of Technology in Delivery of Training

❖ GOAL: By [insert date] have in place refresher aids for OJT training and skills updates

Strategies

- Evaluate most appropriate delivery technologies (CBT, job aids, electronic delivery)
- Identify key areas for this type of training
- Identify standards for technology delivery
- Identify staffing and tech requirements
- Process in [insert date] pilot in [insert date]

❖ GOAL: By [insert date] have in place the technology needed to provide just-in-time training in all plants and continually evaluate new technology

TECHNICAL TRAINING: GOALS AND STRATEGIES (*Continued*)

Ability to Tie Technical Training with Performance Impact

❖ GOAL: By [insert date] have in place the capability to evaluate and confirm skill proficiency provided by training for an individual

Strategies

- Peer evaluation
- Testing
- Demonstration

❖ GOAL: Have in place a process that clearly identifies the dollars spent on training and the return on this investment (ROI)

Strategies

- IS system for accounting
- Accountability for ROI

IS System That Supports Tracking of all Training Requirements

❖ GOAL: By [insert date] tracking systems in place that track a person's training and signal retraining needs

❖ GOAL: Have in place the capability for an individual to schedule himself or herself into needed training

Strategies

- Checks and balances of when they can schedule
- Ties into development plans

❖ GOAL: Have in place IS capability to track dollars spent on training

❖ GOAL: By [insert date] we are using information technology to share training materials, modules, courses between plants

❖ GOAL: By [insert date] have in place a skills database that defines the skills an individual has and an automated system for access

Strategies

- Individuals have ability to enter their own information

Individuals Have Responsibility and Control Over Their Skill Development Needs

❖ GOAL: By [insert date] every employee has a development plan in place

Strategies

- Development plan includes:
  - Present abilities
  - Gap analysis of where they should be
  - Job skills, basic skills, etc.

TECHNICAL TRAINING: GOALS AND STRATEGIES (*Continued*)

- Evaluate labor negotiation impact
- Individuals self-identify needs, establish agreement with manager, make commitment
- Establish ability to measure proficiency

❖ GOAL: By [insert date] every employee knows how they can obtain the training needed for their job

Strategies

- Published training schedules

❖ GOAL: Developmental needs (from development plans) are driving the training we are developing and delivering

Involvement and Ownership Across All Levels in Design, Development, and Delivery of Training

❖ GOAL: By [insert date] have in place a single point of contact committed in each plant for coordination of tech training

Strategies

- Plant steering committees also possible

❖ GOAL: By [insert date] establish a coordinated approach and strategy of what is being developed in training across all plants and how it can be shared

Strategies

- Potential for plant steering committees coordinated by corporate technical training

❖ GOAL: By [insert date] have in place a cross-functional group of people with technical training skills in all plants

Strategies

- Incentives for involvement in training
- Early involvement in new line and line modifications
- Train the Trainer to teach process

❖ GOAL: By [insert date] all peer-to-peer training will follow a structured OJT approach

Strategies

- People trained on OJT techniques
- Qualifications of trainers

STEERING COMMITTEE INVOLVEMENT AFTER THE IMPLEMENTATION

	Strategy		
Competitive Analysis	Environmental Scan	Benchmarking	Focus Groups
Analysis of competition's current state and future direction and the impact on technical training	Analysis of the elements that affect (customers, stakeholders, influencers)	List of companies benchmarked	Conduct at each plant location to determine the current sate of technical training and the future needs of internal customers

VISION FOR TECHNICAL TRAINING

Management Commitment of Resources to Learning That Drives Business Results	Culture Is One of Learning Organization	Standardized Approach to Technical Training Used Throughout the Company	Job Descriptions That Identify Required skills

Develop a Continuous Learning Process as a Strategy for Business Improvement Activity

Activity	Who	When	Resources
1. Select and adopt a standard approach to technical learning	Subgroup of Technical Learning Task Force	[Insert Date]	[Insert Costs]
2. Orient all personnel on the standard approach	Corporate, technical training at corporate; appropriate plant personnel	[Insert Date]	[Insert # Resources]
3. Vendors/OEM oriented and informed of expectations on standard approach	Purchasing, Corporate Engineering, IS, and plant personnel	[Insert Date]	[Insert # Resources]
4. Develop a method for plants to assess and prioritize needs	Corporate and plant training	[Insert Date]	[Insert # Resources]
5. Identify a core curriculum for regulatory, safety, and quality skill training	Corporate training, safety	[Insert Date]	[Insert # Resources]
6. Complete the development courses using standard approach ? Quality (courses/training) ? Safety (courses)	Corporate training and user operating departments	[Insert Dates]	[Insert Costs]
7. Complete train the trainer for core group	Corporate and plant training	[Insert Date]	[Insert # Resources]

8.	Identify a training curriculum for safety and Q.A. professionals	Corporate training, safety	[Insert Date]	[Insert # Resources]
9.	Develop job descriptions that identify required skills: • Complete an inventory of skills that exist within plants • Complete list of job skills needed to operate and maintain all equipment in plants	Corporate technical training and plants	[Insert Dates]	[Insert Costs]
10.	Develop and install electronic performance support systems for just-in-time training	Corporate technical training and IS	[Insert Date]	[Insert Costs]
11.	Develop and implement a process that identifies dollars spent on training and ROI benefits	Corporate F and A, corporate IS, corporate training	[Insert Date]	[Insert # Resources]

APPENDIX IV

A Written Questionnaire to Assess Technical Training Needs

[Date]

Dear Manufacturing Manager:

What are the training needs of employees in your organization? The answer to this question could be immensely important in clarifying priorities so that money invested in training will be well-spent.

Please take a few minutes to complete this survey about the training needs of employees in your organization. Even if you do not personally feel a need for training in your organization or are not personally involved in observing employees on a daily basis, please take time to complete the survey and return it. When the results are compiled, no individuals or organizations will be identified; only summary statistics will be reported and published. Of course, your participation is voluntary. You are free to withdraw your participation at any time or to decline to answer specific questions.

The results of this survey will be reported to top managers in your organization.

Should you have questions about the survey, call [**insert telephone number**] to receive additional information. Thank you for your cooperation.

Cordially,

A Technical Training Needs Assessment Survey

1. What is your job category? (*Circle the appropriate response code below.*)

   Top manager reporting directly to the president, chief executive   1
   officer, or plant manager

   Manager who supervises supervisors, team leaders, or foremen   2

   Supervisor, team leader, or foreman who oversees   3
   nonsupervisory employees

   Professional or technical worker in engineering or MIS   4

   Salesperson for the organization   5

   Hourly production employee   6

   A different job category (*Specify here:*)

2. How long have you been in your current job? (*Circle the appropriate response code below.*)

   Less than 1 year   1
   More than 1 year through 2 years   2
   More than 2 years through 3 years   3
   More than 3 years through 4 years   4
   More than 4 years through 5 years   5
   More than 5 years   6

3. To meet the challenges of modern manufacturing, employees who work in such settings require certain minimum skill standards. For each skill standard listed in the left column below, circle an appropriate response

code in the middle column to indicate *how important* you consider that skill standard to be for performing work successfully in your organization. Use the following scale for the middle column:

1 = no importance; 2 = some importance; 3 = important; 4 = much importance; 5 = very great importance

Then circle an appropriate response code in the right column to indicate how much training you feel is needed to improve the abilities of employees to *meet this skill standard*. Use the following scale for the right column:

1 = no need; 2 = some need; 3 = needed; 4 = much need; 5 = very great need

Skill Standard	*How Important?*					*How Much Need for Training?*				
A competent and skilled worker can. . .	**No Importance**			**Very Great Importance**		**No Need**			**Very Great Need**	
I Communication and Teamwork										
1. Identify interpersonal characteristics of a team player	1	2	3	4	5	1	2	3	4	5
2. Demonstrate the characteristics of a team player	1	2	3	4	5	1	2	3	4	5
3. Contrast the role of a team with the role of an individual	1	2	3	4	5	1	2	3	4	5
4. Perform techniques used as a team leader	1	2	3	4	5	1	2	3	4	5
5. Demonstrate productive relationships within the work group	1	2	3	4	5	1	2	3	4	5

Note: The list of skill standards in the left column above is adapted from the National Skills Standard Project for Advanced Manufacturing (NACFAM), 1331 Pennsylvania Avenue NW, Suite 1410 North, Washington, DC 2004–1703. Phone: 202–662–1703.

Skill Standard	How Important?					How Much Need for Training?				
A competent and skilled worker can. . .	No Importance			Very Great Importance		No Need			Very Great Need	
6. Apply group dynamic principles to manufacturing situation	1	2	3	4	5	1	2	3	4	5
7. Identify possible electronic communication uses	1	2	3	4	5	1	2	3	4	5
8. Explain the effect of electronic communications versus other communications methods	1	2	3	4	5	1	2	3	4	5
9. Select appropriate communicate methods	1	2	3	4	5	1	2	3	4	5
10. List the characteristics of a good group leader	1	2	3	4	5	1	2	3	4	5
11. Identify various group processes	1	2	3	4	5	1	2	3	4	5
12. Identify components of group dynamics	1	2	3	4	5	1	2	3	4	5
13. Demonstrate good leadership	1	2	3	4	5	1	2	3	4	5
14. Apply facilitation skills in a group setting	1	2	3	4	5	1	2	3	4	5
15. Read process information and follow instructions	1	2	3	4	5	1	2	3	4	5
16. Read material and describe concepts	1	2	3	4	5	1	2	3	4	5
17. Read documentation, such as a computer manual, to determine actions for specific situations	1	2	3	4	5	1	2	3	4	5
18. Write the steps of a manufacturing process using sentences and statements as appropriate	1	2	3	4	5	1	2	3	4	5
19. Use correct punctuation	1	2	3	4	5	1	2	3	4	5
20. Use correct spelling	1	2	3	4	5	1	2	3	4	5

(Continued)

Skill Standard	*How Important?*					*How Much Need for Training?*				
A competent and skilled worker can. . .	**No Importance**				**Very Great Importance**	**No Need**				**Very Great Need**
21. Write with accuracy, brevity, and clarity	1	2	3	4	5	1	2	3	4	5
22. Organize material with a logical flow	1	2	3	4	5	1	2	3	4	5
23. Organize and deliver a persuasive presentation	1	2	3	4	5	1	2	3	4	5
24. Demonstrate good speaking characteristics	1	2	3	4	5	1	2	3	4	5
25. Demonstrate appropriate presentation demeanor	1	2	3	4	5	1	2	3	4	5
26. Interpret and clarify directions prepared by others	1	2	3	4	5	1	2	3	4	5
27. Communicate with customer(s) to establish requirements	1	2	3	4	5	1	2	3	4	5
II Math and Measurement										
1. Add, subtract, multiply, and divide four-digit numbers with the use of a calculator	1	2	3	4	5	1	2	3	4	5
2. Add, subtract, multiply, and divide four digit numbers without the use of a calculator	1	2	3	4	5	1	2	3	4	5
3. Apply basic math functions to solve problems	1	2	3	4	5	1	2	3	4	5
4. Create and interpret basic graphs and charts commonly used in manufacturing	1	2	3	4	5	1	2	3	4	5
5. Match measurement activities to manufacturing process	1	2	3	4	5	1	2	3	4	5
6. Select and use appropriate measurement techniques and instruments	1	2	3	4	5	1	2	3	4	5

Skill Standard	How Important?					How Much Need for Training?				
A competent and skilled worker can. . .	No Importance				Very Great Importance	No Need				Very Great Need
7. Describe measurements' role in manufacturing	1	2	3	4	5	1	2	3	4	5
8. Distinguish between direct and calculated measurements	1	2	3	4	5	1	2	3	4	5
9. Compute calculated measurements	1	2	3	4	5	1	2	3	4	5
10. Demonstrate proper *general* measurement techniques	1	2	3	4	5	1	2	3	4	5
11. Demonstrate proper *precision* measurement techniques	1	2	3	4	5	1	2	3	4	5
12. Describe the appropriate application and use of precision measurements in manufacturing	1	2	3	4	5	1	2	3	4	5
13. Explain calibration requirements of various precision instruments	1	2	3	4	5	1	2	3	4	5
14. Illustrate measurement differences when taken with calibrated and noncalibrated instruments	1	2	3	4	5	1	2	3	4	5
15. Match appropriate measurement tools with various types of measurement requirements	1	2	3	4	5	1	2	3	4	5
16. Demonstrate proper measurement tool usage	1	2	3	4	5	1	2	3	4	5
17. State selection criteria for measurement tools	1	2	3	4	5	1	2	3	4	5
18. Convert between U.S. and metric measurement systems	1	2	3	4	5	1	2	3	4	5
19. Convert fractional measurement to decimal measurement	1	2	3	4	5	1	2	3	4	5

(Continued)

Skill Standard	*How Important?*					*How Much Need for Training?*				
A competent and skilled worker can. . .	No Importance			Very Great Importance		No Need			Very Great Need	
20. Compute within measurement systems	1	2	3	4	5	1	2	3	4	5
21. Document results of measurement activities and calculations	1	2	3	4	5	1	2	3	4	5
22. Interpret results of measurements and calculations	1	2	3	4	5	1	2	3	4	5
23. List steps with rationale of proper measurement procedures	1	2	3	4	5	1	2	3	4	5
24. Distinguish between general and precision measurement	1	2	3	4	5	1	2	3	4	5
25. Distinguish between U.S. and metric measurement systems	1	2	3	4	5	1	2	3	4	5
III Workplace Safety and Health										
1. Assume responsibility for the personal safety of self and others	1	2	3	4	5	1	2	3	4	5
2. Maintain a clean and safe work environment	1	2	3	4	5	1	2	3	4	5
3. Demonstrate a positive personal attitude toward safety	1	2	3	4	5	1	2	3	4	5
4. Comply with established safety practices	1	2	3	4	5	1	2	3	4	5
5. Complete forms/ paperwork as required	1	2	3	4	5	1	2	3	4	5
6. Wear protective safety clothing as required	1	2	3	4	5	1	2	3	4	5
7. Maintain and use protective guards and equipment on machinery	1	2	3	4	5	1	2	3	4	5
8. Handle/store flammable materials appropriately	1	2	3	4	5	1	2	3	4	5
9. Use electrical devices correctly and safely	1	2	3	4	5	1	2	3	4	5

Skill Standard	How Important?					How Much Need for Training?				
A competent and skilled worker can. . .	No Importance			Very Great Importance		No Need			Very Great Need	
10. Prevent spontaneous ignition by practicing proper waste disposal habits	1	2	3	4	5	1	2	3	4	5
11. Keep marked aisles clear of equipment and materials	1	2	3	4	5	1	2	3	4	5
12. Interpret/display MSDS sheets as required	1	2	3	4	5	1	2	3	4	5
13. Identify fire exits and fire-fighting equipment	1	2	3	4	5	1	2	3	4	5
14. Report unsafe practices to appropriate personnel	1	2	3	4	5	1	2	3	4	5
15. Operate equipment in a safe, prescribed manner	1	2	3	4	5	1	2	3	4	5
16. Locate power shutoff controls for all machinery/equipment	1	2	3	4	5	1	2	3	4	5
17. Report malfunctions to appropriate personnel	1	2	3	4	5	1	2	3	4	5
18. Inspect material/ equipment/fixtures for defects	1	2	3	4	5	1	2	3	4	5
19. Determine weight/ operating limits of equipment	1	2	3	4	5	1	2	3	4	5
20. Perform periodic checks during operation to assure proper function	1	2	3	4	5	1	2	3	4	5
21. Possess valid first aid card	1	2	3	4	5	1	2	3	4	5
22. Determine need for CPR and administer as appropriate	1	2	3	4	5	1	2	3	4	5
23. Apply appropriate first aid techniques	1	2	3	4	5	1	2	3	4	5
24. Define different types of chemical, biological, and physical hazards	1	2	3	4	5	1	2	3	4	5
25. Respond to emergencies in the appropriate manner	1	2	3	4	5	1	2	3	4	5

(Continued)

Skill Standard	How Important?					How Much Need for Training?				
A competent and skilled worker can. . .	No Importance			Very Great Importance		No Need			Very Great Need	
26. Describe ergonomics and its importance to the manufacturing process	1	2	3	4	5	1	2	3	4	5
IV Problem Solving										
1. Explain the value of applying a problem-solving system	1	2	3	4	5	1	2	3	4	5
2. Apply a system of problem solving	1	2	3	4	5	1	2	3	4	5
3. Identify opportunities for applying problem-solving techniques	1	2	3	4	5	1	2	3	4	5
V Quality Assurance										
1. Contrast quality manufacturing systems with other manufacturing systems	1	2	3	4	5	1	2	3	4	5
2. Identify influences of a quality system on specific manufacturing processes	1	2	3	4	5	1	2	3	4	5
3. Explain the effect of quality on profit	1	2	3	4	5	1	2	3	4	5
4. Identify the effects of continuous quality improvement	1	2	3	4	5	1	2	3	4	5
5. Demonstrate the ability to apply continuous quality improvement to manufacturing processes	1	2	3	4	5	1	2	3	4	5
6. Integrate improvement processes	1	2	3	4	5	1	2	3	4	5
7. Define statistical process control (SPC)	1	2	3	4	5	1	2	3	4	5
8. Identify the relationship between SPC steps and specific production processes	1	2	3	4	5	1	2	3	4	5
9. Apply SPC to specific production processes	1	2	3	4	5	1	2	3	4	5
10. Analyze production specific processes	1	2	3	4	5	1	2	3	4	5

Skill Standard	How Important?					How Much Need for Training?				
A competent and skilled worker can. . .	No Importance			Very Great Importance		No Need			Very Great Need	
11. Analyze and interpret test data for compliance to specifications	1	2	3	4	5	1	2	3	4	5
12. Improve production process if indicated by analysis of data	1	2	3	4	5	1	2	3	4	5
13. Maintain production according to instructions	1	2	3	4	5	1	2	3	4	5
14. Identify customer problems	1	2	3	4	5	1	2	3	4	5
15. Classify customer problems	1	2	3	4	5	1	2	3	4	5
16. Determine causes of the problem	1	2	3	4	5	1	2	3	4	5
17. Apply problem-solving system	1	2	3	4	5	1	2	3	4	5
18. Recommend possible solutions	1	2	3	4	5	1	2	3	4	5
19. Develop a plan utilizing a selected quality control system	1	2	3	4	5	1	2	3	4	5
20. Evaluate process selected, versus desired goals	1	2	3	4	5	1	2	3	4	5
VI Blueprint Reading										
1. Identify basic blueprint terminology	1	2	3	4	5	1	2	3	4	5
2. Identify different types of dimensions	1	2	3	4	5	1	2	3	4	5
3. Identify general note symbols	1	2	3	4	5	1	2	3	4	5
4. Locate notes on a print	1	2	3	4	5	1	2	3	4	5
5. Interpret commonly used abbreviations and terminology	1	2	3	4	5	1	2	3	4	5
6. Determine tolerances associated with dimensions on a drawing	1	2	3	4	5	1	2	3	4	5

(Continued)

Skill Standard	*How Important?*					*How Much Need for Training?*				
A competent and skilled worker can. . .	No Importance				Very Great Importance	No Need				Very Great Need
7. Determine the tolerance for a reference dimension	1	2	3	4	5	1	2	3	4	5
8. Identify types of lines within a drawing	1	2	3	4	5	1	2	3	4	5
9. List the essential components found in the title block	1	2	3	4	5	1	2	3	4	5
10. List the essential components found in the revision block	1	2	3	4	5	1	2	3	4	5
11. Identify orthographic views	1	2	3	4	5	1	2	3	4	5
12. Identify isometric views	1	2	3	4	5	1	2	3	4	5
13. Identify position of views (top, front, side, and auxiliary)	1	2	3	4	5	1	2	3	4	5
14. Visualize one or more views from a given view	1	2	3	4	5	1	2	3	4	5
15. Determine the scale of the view or section	1	2	3	4	5	1	2	3	4	5
16. Check for revisions	1	2	3	4	5	1	2	3	4	5
VII Manufacturing Fundamentals										
1. Perform the basic arithmetic functions	1	2	3	4	5	1	2	3	4	5
2. Use measuring instruments	1	2	3	4	5	1	2	3	4	5
3. Use hand calculators	1	2	3	4	5	1	2	3	4	5
4. Calculate percents, rate, ratio, and proportion with the use of a calculator	1	2	3	4	5	1	2	3	4	5
5. Make reasonable estimates of arithmetic results without the use of a calculator	1	2	3	4	5	1	2	3	4	5
6. Demonstrate basic mechanical skills	1	2	3	4	5	1	2	3	4	5
7. Identify and report equipment malfunctions	1	2	3	4	5	1	2	3	4	5

Skill Standard	How Important?					How Much Need for Training?				
A competent and skilled worker can. . .	No Importance				Very Great Importance	No Need				Very Great Need
8. Follow established safety procedures when around machinery/equipment	1	2	3	4	5	1	2	3	4	5
9. Describe the importance of correct fixturing and work holding devices	1	2	3	4	5	1	2	3	4	5
10. Design and create fixtures or holding devices	1	2	3	4	5	1	2	3	4	5
11. Follow established safety procedures when using machine tools	1	2	3	4	5	1	2	3	4	5
12. Identify a variety of common machine tools	1	2	3	4	5	1	2	3	4	5
13. Describe the function of specific machine tools	1	2	3	4	5	1	2	3	4	5
14. Inspect machine tools for defects	1	2	3	4	5	1	2	3	4	5
15. Maintain company-provided machine tools	1	2	3	4	5	1	2	3	4	5
16. Locate and retrieve production materials specific to process flow and delivery schedule	1	2	3	4	5	1	2	3	4	5
17. Retrieve and communicate process flow instructions and delivery schedules	1	2	3	4	5	1	2	3	4	5
18. Operate hand tools in a safe, prescribed manner	1	2	3	4	5	1	2	3	4	5
19. Inspect hand tools for defects	1	2	3	4	5	1	2	3	4	5
20. Maintain company-provided hand tools	1	2	3	4	5	1	2	3	4	5
21. Interpret prints to determine appropriate tool usage	1	2	3	4	5	1	2	3	4	5

(Continued)

Skill Standard	How Important?					How Much Need for Training?				
A competent and skilled worker can...	No Importance				Very Great Importance	No Need				Very Great Need
22. Follow electrical troubleshooting procedures	1	2	3	4	5	1	2	3	4	5
23. Identify types of work-saving devices used in manufacturing	1	2	3	4	5	1	2	3	4	5
24. Describe scenarios in which work-saving devices can be used	1	2	3	4	5	1	2	3	4	5
VIII Business Planning and Operation										
1. Identify the organizational need for profit	1	2	3	4	5	1	2	3	4	5
2. Identify opportunities for profit in manufacturing processes	1	2	3	4	5	1	2	3	4	5
3. Identify possible barriers to profit in manufacturing processes	1	2	3	4	5	1	2	3	4	5
4. Identify strategies that may maximize profit potential in manufacturing processes	1	2	3	4	5	1	2	3	4	5
5. Recognize a business plan that provides for an acceptable profit	1	2	3	4	5	1	2	3	4	5
6. Identify the components that lead to customer satisfaction	1	2	3	4	5	1	2	3	4	5
7. Identify possible actions that may lead to customer dissatisfaction	1	2	3	4	5	1	2	3	4	5
8. Identify the ways that the level of customer satisfaction may affect company success	1	2	3	4	5	1	2	3	4	5
9. Explain the importance of a business reputation	1	2	3	4	5	1	2	3	4	5
10. Identify the ways that customer satisfaction influences a business reputation	1	2	3	4	5	1	2	3	4	5

Skill Standard	How Important?					How Much Need for Training?				
A competent and skilled worker can. . .	No Importance			Very Great Importance		No Need			Very Great Need	
11. Identify possible actions that may be used to correct customer dissatisfaction	1	2	3	4	5	1	2	3	4	5
12. Define a safe work environment	1	2	3	4	5	1	2	3	4	5
13. Identify immediate and real costs of an accident	1	2	3	4	5	1	2	3	4	5
14. Identify methods of preventing accidents in the workplace	1	2	3	4	5	1	2	3	4	5
15. Define the term *value added*	1	2	3	4	5	1	2	3	4	5
16. Explain why cost factors are not constant	1	2	3	4	5	1	2	3	4	5
17. Identify steps within manufacturing processes that determine cost	1	2	3	4	5	1	2	3	4	5
18. Define the term *profit*	1	2	3	4	5	1	2	3	4	5
19. List benefits that are employer paid or provided	1	2	3	4	5	1	2	3	4	5
20. List benefits that are offered to employees for their optional participation	1	2	3	4	5	1	2	3	4	5
IX Computer Use										
1. List possible computer applications in manufacturing processes	1	2	3	4	5	1	2	3	4	5
2. Identify possible effects of introducing computers into manufacturing processes	1	2	3	4	5	1	2	3	4	5
3. List various methods of tracking inventory quantities	1	2	3	4	5	1	2	3	4	5
4. List factors that determine inventory demand	1	2	3	4	5	1	2	3	4	5
5. Demonstrate use of an industry-accepted word processing software package	1	2	3	4	5	1	2	3	4	5

(Continued)

Skill Standard	How Important?					How Much Need for Training?				
A competent and skilled worker can. . .	No Importance				Very Great Importance	No Need				Very Great Need
6. Demonstrate use of an industry-accepted spreadsheet software package	1	2	3	4	5	1	2	3	4	5
7. Demonstrate use of an industry-accepted database software package	1	2	3	4	5	1	2	3	4	5
8. Demonstrate use of an industry-accepted statistical processing software package	1	2	3	4	5	1	2	3	4	5
9. Demonstrate use of an industry-accepted graphic software package	1	2	3	4	5	1	2	3	4	5
X Product and Process Control										
1. List a variety of process control applications	1	2	3	4	5	1	2	3	4	5
2. Collect and analyze information to determine and improve work processes	1	2	3	4	5	1	2	3	4	5
3. Explain the advantages and disadvantages of a just-in-time inventory	1	2	3	4	5	1	2	3	4	5
4. Create a project plan	1	2	3	4	5	1	2	3	4	5
XI Workforce Issues										
1. Recognize the difference between a team environment workplace and a conventional workplace	1	2	3	4	5	1	2	3	4	5
2. Explain how organizational structure affects a manufacturing process	1	2	3	4	5	1	2	3	4	5
3. Identify the characteristics of a diverse workforce	1	2	3	4	5	1	2	3	4	5
4. List steps of a grievance or dispute resolution procedure	1	2	3	4	5	1	2	3	4	5

Skill Standard	How Important?					How Much Need for Training?				
A competent and skilled worker can...	No Importance			Very Great Importance		No Need			Very Great Need	
5. Identify good personal ethical characteristics and behaviors	1	2	3	4	5	1	2	3	4	5
6. Demonstrate good personal ethics	1	2	3	4	5	1	2	3	4	5
7. Identify good ethical business behavior	1	2	3	4	5	1	2	3	4	5
8. Differentiate between good and poor business ethic practices	1	2	3	4	5	1	2	3	4	5
9. Match employee responsibilities to employer expectations	1	2	3	4	5	1	2	3	4	5
10. Define discrimination, harassment, and equity	1	2	3	4	5	1	2	3	4	5
11. Demonstrate nondiscriminatory behavior	1	2	3	4	5	1	2	3	4	5
XII Workplace Skills										
1. Demonstrate consistently punctual arrival	1	2	3	4	5	1	2	3	4	5
2. Document regular attendance	1	2	3	4	5	1	2	3	4	5
3. Demonstrate enthusiasm and confidence about work and learning new tasks	1	2	3	4	5	1	2	3	4	5
4. Demonstrate safe, careful use, treatment, and maintenance of tools, equipment, and machines	1	2	3	4	5	1	2	3	4	5
5. Demonstrate appropriate dress and hygiene for successful employment	1	2	3	4	5	1	2	3	4	5
6. Demonstrate the ability to act in polite and respectful ways toward co-workers	1	2	3	4	5	1	2	3	4	5

(Continued)

Skill Standard	*How Important?*					*How Much Need for Training?*				
A competent and skilled worker can. . .	**No Importance**				**Very Great Importance**	**No Need**				**Very Great Need**
7. Demonstrate the ability to complete tasks on time and accurately	1	2	3	4	5	1	2	3	4	5
8. Demonstrate the ability to make career decisions	1	2	3	4	5	1	2	3	4	5
9. Demonstrate the ability to use labor market information	1	2	3	4	5	1	2	3	4	5
10. Prepare a resume and letter of application/ interest	1	2	3	4	5	1	2	3	4	5
11. Fill out an application for employment	1	2	3	4	5	1	2	3	4	5
12. Participate in an employment interview	1	2	3	4	5	1	2	3	4	5
13. Follow directions and procedures	1	2	3	4	5	1	2	3	4	5
14. Be depended on not to steal equipment and materials	1	2	3	4	5	1	2	3	4	5
15. Be truthful in communications with co-workers and supervisors	1	2	3	4	5	1	2	3	4	5
16. Accept constructive criticism	1	2	3	4	5	1	2	3	4	5
17. Demonstrate an ability to learn new skills and behaviors	1	2	3	4	5	1	2	3	4	5
18. Demonstrate a willingness to work	1	2	3	4	5	1	2	3	4	5
19. Demonstrate a willingness to learn	1	2	3	4	5	1	2	3	4	5
20. Work with minimal supervision	1	2	3	4	5	1	2	3	4	5
21. Plan and organize work	1	2	3	4	5	1	2	3	4	5
XIV Learning Skills										
1. Identify personal preferred learning styles	1	2	3	4	5	1	2	3	4	5

Skill Standard	How Important?					How Much Need for Training?				
A competent and skilled worker can. . .	No Importance			Very Great Importance		No Need			Very Great Need	
2. Demonstrate ability to learn new process steps	1	2	3	4	5	1	2	3	4	5
3. Implement new process steps given oral instructions	1	2	3	4	5	1	2	3	4	5
4. Read process instructions and implement appropriate steps	1	2	3	4	5	1	2	3	4	5
5. Participate in product- or process-specific training and report significant information	1	2	3	4	5	1	2	3	4	5

In what other areas do you feel a need for professional development? Please list them in order of priority below, with 1 = greatest area of need.

Importance	Area
1.	
2.	
3.	

Please add any other comments you would like to make.

REFERENCES

Adams, R. (1975). *DACUM approach to curriculum, learning, and evaluation in occupational training.* Halifax, NC: A Nova Scotia Newstart Report, Department of Regional Economic Expansion.

Agrawal, A. (1995). Technology learning laboratories. In L. Kelly (Ed.), *The ASTD technical and skills training handbook* (pp. 369–384). New York: McGraw-Hill.

Allen, R. (1997). Playing it safe. *Human Resource Executive, 11*(11), 1, 26–30.

Allum, J., and Hofstader, R. (1998). Business and education connect. *Technical Training, 9*(3), 16–20.

American Society for Training and Development. (1994a). *Practical guide for technical and skills trainers* (2 vols.). Alexandria, VA: Author.

American Society for Training and Development. (1994b). *The best of case studies in technical training.* Alexandria, VA: Author.

American Society for Training and Development. (2000). *State of the industry report.* Alexandria, VA: Author.

Arkin, A. (1996). Safer workplaces are no accident. *People Management, 2*(15), 37–38.

Barnshaw, J. (1992). Educational resources in your own back yard. *Technical and Skills Training, 46*(5), 53–57.

Barron, T. (1997a). Streamlined or oversized? Conflicting views of OSHA training rules. *Technical and Skills Training, 8*(2), 7–8.

Barron, T. (1997b). The new universe of multimedia courseware. *Technical and Skills Training, 8*(4), 8–11.

Barron, T. (1999a). A tangled web of partnerships. *Technical Training, 10*(5), 14–19.

Barron, T. (1999b). Simulation gets real. *Technical Training, 10*(6), 12–17.

Barron, T. (1999c). Whither skill standards? *Technical Training, 10*(2), 18–23.

Bartel, A. (1989). *Formal employee training programs and their impact on labor productivity: Evidence from a human resource survey.* NBER (Working paper No. 3026).

Bass, R. (1996). Developing legally defensible tests. In L. Kelly (Ed.), *Supplement 1 to the ASTD technical and skills training handbook* (pp. 149–164). New York: McGraw-Hill.

Bassi, L., Buchanan, L., and Cheney, S. (1997). *Trends that affect learning and performance improvement: A report on the members of the ASTD benchmarking forum.* Alexandria, VA: ASTD.

Bassi, L., and Van Buren, M. (1998). Investments in intellectual capital: Developing methods for measuring the impact and value of HRD. *Academy of Human Resource Development* (Outstanding papers from the 1998 Annual Research Conference, 15–21.)

Beibel, M. (1995). Instructional design basics. In L. Kelly (Ed.), *The ASTD technical and skills training handbook* (pp. 243–266). New York: McGraw-Hill.

Berik, G., and Bilginsoy, C. (2000). Do unions help or hinder women in training? Apprenticeship programs in the United States. *Industrial Relations, 39*(4), 600–624.

Bersani, M. (1999). A revolution in sales training. *Technical Training, 10*(3), 25–27.

Blair, D., and Giles, S. (1996). Evaluating test questions: More than meets the eye. *Technical and Skills Training, 7*(4), 23–24.

Bloch, M. (2000). The changing face of the workforce. *Training, 37*(12), 73–78.

Bluestone, B., and Harrison, B. (1982). *The deindustrialization of America: Plant closings, community abandonment and the dismantling of basic industry.* New York: Basic Books.

Blume, E. (1991). Finding and training machinists. *Technical and Skills Training, 2*(1), 40–45.

Boling, N., and Lee, C. (1999). A new workplace strategy for Taiwan. *Technical Training, 10*(3), 37.

Boyd, S. (1999). Breathing life into dull safety training sessions. *Technical Training, 10*(2), 37.

Braddock, D. (1999, November). Employment outlook: 1998–2008: Occupational employment projections to 2008. *Monthly Labor Review,* pp. 51–77.

Brinkerhoff, R. (1995). Using evaluation to improve the quality of technical training. In L. Kelly (Ed.), *The ASTD Technical and Skills Training Handbook* (pp. 385–410). New York: McGraw-Hill.

Brown, J. (1983). *Are those paid more really no more productive? Measuring the relative importance of tenure as on-the-job training in explaining wage growth.* Princeton, NJ: Princeton Industrial Relations (Working Paper).

Brown. J. (1988). *Why do wages increase with tenure? On-the-job training and life cycle wage growth observed within firms.* Stony Brook, NY: SUNY at Stony Brook.

Brown, S., and Seidner, C. (Eds.) (1998). *Evaluating corporate training: Models and issues.* Boston, MA: Kluwer.

Brunelli, M. (2000). Net streamlines search for IT training. *Purchasing, 128*(6), 97.

Built to work: A common framework for skill standards. (2000). Washington, DC: National Skills Standards Board.

Burgoyne, J. and Cooper, C. (1975). Evaluation methodology. *Journal of Occupational Psychology, 48,* 53–62.

Caiazza, K. (1999). The big splash: Training for a new product rollout. *Technical Training, 10*(2), 29–31.

Cantor, J. (1994). Apprenticeships and community colleges: Linkages in America's defense. *Journal of Industrial Teacher Education, 31*(3), 8–27.

Cantor, J. (1997). Registered pre-apprenticeship: Successful practices linking school to work. *Journal of Industrial Teacher Education, 34*(3), 35–58.

Carnevale, E. (1993a). On target: This is your career. *Technical and Skills Training, 4*(4), 27–31.

Carnevale, E. (1993b). On target: Translating technical information and training. *Technical and Skills Training, 4*(1), 30–32.

Carnevale, E. (1995). Trends in technical jobs, skills, and training. In L. Kelly (Ed.), *The ASTD technical and skills training handbook* (pp. 567–580). New York: McGraw-Hill.

Cellich, C. (1992). Mexico's Institute of Technical Training: An innovative approach. *International Trade Forum, 4,* pp. 16–23.

Chakris, B.J., and Rolander, R. (1986). *Careers in training and development.* Washington, DC: ASTD.

Chance, P. (1995). The technical training function: Growth of technical training professionalism. In L. Kelly (Ed.), *The ASTD technical and skills training handbook* (pp. 97–116). New York: McGraw-Hill.

Cheney, S., and Jarrett, L. (Eds.). (1997). *Excellence in practice, Vol. 1.* Alexandria, VA: ASTD.

Clark, C. (1995). Instructional system development: Evaluation phase, chapter VI [36 paragraphs]. *www.nwlink.com/~donclark/hrd/sat6.html* [On-line]

Clark, R. (1989). *Developing technical training: A structured approach for the development of classroom and computer-based instructional materials.* Reading, MA: Addison-Wesley.

Clinton, M. (1998). Uncertain effects: Can basic skills education improve motivation? *Technical Training, 9*(6), 35–37.

Cooke, W. (1990). *Labor-management cooperation: New partnerships or going in circles?* Kalamazoo, MI: W.E. Upjohn Institute.

Del Gaizo, E. (1984). Proof that supervisory training works. *Training and Development, 38,* 30–31.

Delisle, R. (2001). *Measuring the impact of training.* Paper presented at the 2001 International Performance Improvement Conference, International Society for Performance Improvement, San Francisco, CA.

Dent, J., and Weber, D. (1999). Technical training. *Info-Line,* 9909. Alexandria, VA: ASTD.

Devarics, C. (1995). On target: Managing technical training. *Technical and Skills Training, 6*(7), 6–8.

Dolainski, S. (1997). Partnering with the (school) board. *Workforce, 76*(5), 28–37.

Dowling, E. (1996). Taking the "zzz" out of technical training. *Technical and Skills Training, 7*(6), 9–13.

Doyle, E. (1999). Project management for trainers. *Technical Training, 10*(3), 8.

Doyle, E., and Van Tiem, D. (1995). Technical and skills training suppliers. In L. Kelly (Ed.), *The ASTD technical and skills training handbook* (pp. 537–566). New York: McGraw-Hill.

Dubois, D., and Rothwell, W. (2000). *The competency toolkit.* (2 vols.). Amherst, MA: HRD Press.

Durham, J. (1992). Southwestern power administration's in-house technical training program. *Transmission and Distribution, 44*(13), 28–32.

Ekkebus, C. (1996). Starting from scratch: Designing training for new plants and modernizations. *Technical and Skills Training, 7*(8), 14–18.

Eline, L. (1998a). A virtual reality check for manufacturers. *Technical Training, 9*(1), 10–14.

Eline, L. (1998b). International standards provide new niche for trainers. *Technical Training, 9*(2), 36.

Eline, L. (1998c). Multimedia: Better supplement than substitute. *Technical Training, 9*(2), 6–7.

Eline, L. (1998d). Training by request only. *Technical Training, 9*(1), 4.

Eline, L. (1999a). Barriers for the breaking: Women in IT training. *Technical Training, 10*(2), 12–16.

Eline, J. (1999b). IT training and certification resources. *Technical Training, 10*(6), 10–11.

Eline, J. (1999c). The training side of ERP. *Technical Training, 10*(3), 12–16.

Elsenheimer, J. (1999). Implementation training for EPSS. *Technical Training, 10*(3), 32–35.

Evanciew, C., and Rojeweski, J. (1999). Skills and knowledge acquisition in the workplace: A case study of mentor-apprentice relationships in youth apprenticeship programs. *Journal of Industrial Teacher Education, 36*(2), 24–54.

Eyres, P. (1998). Seven requirements for effective safety training. *Technical Training, 9*(4), 35–36.

Falletta, S., and Combs, W. (1997). Evaluating technical training: A functional approach. *Info-Line,* No. 9709. Alexandria, VA: ASTD.

Fertal, A. (1996). Specify training by performance—not by the pound. *Technical and Skills Training, 7*(3), 5–8.

Filling the skills gap. (2000). *Business Europe, 40*(10), 6.

Fister, S. (2000). Reinventing training at Rockwell Collins. *Training, 37*(4), 64–70.

Frantz, N. (1994). Youth apprenticeships in the United States: Transmission or transformation of the German apprenticeship system. *Journal of Industrial Teacher Education, 31*(3), 28–39.

Galagan, P. (1983). The numbers game: Putting value on human resource development. *Training and Development, 37,* 48–51.

Garvin, D. (1993). Building a learning organization. *Harvard Business Review, 71,* 78–91.

Gery, G. (1991). *Electronic performance support systems.* Boston: Weingarten.

Gettle, M. (Ed.). (1998). *In action: Managing the small training staff.* Alexandria, VA: ASTD.

Gilley, J., and Maycunich, A. (1998). *Strategically integrated HRD: Partnering to maximize organizational performance.* Reading, MA: Addison-Wesley.

Gittlen, S. (2000). Training at its best. *Network World, 17*(46), 123–126.

Glister, P. (2000). Legislating an IT fix. *Workforce, 79*(7), 34–38.

Gottlieb, J. (1999). Adding value: Product training for external customers. *Technical Training, 10*(4), 34–37.

Hallberg, C., and DeFiore, R. (1997). Curving toward performance. *Technical and Skills Training, 8*(1), 9–11.

Hamilton, M., and Hamilton, S. (1997). Turbo OJT can redefine workplace learning. *Technical Training, 8*(8), 8–12.

Hardinger, S. (2001). Measuring the effects of training: The Prudential launchpad case study. In J. Woods and J. Cortada (Eds.), *The 2001 ASTD training and performance yearbook* (pp. 334–340). New York: McGraw-Hill.

Harris, D., and DeSimone, R. (1994). *Human resource development.* New York: Dryden Press.

Hays, S. (1999). The ABCs of workplace literacy. *Workforce, 78*(4), 70–74.

Herschbach, D. (1998). Reconstructing technical instruction. *Journal of Industrial Teacher Education, 36*(1), 36–61.

Hight, J. (1998, June). Young workers participation in post-school education and training. *Monthly Labor Review,* pp. 14–21.

Hong Vo, C. (1996). Selling self-interest. *Vocational Education Journal, 71*(2), 22–25.

Houle, C. (1961). *The inquiring mind.* Madison, WI: University of Wisconsin Press.

Huey, T., and McCallar, S. (2000). Is there anyone out there who does not have a shortage of skilled labor? *Plant Engineering.*

Information technology training. (1998). *National HRD executive survey,* presented at www.astd.org/virtual_community/research/nhrd_executive_survey_98it.html

Jasinowski, J. (1998). State, federal (and boardroom) level training. *Technical Training, 9*(3), 40.

Johnson, D. (1993). Cost-effectiveness evaluation of decentralized international technical training. *Human Resource Development Quarterly, 4*(3), 265–275.

Johnson, S., and Ferej, A. (1997). Apprenticeship training as preparation for self-employment. *Journal of Industrial Teacher Education, 35*(1), 48–72.

Johnston, W. (1987). *Workforce 2000: Work and workers for the 21st century.* Indianapolis, IN: The Hudson Institute.

Kazis, R. (1995). School-to-work programs. *Info-Line,* 259509. Alexandria, VA: The American Society for Training and Development.

Kelly, R. (1995). Apprenticeship training pays big dividends. *Technical and Skills Training, 6*(5), 22–24.

Kemp, J., and Cochern, G. (1994). *Planning for effective technical training: A guide for instructors and trainers.* Englewood Cliffs, NJ: Educational Technology.

King, S., King, M., and Rothwell, W. (2000). *The complete guide to training delivery: A competency-based approach.* New York: Amacom.

King-Taylor, L. (1999). Coaching the new technical trainer. *Technical Training, 10*(5), 10–13.

Kirk, J. (1998). Online web-based training resources. *Technical Training, 9*(2), 4–5.

Kirkpatrick, D. (1994). *Evaluating training programs: The four levels.* San Francisco: Berrett-Koehler.

Knowles, M. (1980). *The modern practice of adult education* (rev. ed.). Chicago: Follett.

Knowles, M., and Hartl, D. (1995). The adult learner in the technical environment. In L. Kelly (Ed.), *The ASTD technical and skills training handbook* (pp. 211–242). New York: McGraw-Hill.

Koury, J. (1996). Case study: Industrial retraining in the Canadian outback. *Technical and Skills Training, 7*(6), 27–29.

Kristof, B. (1999). Build it, break it, restore it: Bringing the real world to the classroom. *Technical Training, 10*(2), 8–11.

Laabs, J. (1997). Cashing in on safety. *Workforce, 76*(8), 53–57.

Langdon, D., Whiteside, K., and McKenna, M. (Eds.). (1999). *Intervention resource guide: 50 performance improvement tools* (pp. 15–25). San Francisco: Jossey-Bass/Pfeiffer.

Latimer, J. (1999). Cross-border knowledge transfer. *Technical Training, 10*(5), 49–51.

Lee, H. (1990). *DACUM technique, task analysis.* CET Handout. Menomonie, WI: University of Wisconsin-Stout.

Lee, R. (1996). The pay-forward view of training. *People Management, 2*(3), 30.

Leigh, J. (1995). *Causes of death in the workplace.* Westport, CT: Quorum Books.

Lermack, H. (1999). A team approach to risk management and safety training. *Technical Training, 10*(5), 53.

Lillard, L., and Tan, H. (1986). Private sector training: Who gets it and what are its effects? *Rand Monograph* R-3331-DOL/RC.

Loew, C. (1999). How teams transform corporate cultures. *Technical Training, 10*(2), 32–35.

Lucadamo, L., and Cheney, S. (1997). Best practices in technical training. *Technical Training, 8*(7), 21–26.

Lynch, L. (1990). Utilizing human resources for strategic advantage: The role of training. Prepared for the BPS conference: *Achieving Systemic Organizational Change.*

Mager, R. (1997). *Preparing instructional objectives: A critical tool in the development of effective instruction* (3rd ed.) Atlanta, GA: Center for Effective Performance.

Mallory, W., and Steele, J. (1995). Assessment of the options. In L. Kelly (Ed.), *The ASTD technical and skills training handbook* (pp. 267–288). New York: McGraw-Hill.

Mancuso, J. (1995). Anatomy of a training program: A start-to-finish look. In L. Kelly (Ed.), *The ASTD technical and skills training handbook* (pp. 431–450). New York: McGraw-Hill.

Marrelli, A. (1993). Ten evaluation instruments for technical training. *Technical and Skills Training, 4*(5), 7–14.

Marsh, P. (1996). On-the-job learning: A look at the papermaking industry. In L. Kelly (Ed.), *Supplement 1 to the ASTD technical and skills training handbook* (pp. 165–190). New York: McGraw-Hill.

Marx, R. (1999). *The ASTD media selection tool for workplace learning.* Alexandria, VA: ASTD.

McCain, M. (1994). Apprenticeship lessons from Europe. *Training and Development, 48*(11), 38–41.

McMurrer, D.P., Van Buren, M.E., and Woodwell, W.H., Jr. (2000). *The 2000 ASTD state of the industry report.* Alexandria, VA: ASTD.

Meyer, M. (1993). Selling technical training to top management. *Technical and Skills Training, 4*(2), 14–16.

Miller, L. (1999). The IT certification binge. *Technical Training, 10*(6), 22–25.

Mincer, J. (1983). Union effects: Wages, turnover, and job training. *Research in Labor Economics.*

Mincer, J. (1988). *Job training, wage growth and labor turnover.* NBER working paper No. 2690.

Mitchell, J. (1997). Genus: Training-species: Technical. *Technical and Skills Training, 8*(4), 3.

Morgante, J. (2000). Fun, games, and safety? Sometimes they do mix. *Learning Circuits, 1*(6).

Mueller, N. (1997). Using SMEs to design training. *Technical Training, 8*(8), 14–19.

Nathan, A., Santi, D., and Chisholm, B. (1995). Managing the technical training function. In L. Kelly (Ed.), *The ASTD technical and skills training handbook* (pp. 49–96). New York: McGraw-Hill.

National Skills Standards Board. (2001). *Getting started on assessment: Developing a voluntary system of assessment and certification based on skill standards.* Washington, DC: Author.

Nelson, O. (1988). *DACUM approach, CVATE handout.* Menomonie, WI: University of Wisconsin-Stout.

Newman, A., Pallesen, P., and Visk, A. (1999). Moving target: Designing training for new system rollouts. *Technical Training, 10*(4), 10–13.

Nickols, F. (2001). Evaluating training: There is no "cookbook" approach. In J. Woods and J. Cortada (Eds.), *The 2001 ASTD training and performance yearbook* (pp. 322–333). New York: McGraw-Hill.

Norton, R. (1997). *DACUM handbook* (2nd ed.). Columbus, OH: Center on Education and Training for Employment, College of Education, The Ohio State University.

Olesen, M. (1999). What makes employees stay. *Training and Development, 53*(10), 48–52.

O'Roark, H. (1998). Basic skills get a boost. *Technical Training, 9*(4), 10–13.

Paquin, D. (1995). Skilled trades programs: Apprentice to master. In L. Kelly (Ed.), *The ASTD technical and skills training handbook* (pp. 411–430). New York: McGraw-Hill.

Parker, E. (1994). *Room to maneuver: The institutional conditions of regional industrial restructuring.* Unpublished doctoral dissertation. Ann Arbor, MI: University of Michigan Dissertation Services.

Parry, S. (1998). Organizing a lesson plan by objectives. *Technical Training, 9*(4), 8–9.

Phoon, A. (1996). Putting some fun in your technical training. In L. Kelly, *Supplement 1 to the ASTD technical and skills training handbook* (pp. 191–210). New York: McGraw-Hill.

Piskurich, G. (1999). Now-you-see 'em, now-you-don't learning centers. *Technical Training, 10*(1), 18–21.

Pollock, L. (2000). Ground force. *People Management, 6*(2), 44–46.

Reid, R. (1993). On target: Training to work safely. *Technical and Skills Training, 4*(7), 29–33.

Reynolds, A. (1993). The basics: Exporting technical training. *Technical and Skills Training, 4*(4), 32–33.

Reynolds, A. (1995). Individualized instructional approaches. In L. Kelly (Ed.), *The ASTD technical and skills training handbook* (pp. 289–318). New York: McGraw-Hill.

Reynolds, A. (1998). Job aids: Still a performance support essential. *Technical Training, 9*(1), 6–7.

Rosow, J.M., and Zager, R. (1988). *Training for new technology: Part V. Partners in learning: Manufacturers and users.* Scarsdale, NY: Work in America Institute.

Rothwell, W. (1996a). *The just-in-time training assessment instrument: Administrator's handbook.* Amherst, MA: HRD Press.

Rothwell, W. (1996b). *The just-in-time training assessment instrument: Data collection instrument.* Amherst, MA: HRD Press.

Rothwell, W. (1999). *The action learning guidebook: A real-time strategy for problem solving, training design, and employee development.* San Francisco: Jossey-Bass/Pfeiffer.

Rothwell, W. (2000a). *Effective succession planning: Ensuring leadership continuity and building talent from within* (2nd ed.). New York: Amacom.

Rothwell, W. (2000b). *The analyst.* Alexandria, VA: ASTD.

Rothwell, W. (2000c). *The evaluator.* Alexandria, VA: ASTD.

Rothwell, W. (2000d). *The intervention selector, intervention designer and developer, intervention implementor.* Alexandria, VA: ASTD.

Rothwell, W. (2000e). *The manager and change leader.* Alexandria, VA: ASTD.

Rothwell, W., and Cookson, P. (1997). *Beyond instruction: Comprehensive program planning for business and education.* San Francisco: Jossey-Bass.

Rothwell, W., Hohne, C., and King, S. (2000). *Human performance improvement: Building practitioner competence.* Woburn, MA: Butterworth-Heinemann.

Rothwell, W., and Kazanas, H.(1994a). *Improving on-the-job training.* San Francisco: Jossey-Bass.

Rothwell, W., and Kazanas, H. (1994b). *Human resource development: A strategic approach* (rev. ed.). Amherst, MA: HRD Press.

Rothwell, W., and Kazanas, H. (1998). *Mastering the instructional design process: A systematic approach* (2nd ed.) San Francisco: Jossey-Bass.

Rothwell, W., and Kazanas, H. (2000). *Building in-house leadership and management development programs.* Westport, CT: Quorum Books.

Rothwell, W., Sanders, E., and Soper, J. (1999). *ASTD models for workplace learning and performance: Roles, competencies, work outputs.* Alexandria, VA: ASTD.

Rothwell, W., and Sensenig, K. (Eds.). (1999). *The self-directed learning sourcebook.* Amherst, MA: HRD Press.

Rothwell, W., and Sredl, H. (2000). *The ASTD reference guide to workplace learning and performance* (3rd. ed.). (2 vols.). Amherst, MA: HRD Press.

Rousseau, D., and Libuser, C. (1997). Contingent workers in high risk environments. *California Management Review, 39*(2), 103–123.

Rowley, W., Crist, T., and Presley, L. (1995). Partnerships for productivity. *Training and Development, 49*(1), 53–55.

Ruber, P. (1996). The high cost of technical training. *Computer Reseller News, 710,* 27–28.

Russell, T., and Driscoll, M. (1998). Creating international course development teams. *Technical Training, 9*(1), 16–19.

Russo, C. (1998). ISO standards: How does your training measure up? *Technical Training, 9*(3), 30–34.

Ruyle, K. (1999). Analyzing tasks to improve performance. *Technical Training, 10*(2), 24–28.

Ruyle, K. (1995). Group training methods. In L. Kelly (Ed.), *The ASTD technical and skills training handbook* (pp. 319–338). New York: McGraw-Hill.

Salopek, J. (1998). Outsourcing, insourcing, and in-between sourcing. *Training and Development, 52*(7), 51–56.

Sample, J. (1993). Legal liability and HRD: Implications for trainers. *Info-Line,* 259309. Alexandria, VA: ASTD.

Sample, J. (1995). Liability and the technical trainer. In L, Kelly (Ed.), *The ASTD technical and skills training handbook* (pp. 175–210). New York: McGraw-Hill.

Sample, J. (1996). Liability and the technical trainer. *Technical and Skills Training, 7*(1), 17–22.

Sanders, E. (1999). Coming to terms with learning technologies. *Technical Training, 10*(1), 34–35.

Schaaf, K. (1999). Combining tools and techniques to enhance training. *Technical Training, 10*(4), 6.

Schedlbauer, M. (1998). Recruiting techies from within. *Technical Training, 9*(2), 16–19.

Schriver, R., and Giles, S. (1997). Proficiency "testouts" streamline annual compliance training. *Technical Training, 8*(8), 5.

Schriver, R., and Giles, S. (1998). Web-based regulatory training. *Technical Training, 9*(3), 36.

Segall, L. (1995). Selecting and supporting the technical trainer. In L. Kelly (Ed.), *The ASTD technical and skills training handbook* (pp. 49–96). New York: McGraw-Hill.

Selden, S. (1996). Multiple approaches for meeting workforce needs: Technical training in the United States postal service. *Review of Public Personnel Administration, 16*(3), 59–73.

Sharpe, C. (Ed.). (1998). *The complete guide to technical and skills training.* Alexandria, VA: ASTD.

Sheets, R. (1995). Colleges, universities, and vocational and technical institutes. In L. Kelly (Ed.), *The ASTD technical and skills training handbook* (pp. 517–536). New York: McGraw-Hill.

Sieloff, D. (2001). The bridge evaluation model. In J. Woods and J. Cortada (Eds.), *The 2001 ASTD training and performance yearbook* (pp. 314–321). New York: McGraw-Hill.

Silverstein, N. (1997). Duracell's integrated training approach. *CBT Solutions,* pp. 49–52.

Simpson, K. (1996). Should you outsource technical training or keep it in-house? *Technical and Skills Training, 7*(6), 25–27.

Sooy, N. (1993). The power of training at PStaley, C. (1999). Good and cheap: No frills WBT. *Technical Training, 10*(5), 29–33.

Stair, R.M., and Reynolds, G.W. (2001). *Principles of information systems: A managerial approach* (5th ed.). Boston, MA: Course Technology-Thompson Learning.

Stamps, D. (1998). Blue-collar blues. *Training, 35*(5), 32–40.

SE and G. *Technical and Skills Training, 4*(6), 16–20.

Stevens, G., and Stevens, E. (1995). *Designing electronic performance support tools: Improving workplace performance with hypertext, hypermedia and multimedia.* Englewood Cliffs NJ: Educational Technology.

Stone, S. (2001). Figure$ never lie—Or do they? *Computer User, 20*(1), 22.

Stormes, J. (1997). Restructuring technical training using ISD. *Technical and Skills Training, 8*(2), 23–27.

Swanson, R., and Torraco, R. (1995). The history of technical training. In L. Kelly (Ed.), *The ASTD technical and skills training handbook* (pp. 1–48). New York: McGraw-Hill.

Tampson, P. (1998). Training ties that bind. *Technical Training, 9*(2), 10–14.

Thompson, C. (2001). Ten steps to determining the return on your training investment. In J. Woods and J. Cortada (Eds.), *The 2001 ASTD training and performance yearbook* (pp. 341–354). New York: McGraw-Hill.

Tompkins, N. (1996). Lessons in many languages. *HRMagazine, 41*(3), 94–96.

Tough, A. (1971). *The adult's learning projects.* Toronto: Ontario Institute for Studies in Education.

Tough, A. (1979). *The adult's learning projects* (2nd ed.). Toronto: Ontario Institute for Studies in Education.

Training trends 2000–2005: Training and education industry leaders. (2000). *The Microcomputer Trainer, 87,* 3–6.

Treese, W. (1999). *The Internet index: Number 24* [On-line], 1999. Available: http://new-website.openmarket.com/intindex/99–05.htm

Treichler, D., and Carmichael, R. (1999). Raytheon's accelerated needs analysis process. *Technical Training, 10*(1), 22–25.

Treinen, D., and Douglas, C. (1995). Financing the technical training function. In L. Kelly (Ed.), *The ASTD technical and skills training handbook* (pp. 143–174). New York: McGraw-Hill.

U.S. Department of Labor. (1989). *Setting up an apprenticeship program, a step-by-step guide in training apprentices for skilled occupations* (rev. ed.). Washington, DC: U.S. Department of Labor, Bureau of Apprenticeship and Training.

U.S. Department of Labor. (1991). *Apprenticeships: Past and present* (rev. ed.). Washington, DC: U.S. Department of Labor, Bureau of Apprenticeship and Training.

U.S. Department of Labor. (1993). *High performance work practices and firm performance.* Washington, DC: Office of the American Workplace.

Using a collaborative training tool. (1999). *Knowledge Management, 4.*

Van Buren, M. (1998). Mainstreaming learning technologies. *Technical Training, 9*(1), 24–28.

Van Buren, M. (2001). *State of the industry: Report 2001.* Alexandria, VA: ASTD.

Verespej, M. (1996). The education difference. *Industry Week, 245*(9), 11–14.

Walter, D. (1998). Training and certifying on-the-job trainers. *Technical Training, 9*(2), 32–35.

Warr, P., Allan, C., and Birdi, K. (1999). Predicting three levels of training outcome. *Journal of Occupational and Organizational Psychology, 72,* 351–375.

Watson, G.H. (1994). *Business systems and engineering: Managing breakthrough changes for productivity and profits.* New York: Wiley.

West, E. (1995). Technical training facilities and equipment. In L. Kelly (Ed.), *The ASTD technical and skills training handbook* (pp. 339–368). New York: McGraw-Hill.

Whitmore, W. (1992). Transferring tecknowledgy. *Technical and Skills Training, 3*(8), 6–9.

Wicklein, R., and Rojewski, J. (1999). Toward a "unified curriculum framework" for technology education. *Journal of Industrial Teacher Education, 36*(4), 38–56.

Wircenski, J., Robertson, R., and Sullivan, R. (1993). Training for ironworker instructors. *Technical and Skills Training, 4*(6), 23–26.

Zemke, R. (1986). What is technical training anyway? *Training, 23*(7), 18–21.

ABOUT THE AUTHORS

William J. Rothwell, Ph.D., is professor of human resource development in the Department of Adult Education, Instructional Systems and Workforce Education and Development, on the University Park Campus of The Pennsylvania State University. He is also president of Rothwell & Associates, a human resource development consulting firm. He was previously assistant vice president and management development director for The Franklin Life Insurance Company in Springfield, Illinois, and training director for the Illinois office of Auditor General. He has worked full-time in human resource management and employee training and development from 1979 to the present. He thus combines real-world experience with academic and consulting experience. His client list includes over thirty multinational corporations, as well as numerous government and nonprofit organizations.

Dr. Rothwell's latest publications include *The Manager and Change Leader* (ASTD, 2001); *Intervention Selector, Designer and Developer, and Implementor* (ASTD, 2000); *The Analyst* (ASTD, 2000); *The Evaluator* (ASTD, 2000); *The ASTD Reference Guide to Workplace Learning and Performance* (3rd ed., 2 vols.; HRD Press, 2000, with H. Sredl); *The Complete Guide to Training Delivery: A Competency-Based Approach* (Amacom, 2000, with S. King and M. King); *Human Performance Improvement: Building Practitioner Competence* (Butterworth-Heinemann, 2000, with C. Hohne and S. King); *Effective Succession Planning: Ensuring Leadership Continuity and Building Talent from Within* (2nd ed.; Amacom, 2000); *The Competency Toolkit* (2 vols.; HRD

Press, 2000, with D. Dubois); and *ASTD Models for Human Performance* (2nd ed.; ASTD, 2000).

Dr. Rothwell is also first editor of the Jossey-Bass/Pfeiffer series, Practicing Organization Development, and first editor of the Jossey-Bass series, Using Technology in Learning and Instruction.

Joseph A. Benkowski, Ph.D., has over thirty years' experience in technical training. He served an apprenticeship in tool and die making and is a journeyperson tool and die maker. He taught apprentice program courses and machine shop at the Fox Valley Technical College in Wisconsin and was later apprenticeship coordinator at the same school. He was then employed for eighteen years at Miller Brewing Company, a Fortune 500 company, where he was technical training coordinator and then manager of corporate technical training. He earned his Ph.D. at Penn State University just before retiring from Miller Brewing Company, and he thereupon accepted a teaching position in training and development at the University of Wisconsin-Stout. He is currently associate dean for outreach, program director for the master's program in training and development, and director of the Stout Technology Transfer Institute.

HOW TO USE THE CD-ROM

System Requirements

Windows PC

- 486 or Pentium processor-based personal computer
- Microsoft Windows 95 or Windows NT 3.51 or later
- Minimum RAM: 8 MB for Windows 95 and NT
- Available space on hard disk: 8 MB Windows 95 and NT
- 2X speed CD-ROM drive or faster

Netscape 3.0 or higher browser or MS Internet Explorer 3.0 or higher

Macintosh

- Macintosh with a 68020 or higher processor or Power Macintosh
- Apple OS version 7.0 or later
- Minimum RAM: 12 MB for Macintosh
- Available space on hard disk: 6MB Macintosh
- 2X speed CD-ROM drive or faster

Netscape 3.0 or higher browser or MS Internet Explorer 3.0 or higher

NOTE: This CD requires Netscape 3.0 or MS Internet Explorer 3.0 or higher. You can download these products using the links on the CD-ROM Help Page.

Getting Started

Insert the CD-ROM into your drive. The CD-ROM will usually launch automatically. If it does not, click on the CD-ROM drive on your computer to launch. You will see an opening page. You can click on this page or wait for it to fade to the Copyright Page. After you click to agree to the terms of the Copyright Page, the Home Page will appear.

Moving Around

Use the buttons at the left of each screen or the underlined text at the bottom of each screen to move among the menu pages. To view a document listed on one of the menu pages, simply click on the name of the document. To quit a document at any time, click the box at the upper right-hand corner of the screen.

Use the scrollbar at the right of the screen to scroll up and down each page.

To quit the CD-ROM, you can click the Quit option at the bottom of each menu page, hit Control-Q, or click the box at the upper right-hand corner of the screen.

To Download Documents

Open the document you wish to download. Under the File pulldown menu, choose Save As. Save the document onto your hard drive with a different name. It is important to use a different name; otherwise the document may remain a read-only file.

You may also click on your CD drive in Windows Explorer and select a document to copy to your hard drive and rename it.

In Case of Trouble

If you experience difficulty using the *Building Effective Technical Training* CD-ROM, please follow these steps:

1. Make sure your hardware and systems configurations conform to the systems requirements noted under "System Requirements" above.
2. Review the installation procedure for your type of hardware and operating system. It is possible to reinstall the software if necessary.
3. You may call Jossey-Bass/Pfeiffer Customer Service at (800) 956-7739 between the hours of 8 A.M. and 5 P.M. Pacific Time, and ask for Technical Support. It is also possible to contact Technical Support by e-mail at *techsupport@JosseyBass.com*.

Please have the following information available:

- Type of computer and operating system
- Version of Windows or Mac OS being used
- Any error messages displayed

Complete description of the problem.

(It is best if you are sitting at your computer when making the call.)

INDEX

A

Action learning team, 190
Adams, R., 158, 159
ADDIE model: analyze step of, 124–133, 134e–135e; design step of, 133, 136–138; development step of, 138–141; evaluation step of, 141; implementation step of, 141; steps listed, 124, 125e
Adult learners: characteristics of, 66; learn in digestible pieces, 181–184; learn with easy to understand/detailed information, 185; learn visually, 184–185; learn when information is consistent, 184, 233

Agrawal, A., 237
Allen, R., 259
Allen, S., 51, 52
American Society for Training and Development, 16, 31, 108, 220
Analyze step (ISD model): described, 124–125; instructional setting, 131; job, 131, 133, 134e–135e; learner, 127, 129e; performance, 125–127, 128e, 150, 151; results of analysis, 133; types of analysis listed, 126e; work, 131; work setting, 127, 130e
Apprenticeship committee, 249
Apprenticeship—Past and Present (U.S. Department of Labor), 245

Apprenticeships: benefits of using, 245–246; classroom instruction during, 252; current programs using, 244–245; DACUM method used in, 249, 250–251, 252; developing competencies/tasks list for, 250–251; developing train-the-trainer program for, 251–252; family tradition of craft, 242–243; history of, 241–242; legislation governing, 243–244; starting a program for, 246–249; technical trainer's role in, 250
Assessing the Perceived Effectiveness of Your Organization's Technical Training, 59e–60e

Assessing technical training needs: building effective training from, 156; case study on, 144–146; DACUM method for, 145–146, 156–168; methods for, 152–156

ASTD (American Society for Training and Development), 17, 220

B

Bamforth, K. W., 33
Barron, T., 73, 193, 230
Bartel, A., 11
Bass, R., 137
Bassi, L., 220
Behavior change evaluation level, 221–222
Beibel, M., 123
Benchmarking: determining what needs, 94–95; overview of, 93; prerequisites and guiding principles for, 94; reporting data of, 95, 98; selecting companies for, 95
Benchmarking Data Guide, 96e–98e
Berik, G., 242
Bersani, M., 63
Bilginsoy, C., 242
Blair, D., 137
Bloch, M., 13
Bluestone, B., 11
Blume, E., 245
Booth, W. S., 34
Boyd, S., 259
Brown, J., 264
Brown, S., 222
Brunelli, M., 210

Budgeting technical training, 88
Burgoyne, J., 220
Butler, C., 49

C

CAD (computer-aided design), 168
Caiazza, K., 74
Cantor, J., 245
Carmichael, R., 152
Carnevale, A., 24, 34, 35, 67, 79, 178
Catanello, 220
CBT (computerized-based training) systems, 167–170. *See also* Online training delivery
Cellich, C., 10
Center for Vocational, Technical, and Adult Education (University of Wisconsin– Stout), 156
Centralized training structure, 35–36
Chakiris, B. J., 219
Champions, 80–82
Chance, P., 58
Cheney, S., 245
Clark, 16, 58
Clark, C., 224
Clark, R., 123
Classroom delivery: apprenticeship program use of, 252; described, 195; technical trainer as facilitator in, 198–199; technical trainer as instructor in, 197–198
Clinton, M., 66
Cochern, G., 16
Code of Hammurabi, 242

Collective bargaining status, 18
Combined Structural Arrangement, 36
Combs, W., 219
Communication: management skills in, 118, 120; strategic planning process role by, 98–99
Competencies Essential for Technical Trainers, 63e
Competitive analysis, 100
Contractual technical trainers, 20
Cooke, W., 265
Cookson, P., 124
Cooper, C., 220
Course Descriptions Linked To The Training Curriculum, 149e
Creating A Job Aid Cover Sheet, 184e
Crist, T., 245
CST (computer-based training), 48–49
CTT+ (Certified Technical Trainer) certification, 197

D

DACUM charts, 160, 161e–163e
DACUM facilitator, 158–159
DACUM method: apprenticeship program use of, 249, 250–251, 252; used in case study, 145–146, 165, 167; defining, 157–158; overview of, 156–157
DACUM process: defining area or occupation, 160;

identifying general areas of competency, 160; identifying major duty statements, 160, 164; room setup during, 159; sequence tasks in major duties, 164–165; seven steps in, 159; type of systems used with, 167–168

Decentralized training structure, 36

Decision Tables, 186e–187e

DeFiore, R., 268

Del Gaizo, E., 220

Delisle, R., 220

Delivery. *See* Training delivery methods

Dent, J., 16, 123

Dervarics, C., 108

Design step: described, 133, 136; formulating training objectives during, 136–137; preparing course specifications during, 137–138; preparing evaluation procedures, 137

Development step, 138–141

Distance learning (TTC), 39–40

Dolainski, S., 245

Douglas, C., 74

Douglas (company), 230

Dowding, 57

Dowling, E., 198

Doyle, E., 64, 229

Dubois, D., 27, 58

E

E-learning, 29

Eline, J., 24

Eline, L., 27, 125, 192

Employees: exemplary, 171; feedback systems for, 273–274; human performance problems by, 270e–272; job aids to, 272; recognition/reward programs for, 274–275; Skilbase Charts recordkeeping on, 172e; work redesign efforts for, 275–276. *See also* Workforce

Environmental scanning, 89–91, 93

EPPS (electronic performance support systems), 168, 171, 173–175

ERP (enterprise resource planning), 73

ERPs (enterprise resource programs), 28

Evaluating technical training: based on process, 222–223; based on time, 222; defining unique aspects of, 218–219; effort devoted to, 220–221; as final ISD model step, 141; importance of, 219–220; issues influencing, 223–224; Kirkpatrick's hierarchy of, 221–222; of OJT (on-the-job training), 204; preparing procedures for, 137; problems plaguing, 224; of safety training, 262–263

Evanciew, C., 245

Exemplary employees, 171

External consultants: interviewing, 84–85; selecting/

contracting with, 85; sourcing qualified, 83–84

F

"Fact Sheet," 84

Falletta, S., 219

Federal Committee on Apprenticeships, 244

Feedback systems, 273–274

Fertal, A., 268

Filling the Skills Gap, 13

Fister, S., 58

Ford, H., 230, 243

Franklin, B., 242

Franklin, J., 242

Frantz, N., 245

Full-time technical trainers, 19–20

G

Gainer, L. J., 35, 79

Galagan, P., 220

Garvin, D., 27

Geographic sector, 91

Gery, G., 168, 170

Getting Started (NSSB website document), 155

Giles, S., 137

Gilley, J., 73, 79, 82

Gitter,, 245

Gittlen, S., 12

Glackens, D. S., 242

Glackens, H. O., 243

Glackens, W. J., 243

Glister, P., 13

Goldstein, H., 34

Groove software (www.groove.net), 190

Group facilitators, 198–199

Group-based technology delivery, 208

A Guide In Gathering Necessary Competitive Information Of Value For Planning Technical Training, 101*e*

H

Hallberg, C., 268
Hamilton, M., 202
Hamilton, S., 202
HandK, 230
Hard skills, 219
Hardinger, S., 223
Harrison, B., 11
Hartl, D., 66
Hays, S., 7
Herschbach, D., 27
Hight, J., 11
Hohne, C., 26, 116, 269
Hong Vo, C., 245
Houle, C., 66
How To Write Decision Tables, 186*e*–187*e*
HPW (high performance workplace), 270
HR (human resources), 16
HRD (human resources development): computerized technical training system used in, 167–170; growing investment in, 220; key trends influencing, 25; strategic planning by, 82. *See also* Technical training
Hudson Institute, 30
Huey, T., 246
Human performance improvement specialists, 268. *See also* Technical trainers

Human performance problems, 270*e*–272
Human Resources Development Institute, 264

I

IDEs (instructional design experts), 58
IDPs (individual development plans), 27
Individualized technology-based delivery, 208–209
Information: adult learning and consistent, 184; adult learning with easy/detailed, 185; available electronically, 171, 173–175
"Information mapping," 181
Instructional setting analysis, 131, 132*e*
International Society for Performance Improvement, 95
An Interview Guide To Examine Strategic Issues In Technical Training, 92*e*
Interviewing process: for environmental scanning, 91–93; of external consultants, 84–85
Is Technical Training A Separate Department In Your Organization?, 65*e*
ISD (instructional systems design): ADDIE model of, 124, 125*e*; analyze step of, 124–133; described, 116, 124; design step of, 133, 136–138; development step of, 138–141; evaluation step

of, 141; implementation step of, 141; proven steps of, 123
ISO (International Standards Organization), 114
IT (information technology): partnership between training and, 212–214; percentage of training done in, 12–13; technical training to use, 8–9

J

Jarrett, L., 245
Job aids, 272
Job analysis, 131, 133, 134*e*–135*e*
Job Chart, 183*e*
Job Description of a Technical Training Coordinator, 61*e*
Job Description of a Technical Training Instructor, 61*e*
Job Hazard Analysis, 260–261
Johnson, D., 222
Johnston, W., 10
Joint training committee, 265–266
Junion, S., 51

K

Katz, R., 35
Kazanas, H., 11, 73, 89, 107, 124, 137, 201
Kazis, R., 245
Kelly, R., 245
Kemp, J., 16
King, S., 26, 116, 269
King-Taylor, L., 58

Kirkpatrick, D., 220, 221–222

Kirkpatrick's hierarchy of training evaluation, 221–222

Knowledge tests, 137, 224

Knowles, M., 66

Kosse, J., 51–52

Koury, J., 259

Krones, 230

L

L and D (learning and development) teams [Rockwell Collins], 50–51, 52

Laabs, J., 198, 259

The Lafayette (newspaper), 242

Langdon, D., 62

Latimer, J., 141

Layout Of A Job Chart, 183*e*

Leader/leadership: management vs., 107–108; technical training responsibilities of, 111–113*e*; vision established by, 108. *See also* Management

Leadership training responsibilities: applying effective instructional design principles, 116; appropriate staffing/ management of trainers, 118; continuous development of oneself, 120; effective interpersonal/communication skills, 118, 120; establishing policies, standards, procedures,

114; listing of key, 111–112*e*; managing outsourced vs. in-house training, 117–118; offering consulting advice, 115–116; organizing technical training function, 116–117; worksheet to brainstorm activities supporting, 113*e*

Learner analysis, 127, 129*e*

Learning centers, 208–209

Learning evaluation level, 221

Lee, H., 157

Lee, R., 223

Lermack, H., 259

Libuser, C., 260

Lillard, L., 264

Lindeman, E. C., 66

Lucadamo, L., 245

Lynch, L., 264

M

McCain, M., 245

McCallar, S., 246

McKenna, M., 62

McNamara, P. V., 243

Mager, R., 136

Malcolm Baldrige National Quality Award, 27

Mallory, W., 194

Management: effective technical training and support of, 53–54*e*; human problems solved through intervention by, 269, 271*e*; leadership vs., 107–108; reporting relationship to, 17–18; technical training respon-

sibilities of, 111–120; technical training support by, 13–14; training steering committee composed of, 85–86; worksheet assessing level of training support by, 15*e*. *See also* Leader/leadership

Management training responsibilities: applying effective design principles, 116; appropriate staffing/ management of trainers, 118; continuous development of oneself, 120; effective interpersonal/communication skills, 118, 120; establishing policies, standards, procedures, 114; listing of key, 111–112*e*; managing outsourced vs. in-house training, 117–118; offering consulting advice, 115–116; organizing technical training function, 116–117; worksheet to brainstorm activities supporting, 113*e*

Mancuso, J., 123

Market sector, 90–91

Marsh, P., 202

Marx, R., 193

Mayberry, 213, 214

Maycunich, A., 73, 79, 82

The Meaning of the Adult Learner (Lindeman), 66

Miller, L., 24

Mincer, J., 264

MIS (management information systems), 16

Mitchell, J., 8, 35

A Model To Depict The
   Key Responsibilities Of
   A Leader/Manager Of
   Technical Training, 112*e*
Mueller, N., 117, 177

N

NAFTA (North American
   Free Trade Agreement),
   27
Naisbitt, 210
National Center (Ohio State
   University), 156
National Recovery Adminis-
   tration Act, 244
Nelson, O., 159
Newman, A., 74
Nickols, F., 222
NJT (near-the-job training),
   199–201
Norton, R., 158
NPS (www.nps.mavy.mil),
   222
NSSB (National Skills Stan-
   dards Board), 153

O

OEMs (original equipment
   manufacturers): certification program through,
   233, 235–236; developing
   instructional materials
   using, 238–240; managing
   and working with, 230;
   planning training for
   equipment installation
   and, 234*e*; safety training
   related to, 260; technical
   trainer's role with,
   230–231; training and
   large, 231–232; training

and small, 232–233; work-
   ing with hands-on,
   236–238. *See also* Vendors
OJT (on-the-job training):
   case study on effective,
   204–207; described,
   201–202; design, development, delivery of, 202,
   204; evaluating, 204;
   when to use, 202
Oleson, M., 12
Online training delivery:
   generally structured experiences using, 209–212;
   storyboard format for,
   190
Organizational goals, technical training supporting,
   56
Organizational impact evaluation level, 222
Organizational needs: predicting long-term and
   short-term, 57; technical
   training supporting, 56.
   See also Technical training
   needs
Organizational strategic
   plan: background prior to
   formulating, 74–75; creating the schedule for,
   77–78; formulated to
   build partnerships,
   82–83; need for cham-
   pion in, 80–82; new approach for, 76–77;
   questions to be addressed
   by, 78–79; reasons to develop, 79; revisiting the
   training strategy, 75–76;
   trainer's role in, 80
Organizational technical
   training: collective bar-

gaining status and, 18;
   level of management
   support for, 13–14; organizational benefits of supporting, 21–23e, 22e;
   perceived reasons for supporting, 25*e*; reporting relationship as factor in,
   17–18; size of organization and, 16–17; source
   for technical trainers and,
   18–20; type of company
   and, 14
Organizations: assessing
   perceived effectiveness
   of training in your,
   59*e*–60*e*; development of
   technical training in
   your, 64*e*; environmental
   scanning of, 89–91, 93;
   formulating/implement-
   ing strategic plan by,
   74–78; rating the technical training in your,
   58; technical training as
   separate department in,
   65*e*
O'Roark, H., 27
OSHA (Occupational Safety
   and Health Administra-
   tion): developing safety
   training plan and, 256,
   258; on issues linked to
   injuries/illnesses by, 263;
   listing safety training requirements and,
   254–256; safety training
   guidelines following,
   258–259; safety training
   recommendations com-
   pliance with, 258; safety
   training to comply with,
   144, 252–253

OSHA (Occupational Safety and Health Administration) Act of 1970, 263
OSHA Office of Training and Education, 261
Our Turn-of-the-Century Trend Watch, 24

P

"Page turners" programs, 212
Pallesen, P., 74
Paquin, D., 245
Parry, S., 136
Part-time technical trainers, 18–19
Particpant evaluation, 262–263
PATN (Postal Audio Training Network), 39
PEG (Performance Engineering Group Inc.), 49
Peloquin, J. J., 8
Performance analysis, 125–127, 128e, 150, 151
Performance consultants, 268. *See also* Technical trainers
Performance Control Corporation, 8
Performance management system, 270
Performance tests, 137
PERMISS, 222
Phoon, A., 199
Piskurich, G., 208
Political sector, 90
Pollock, L., 259
Presley, L., 245
Principles of Procedures Mapping, 182e

Productivity paradox, 231–232
PSTN (Postal Satellite Training Network), 39–40
Purington, C., 49, 50, 51, 52

Q

"Question Sheet," 84
Quick changeover training program, 80–81

R

R.A. Jones, 230
Reaction evaluation level, 221
Reaction sheet, 262–263
Recognition/reward programs, 274–275
Reid, R., 245
Resident training (TTC), 39
Revere, P., 242
Reynolds, A., 208
Reynolds, G. W., 215
RFP (request for a proposal), 84
Riccucci, N. M., 34
Robertson, R., 252
Rockwell Collins technical training: history lessons of, 49–50; map for the future of, 50–51; new and improved, 52; overview of, 48–49; teaming up vendors for, 51–52
Rohe, C. A., 34
ROI (return on investment), 222
Rojewski, J., 245
Rolander, R., 219
Rosow, J. M., 265

Rothwell, W., 11, 23, 26, 27, 29, 30, 57, 58, 62, 73, 82, 89, 107, 116, 117, 124, 137, 190, 197, 198, 201, 209, 269
Rousseau, D., 260
Rowley, W., 245
Ruber, P., 9
Russo, C., 27
Ruyle, K., 195

S

SACs (state apprenticeship councils), 244
Safety training: clarifying requirements for, 254–256; conducting, 262; determining need for, 259–260; developing learning activities for, 261–262; developing plan for, 256, 258; developing safety strategy for, 253; evaluating program effectiveness, 262–263; identifying goals and objectives of, 261; identifying needs of, 260–261; making recommendations for, 258; model guide to, 258–259; OSHA requirements for, 252–253; sample safety matrix for, 257e; selecting task force for, 253–254
Salopek, J., 138
Sample Checksheet Format To Guide On-The-Job Training, 203e
Sample Cover Page, 185e
Sample DACUM Chart Of An Entry-Level Trainer In China, 161e–163e

Sample, J., 259
Sample Safety Matrix, 257*e*
Sanders, E., 26, 62, 108
Schaaf, K., 198
Schmidt, M. R., 41, 42
Schoen, D. A., 41, 42
Schriver, R., 137
Schulz, E. R., 35
Schwen, 58
Self-directed learning, 209
Sensenig, K., 26, 209
Sequencing by problem, 137
Sequencing by procedure,
  137
Sharpe, C., 16
Short-term training need,
  147
Sieloff, D., 223
Silverstein, N., 185
Simpson, K., 238
The Skilbase Chart Con-
  cept, 169*e*, 172*e*
Skills standards, 152–153
SMEs (subject-matter ex-
  perts), 58, 177
Smile sheet, 262–263
Social sector, 90
Sooy, N., 245
Soper, J., 26, 62, 108
Sorensen, C. E., 243
Southwestern Power techni-
  cal training: for construct-
  ing support-engineering
  infrastructure, 44–45; de-
  scription of, 46–47; design
  courses needed for,
  45–46; future for, 47–48;
  overview of, 44
Sredl, H., 57, 62, 197, 198
Stair, R. M., 215
Stamps, D., 12
Steele, J., 194

Steering committee, 85–86
Stevens, E., 174, 175
Stevens, G., 174, 175
Stone, S., 13
Stormes, J., 123
Storyboard format: built for
  online training, 190; described, 188; live group
  and, 189–190; questions
  addressed by, 188–189
Strategic planning committee: planning/managing
  meetings for, 87–88;
  when to use a, 86–87
Strategic planning process:
  assessing need for champion for, 80–82; assessing
  training needs as part of,
  144–146; for budget
  process, 88; competitive
  analysis in, 100; designed
  to know build partner-
  ship, 82–83; developed for
  technical training,
  100–101*e*; development
  of, 79; for using environmental scanning, 89–91,
  93; using external consultant in, 83–85; imple-
  mented for technical
  training, 101; questions to
  ask during, 78–79; role
  played by communication
  in, 98–99; role of technical trainers in, 80; using
  steering committee for,
  85–86; using strategic
  planning committee in,
  86–88; union involvement
  in, 99–100; worksheet for
  organizing technical
  training, 102*e*–105*e*

Structured experience,
  209–212
Sugar, 58
Sullivan, R., 252
Swanson, R., 8

T

Tan, H., 264
Task analysis, 133
Technical Instructor Institute (University of Wisconsin-Stout), 21
Technical occupations: basic
  skills training prerequisite
  to, 7; expected job
  growth (1998-2008) in,
  6–7; listed, 5–6; technical
  training enhancement of,
  11–12
Technical Skills Professional
  Practice Area of the
  American Society for
  Training and Develop-
  ment, 95
Technical trainers: classroom roles of, 197–199;
  competencies essential
  for, 63e; contractual, 20;
  full-time, 19–20; IDEs as,
  58; job descriptions of
  coordinator and instructors of, 61*e*; part-time,
  18–19; performance
  analysis by, 150, 151;
  pilot-testing course, 138,
  141; role in apprenticeships by, 250; role with
  OEMs, 230–231; role in
  strategic planning by, 80;
  SMEs as, 58, 177;
  staffing/management of,

118; unique competencies of, 58, 62–67; working in union environment, 266–267; workplace performance outcome focus by, 268–270, 272

Technical training: alternatives to, 272–276; benefits of organizational support for, 21–23e, 22e; characteristics of effective, 52–58; defining, 4–9; examples of standards for, 115e; factors influencing organizations and, 13–20; implementing strategic planning for, 101; importance of, 9–13; as including people to use technology, 8–9; involvement of unions in, 99–100, 264–267; lessons learned from experience in, 281–285; meaning based on definitions, 7–9; meaning based on work, 5–7; as percentage of all work training, 12–13; quick changeover, 80–81; strategic planning process developed for, 100–101e; vignettes illustrating need for, 3–4

Technical training alternatives: feedback systems as, 273–274; job aids as, 272; recognition/reward programs as, 274–275; work redesign efforts as, 275–276

Technical training case studies: effective characteristics derived from, 55–58; Rockwell Collins, 48–52; Southwestern Power, 44–48; U.S. Postal Service (USPS), 33–42

Technical training characteristics: derived from the case studies, 55–58; management support, 53–54e; perceptions of, 53e; survey respondents on effective, 54–55e

Technical training department: leadership vs. management of, 107–108; roles of leader and manager of, 108, 111

Technical training lessons: aligning training with goals/needs, 282; building partnerships, 283–284; demonstrating sense of urgency, 284; listed, 281; making the focus results, 282; as means for continuous improvement, 284–285; striking balance in training materials, 285; work as part of strategic planning process, 282–283

Technical training materials: case study on preparing, 179–181; developed with OEMs, 238–240; make-or-buy decision on, 176–178; preparing, 178–179; using storyboard format to develop, 188–190

Technical training needs: building course from assessment of, 156; case study on assessing, 144–146; DACUM method for assessing, 145–146, 156–168; defining, 146–147, 150; distinguished from other needs, 150–152; issues of, 143–144; methods used to assess, 152–156; understanding, 153e; wants vs., 147. See also Organizational needs

Technical training planning: case study on formulating/implementing, 74–78; importance of, 73–74. See also Strategic planning process

Technical training preparation: adult learning principles and, 181–185; case study on, 179–181; make-or-buy materials decision, 176–178; using storyboard format, 188–190; of training materials, 178–179

Technical training standards, 115e

Technical training trends: changing training focus, 26–27; focus on value of workers as, 30; globalization focus as, 27–28; history of, 23–24; impact of technology on, 28–29; indications of future, 24–26; involvement of workers as, 29–30

Technological sector, 90

Technology: EPPS (electronic performance

Technology (*Continued*)
support systems), 168,
171, 173–175; impact on
technical training trends
by, 28–29; productivity
paradox and, 231–232
Template For A Lesson Plan
For A Classroom-Based
Technical Training
Course, 139*e*–140*e*
Torraco, R., 8
Tough, A., 66
*Toward Continuous Learning
Outlines* (Rosow and
Zager), 265
"Town hall meeting" ap-
proach, 99
Training course: descriptions
linked to curriculum,
149*e*; developing specifications for, 137–138;
template for lesson plan
for, 139*e*–140*e*
Training curriculum: course
descriptions linked to,
149*e*; as effective training
characteristics, 57; matrix
for, 148*e*; of the TTC
(USPS), 38–39. *See also*
ISD (instructional systems
design)
Training Curriculum Ma-
trix, 148*e*
Training delivery methods:
characteristics of effec-
tive, 56–57; classroom,
195, 197–199, 252; foun-
dation for partnership
between IT and, 212–214;
generally structured experiences, 209–212; group-
based technology, 208;
individualized technology-

based, 208–209; issues in
determining, 193–195;
key issues in system development of, 214–216;
mechanisms of, 37; NJT
(near-the-job training),
199–201; OJT (on-the-
job training), 201–207;
self-directed, 209; used by
TTC, 39–40; types listed,
194*e*
Training and Development (magazine), 95
Training Evaluation Ser-
vices, 222
Training (magazine), 95
Training objectives,
136–137
Training request, 150
Transfer climate, 223
Treese, W., 193
Treichler, D., 152
Treinen, D., 74
Trist, E. L., 33
TTC (National Technical
Training Center) [USPS]:
opening of, 38–39; struc-
ture, organization, cur-
riculum of, 38–39;
training delivery ap-
proaches used by, 39–40

U

UBC (United Brotherhood
of Carpenters), 245
Unions: involved in strategic
planning process,
99–100; involved in tech-
nical training programs,
264–267
Universal training simulators, 237

U.S. Bureau of Labor Statistics, 5
U.S. corporations: research
on benefits of technical
training to, 10–11; tech-
nical training percentage
of all training in,
12–13
U.S. Department of Labor,
11, 242, 243, 244, 245,
246
U.S. Department of Labor,
Bureau of Employment
and Training regional of-
fice, 247, 248
U.S. Department of Labor,
Secretary of Employment
of Apprenticeships and
Training, 247
U.S. Postal Service (USPS)
technical training: changing work processes
through, 40–41; delivery
methods of, 37; for delivery methods/ knowledge
acquisition, 41–42; na-
ture of, 34–35, 37–38;
overview of, 33–34;
providers of, 36–37; technical workforce involved
in, 35; work content and
structure of, 35–36

V

Van Buren, M., 12, 220
Van Tiem, D., 229
Vendors: effective management of, 56; Rockwell
Collins teaming up of,
51–52. *See also* OEMs
(original equipment man-
ufacturers)

Ventana for Windows (www.groupsystems.com), 190

Verespej, M., 245

Vestibule (near-the-job) training, 199–201

Vision: defining, 108; worksheet to formulate, 109e–110e

Visk, A., 74

W

Walter, D., 201

WAPA (Western Area Power Administration), 48

Weber, D., 16, 123

West, E., 198

Whiteside, K., 62

Who Develops Technical Training In Your Organization?, 64e

Wicklein, R., 151

Williams, 58

Wircenski, J., 252

WLP (workplace learning and performance), 26

Work analysis, 131

Work redesign efforts, 275–276

Work setting analysis, 127, 130e

Workforce 2000: Work and Workers for the 21th Century (Hudson Institute), 30

Workforce: examining training records of, 144; exemplary members of, 171; human performance problems by, 270e–272; Skilbase Chart record-keeping on, 172e; technical U.S. Postal Service, 35. *See also* Employees

Worksheet For Conducting Instructional Setting Analysis, 132e

Worksheet For Conducting Job Analysis, 134e–135e

Worksheet For Conducting Learner Analysis, 129e

Worksheet For Conducting Performance Analysis, 128e

Worksheet For Conducting Work Setting Analysis, 130e

Worksheet For Considering Interventions, 271e

Worksheet To Assess Level of Management Support for Technical Training, 15e

Worksheet To Brainstorm Activities To Support The Responsibilities Of A Technical Training Manager Or Leader, 113e

Worksheet To Formulate A Vision For The Technical Training Function, 109e–110e

Worksheet To Organize Information For Formating Strategic Planning For Technical Training, 102e–105e

Worksheet To Structure Your Thinking On Delivery Methods, 196e

Worksheet To Structure Your Thinking On Groups With Whom You Come Into Contact, 119e

Worksheet To Structure Your Thinking On Self-Directed Learning Activities, 211e

WST (Web-based training), 48

Z

Zager, R., 265

Zemke, R., 8

Zuboff, S., 41, 42